OTHER BACKWARD CLASSES IN INDIA

OTHER BACKWARD CLASSES IN INDIA

A Case Study of Assam

Pulak Chandra Devnath,

N.B. Biswas

KALPAZ

ISBN: 978-93-5128-085-9
Price : ` 790

First Published, 2015

Published by

Kalpaz Publications
C-30, Satyawati Nagar,
Delhi-110052
Ph. : 9212142040
E-mail: kalpaz@hotmail.com

Laser Typesetting : Abhishek Mandal, Delhi
Printed at : G. Print Process, Delhi

Cataloging in Publication Data—DK
Courtesy: D.K. Agencies (P) Ltd. <docinfo@dkagencies.com>

Biswas, N. B. (Nikunja Behari), author.
Other backward classes in India : a case study of Assam / N.B. Biswas, Pulak Chandra Devnath.
pages cm
Includes bibliographical references (pages) and index.
ISBN 9789351280859

1. Caste—India. 2. Caste—India—Assam. 3. Dalits—Government policy—India. 4. Dalits—Government policy—India—Assam. I. Devnath, Pulak Chandra, author. II. Title.

DDC 305.56880954 23

Contents

Preface

India is a multi-cultural, multi-lingual and a composite racial country. The country which covered Hindu Kush to Himalayan range, naturally had an interaction with the people of culture of the range. In spite of that the Indian society is class and community-based which has come on the way for the progress and development of the country. The vast majority of the people of India consist of those persons who are backward in all fields. The caste system of the country has done a great loss in the upliftment of people of India. There are backward classes, scheduled castes, scheduled tribes and tribal people who are educationallys backward. In Articles 341 and 342 of the Indian Constitution, there is a list of scheduled castes and scheduled tribes. From the educational point of view they are far behind to those who belong to the upper class. Some efforts were made for the education of scheduled castes, scheduled tribes and tribal people in the pre-independence era.

The present volume is an outcome of the in-depth study of the backward communities and backward classes in India through the primary and secondary sources. The authors of the volume have made an attempt to go through the genesis of the emergence of backward classes in India and also have discussed various backward communities in general in India in this volume. Special attempt has been made to look into the backward classes in Assam. The government policy related to backward communities has also be analysed in this book. The significant aspect of the volume is the analysis of socio-economic and educational condition of the backward communities in India and Assam.

The more interesting aspect of this volume is the discussion of the various backward communities such as ahom, asur, baria, basor, baiga, bedia, beldar, bhatta, bhill, chutia, das, ganak, ghosh, hoala, koch rajbongshi, kumar, kurmi, mahishya, mala, mala Christian, Manipuri Brahmin, Manipuri Muslim, matak, moran, nai, nath yogi, chhetri, gurung, rai, magars, lohar, sadgop, tanti are available in the literature and also through the field work.

The volume has highlighted the in-depth study of three hundred backward community families of Assam which will pave the way of the future researchers and of the social scientists to look into the contribution and importance in the era of globalisation. Therefore, the volume will generate or arouse the interest of the students, teachers, researchers, academicians, social scientists etc., in the country and abroad.

Pulak Chandra Devnath,

N.B. Biswas

1

Historical Background of Backward Classes in India

Genesis of Caste System

The origin of caste system cannot be seen in one single authoritative text, nor can it be attributed to one single founder. It developed gradually in a natural way over thousands of years. The experiences and deep-thinking of many learned sages and intellectuals belonging to different communities at different points of time have contributed to evolve this process. It is a very old and indigenous system, conceptualised, developed and practiced exclusively in India.

As Basham has pointed out, caste system may well be called a natural response to many small and primitive groups of people, who were forced to come to terms, with a more advanced economic and social system. It provided a mechanism, by which numerous discrete tribes could be all sorts of groups and associations arising for political, sectarian or other reasons could be internalised and preserved within the whole.

Caste is the development of thousands of years of the association of many racial and other groups in a single cultural system. The arrival of Aryans hereditary kinship and tribal groups in India in waves, from different parts of the world and their mixing up with the indigenous people (popularly known as Hindus) gave birth Varna-system of Vedic culture.

The beginning of the system can be traced from the times of pastoral tribal society, when people started forming small groups mostly living in hilly areas, not far from rivers. Tribal communities were nomadic or semi-nomadic and egalitarian. They depended totally on nature for their means of supporting livelihood.

Gradually pastoral tribal society transformed into a settled agricultural society, confining its activities and life within a small area or territory. Agricultural society leisurely evolved its structures and systems over about 2000 years (roughly between 2000 BC to about 600 BC), and kept on coping with the changes slowly, time had brought in. As it reflected in 'Rigveda' that when people ceased to be a wandering people that heralded the early stages of Vedic Age.

Clans and tribes settled permanently in different parts of the country. The process of possession of land, slaves and hiring of labourers began. People hardly possessed more than what was needed for their very sustenance. After that a new phase started with the practice of cultivation, rise of crafts and iron tools transformed the egalitarian society into fully agricultural and stratified society sometime during the Sixth Century BC.

After entering into India, first Aryans conquered its original inhabitants of northern part of India, colonised and established kingdoms, then Deccan and then south. During the period, it was possible to have high ranks, but not high social classes. Initially, a simple class division was seen in the social structure, i.e., nobility and the ordinary tribesmen. The units of socio-political organisations were family, clan, village, tribe and Jana. Family was the unit of society headed by father. Three or four generations lived together, and probably owned property in common. A number of families living in one locality formed gram (village). A number of such fighting units dwelling in a particular region constituted a canton. Jana (a group of tribes) consisted of a number of such cantons, with a king as their ruler.

In the beginning, Varna - meaning colour - guided the division of the society. Starting with arrival of Aryans in waves and mixing-up of their culture with native culture of the land evolved a social structure based on the principles of "Varna" (giving birth to caste system), "Dharma" and "Karma", which together distributed, organised performance of various functions and contributed to the growth of the Indian society during those period. These principles gave Vedic society a distinct character, defined roles and organised inter-relationship of various sections of society. Fair complexioned Aryans being the conquerors as they kept themselves on the top of the hierarchy and also enjoyed a special status in the society. They had spreaded their language and culture all over the north. In the meantime, many changes started taking place in the life, manners, religion, language and literature of people.

Principle of 'Varna' had stratified Vedic society into four groups - Bramins (intellectuals), Kshatriyas (warriors), Vaishyas (Businessmen) and Shudras (service providers) according to aptitudes, occupation and location of people. Aryans dependents of Brahmins and Kshatriyas were the subject class. Vaishyas followed the profession of agriculture or cattle-raising and constituted also the armed forces of their princes. The three classes were not rigidly separated. People, who were conquered and admitted into the fold of Aryan society, were looked upon as the lowest of the four classes. Conquered Kols and Dravid tribes formed the fourth class of Dasas or Shudras. Aryan princes did not regard Dasa princes as inferior, for they made alliances with them.

The process of possession of land, slaves and hired labourers commenced. People started producing and possessing more than they needed. The kings collected their surplus yields. The power of kings gradually increased. For regular collection, administrative and religious methods were devised.

As more and more indigenous and foreign groups were started merging into the Hindu-fold, Vedic Varna system gave rise to caste system. For making place for new groups, caste system provided a mechanism. Through it, the job of assimilation of different tribal, local and immigrant groups was done cordially, at different points of time. Each new group joining it was given a separate caste identity. It neither disturbed the existing internal social order nor was any new group prevented from joining it and still allowed new groups to preserve its specialties and indigenous culture. It gave each one opportunity to develop within its own parameters. Thousands of endogamous groups were included into it. Each group was allowed to maintain its own rules, regulations, customs, way of living, and power to control conduct of its members. However, principles of Varna, Dharma, and Karma remained the foundation stones of caste system and contributed to its growth in a systematic way.

Castes had its ethnic roots as denoted by Jati, and a ritualistic and symbolic significance in its Varna aspect. Different castes found their place under a Varna on the basis of their being ritually clean or unclean, nature of work and amount of self-discipline they exercised. Numerous castes and sub-castes emerged within each Varna. The four Varnas remained the same. These were never more or less than four. For over 2000 years, their order in precedence remained the same. As far as castes were concerned, they rose and fell in their social order, some died out and new ones were formed from time to time.

Perhaps, the first faint trace of caste is to be found in the careful cataloguing of traders and professions in later Vedic literature. Many traders were organised into guilds around Fifth century AD, in which, some authorities have seen the origin of commercial castes. These can be seen as the castes in making. Even up to Seventh century AD, people showed no clear knowledge of the existence of castes. Huan Tsang, in the Seventh century was well-aware of the existence of Varna, but not of castes.

Later on, caste-system has become a dominant factor, a natural unit of Indian society, running through the entire fabric of its social structure. Slowly but steadily it got inseparably intertwined with Indian way of life. So much and so that, Muslims and Christians, Sikhs and Buddhists, living in India could not remain immune from it for long, though their respective religions believe in egalitarian society. They have, with all their equalitarian faith, formed caste groups within themselves.

Not only in the past, but at present also, caste system appears to be a valid and useful, a natural and inevitable unit of society. It is popular and commands respect and attention of majority of Indian masses of all sects present in India, whether foreign or indigenous. For them following four are fundamental social institutions. An individual is supposed to be a natural member of a family, which is a unit of an extended family, extended family of Kula, Kula of a tribe (Vish) - and a tribe of a Jana or Jati (Caste).

A person's relations with members of his caste are closer than with those, belonging to other castes. Caste values, beliefs, prejudices, injunctions as well as distortions of reality are the indivisible part of a person's psyche and conscience. Internalised caste norms define an individual role in the society. It makes one feel good and loved, when he lives up to these norms, and anxious and guilty, when he transgresses them. In a way, caste is still second only to the family in widening a person's social radius and in getting importance in his/her private and occupational life.

Caste system has travelled a very long distance since its inception. Many changes took place in the system. Once changed, the system never returned to its original form.

A caste is a combined social system of occupation, endogamy, culture, social-class and political power. Caste should not be confused with class, in that members of a caste are deemed to be alike in function or culture, whereas not all members of a defined class may be so alike. Although, Indian society is often now associated with the word "caste", it was first used by the Portuguese to describe inherited class status in their own European society. English caste is from Latin castus "pure, cut off, segregated", and the participle of carere "to cut off".

Application to Hindu social groups originates in the 17th century, via Portuguese casta "breed, race, caste". Discrimination based on caste, as perceived by UNICEF, is prevalent mainly in parts of Asia (India, Sri Lanka, Bangladesh, Nepal, and Japan) and Africa. UNICEF estimates that such yellow discrimination based on caste affects 250 million people worldwide.

Indian society has consisted since ancient times of several thousand tribal and occupational groups, castes or communities called Jati. The phrase "Hindu Caste System" conflates two entirely different concepts – the Varna (class/group), theoretical scheme based on idealised Brahminical traditions, and the Jati system prevalent throughout the Indian society since historical times.

Faced with a confounding array of thousands of autonomous and hierarchically fluid communities (Jatis), the late 19th century British colonial administration decided to categorise and rank the entire Hindu population of India by placing each of the Jatis within the theoretical Varna scheme for the purposes of the decennial census, and ostensibly for eventual administrative convenience. The 1901 census was led by Herbert Hope Risley, an ICS officer with racial beliefs about the Indian population, including the superiority of the Brahmins, whom he saw as descendants of the ancient Aryan invaders, in the light of then prevalent but flawed historical views. Simultaneous with this first ever codification into secular law of Varna-based caste identities, communities (Jatis) sought to place themselves on higher levels of Varna categories. On the other hand, most of the Jatis grouped into the lower caste categories rejected the Varna categories, as they found this arbitrary classification unreasonable, unfair and unacceptable. This newly frozen materialisation of caste created a growing resentment firstly, against the system itself and secondly, against the Brahmins, who were seen as the beneficiaries of an arrangement which now officially anointed their place at the top of the social hierarchy. The revolt of the Justice Party and Periyar in the south, by the Maharaja of Kolhapur and Dr. Ambedkar in western India against this, in the early decades of the 20th century, has had a profound, long-lasting impact on the Indian society and politics, which continues to this day.

The British Colonial melding of the ubiquitous and fluid Jati with the theoretical and rigid Varna scheme starting from the 1901 census has resulted in a wide-spread belief that the entire Hindu society was organised according to the Varna scheme since ancient times. In fact, most of India's diverse population viewed the artificial and rigid scheme as unjust and arbitrary. Modern Indian society has been struggling with the flawed and rigid classification system that British colonial administration left it with.

Some activists, most prominently at the UN conference at Durban, have asserted that the caste is a form of racial discrimination. This view has been disputed by some sociologists such as Andre Béteille, who writes that treating caste as a form of racism is "politically mischievous" and worse, "scientifically nonsense" since there is no discernible difference in the racial characteristics between Brahmins and Scheduled Castes such as the Jatav. He writes that "Every social group cannot be regarded as a race simply because we want to protect it against prejudice and discrimination."

The Indian government, too, has denied the claims of equivalence between caste and racial discrimination, pointing out that the issues of social status is essentially intra-racial and intra-cultural. The view of the caste system as "static and unchanging" is disappearing as people learn to communicate better. The Indian government has been working towards creating equality between castes with affirmative action, such as guaranteed seats in educational institutions, government jobs (and promotions) and even in the Parliament for those of the Scheduled untouchable castes and tribes. Scholarships have also been available to all of these groups, so that they can go on to further education more easily and this has raised their social status. Sociologists describe how the perception of the caste system as a static and textual stratification has given way to the perception of the caste system as a more processional, empirical and contextual stratification. Others have applied theoretical models to explain mobility and flexibility in the caste system in India. According to these scholars, groups of lower-caste individuals could seek to elevate the status of their caste by attempting to emulate the practices of higher castes. The eminent socio-anthropologist M.N. Srinivas has also questioned the rigidity of caste and introduced the concept of Sanskritisation.

Varna

Early Indian texts like the Manusmriti and the Puranas speak of 'Varna,' which means order, type or colour. It groups the society into four main categories as follows: Brahmins (scholars, teachers, and priests); Kshatriyas (warriors, kings, and administrators); Vaishyas (agriculturists and merchants) and Shudras (artisans and service providers).

All others who did not subscribe to the norms of this Hindu society, including foreigners, tribals and nomads were called Mlechhas and even those who had been excommunicated were called "Anaryas" (non-Aryans), who were to be treated as contagious and untouchables. The fear of banishment from the society was seen as a powerful disincentive against violating its norms by its members. A late section of the Shanti Parva of the Mahabharata suggests an origin of this practice: "He who becomes harsh in speech or violent in temper, he who seduces or abducts other people's women or robs the wealth that belongs to others, should be cast off by us".

The hypothetical system provided each group with its own niche, and few individuals were left without a distinct role. According to the Varna system, Brahmins are enjoined to live in poverty and their primary vocation was to learn the Vedas, sacred texts and secular subjects, teach others and pray for the well-being of all. The Kshatriya's main occupation was martial skills, protection of civil society and governance. The Vaishyas were those occupied with trade and agrarian activities including cattle-raising, while the Sudras were other workers, craftsmen and service providers of all types. The reality of thousands of Jatis, which freely did what they pleased and had a variety of roles, was explained away as having been the outcome of mixing of Varnas, or 'Varna Sanskara'. All the Varnas were urged, without exception, to inculcate non-possessiveness, non-stealing, truthfulness, non-violence and benevolence. These too were the very attributes propounded by the Jain and Buddhist doctrines. It was believed that after death, people are reborn into a higher caste if they had led a moral life or a lower caste if they led an immoral life. Thus, it was thought that those, who served undesirable functions, like the untouchables, deserved their lot, because of their past Karma.

As the historian Romila Thapar has pointed out in her 'The Past and Prejudice': "The dynamic of Indian society was the juxtaposition of precept to practice, of the organisation of life as it should be, to the organisation of life as it is. For every aspect of life, from the most mundane to the most exhilarating, there was a theory of functioning which did not necessarily reflect the reality. The theory was the ideal image.....The resulting dichotomies were not forced into confrontation but were adjusted...Such adjustments seem easier in pre-industrial societies whose cultures invariably appear to be more gentle, meditative and less competitive, ...".

Although Brahmins have usually been described as the priestly class, this is not entirely accurate, as a temple priest need not have been a Brahmin, in fact, very few could have been, given the vast number of temples and the sparse population of Brahmins; however, the performers of a Vedic Yajna for others or a public Yajna fire sacrifice usually were Brahmins. All the Dvija (twice born), i.e., Brahmins, Kshatriyas and Vaishyas could and did perform the Homa fire sacrifice for themselves. Even this has not always been followed by all sects within Hinduism - for example, in the Arya Samaj, all castes including Shudras can perform the fire sacrifice. There were several categories among the Brahmins and temple priests were usually at the lower end of the Brahmin social scale. The ancient Greeks, e.g., Megasthenes in his Indika and the Muslims, e.g., Alberuni (1030 CE) described Brahmins as philosophers. Megasthenes calls them Brachmanes and characterises them thus:

"The philosophers are first in rank, but form the smallest class in point of number. Their services are employed privately by persons, who wish to offer sacrifices or perform other sacred rites, and also publicly by the kings at what is called the Great Synod, wherein at the beginning of the new year all the philosophers are gathered together before the king at the gates, when any philosopher who may have committed any useful suggestion to writing, or observed any means for improving the crops and the cattle, or for promoting the public interests, declares it publicly."

According to some researchers, by the 4th century AD, and certainly by the 7th century AD, there were people excluded from society altogether – the group of outcastes now referred to by themselves as Dalits or the "downtrodden." Thus, an untouchable, or an "outcaste", was a person who was deemed to not have any "Varna by those who claimed to possess it."

In any event, now in modern India, with rapid urbanisation and large scale migration, the ensuing crowded living arrangements and public transport, and the broad-based mix of workplace colleagues, there has been a significant change in social attitudes, more in the larger towns and certainly in the metros. Associations of occupations with caste have also been changing, especially as new occupations are developing.

Jatis

Professor Madhav Gadgil (1983), has described the reality of castes, which are called Jatis, in India, based on his research in rural Maharashtra: "The Indian society is even today an agglomeration of numerous castes, tribes and religious communities. The tribal and caste groups are endogamous, reproductively isolated populations traditionally distributed over a restricted geographical range. The different caste populations, unlike tribes, have extensive geographical overlap and members of several castes generally constitute the complex village society. In such a village society, each caste, traditionally self-regulated by a caste council, used to lead a relatively autonomous existence. Each caste used to pursue a hereditarily prescribed occupation; this was particularly true of the artisan and service castes and the pastoral and nomadic castes. The several castes were linked to each other through a traditionally determined barter of services and produce (Ghuye 1961, Karve 1961). These caste groups retained their identity even after conversion to Islam or Christianity. Each of the caste groups was, thus, the unit within which cultural and perhaps genetic evolution occurred, at least for the last 1500 years when the system was fully crystallised and probably much longer. Over this period, the various castes had come to exhibit striking differences in cultural traits like skills possessed, food habits, dress, language, religious observances as well as in a number of genetic traits."

In "A New History of India," Stanley Wolpert states, "a process of expansion, settled agricultural production and pluralistic integration of new people led to the development of India's uniquely complex system of social organisation by occupation....".

Under the Jati system, a person is born into a Jati with ascribed social roles and endogamy, i.e., marriages take place only within that Jati. The Jati provided identity, security and status and has historically been open to change based on economic, social and political influences. In the course of early Indian history, various tribal, economic, political and social factors led to a continuous closing, consolidation and variation in the prevailing social ranks which tended to become traditional, hereditary system of social structuring. This system of thousands of exclusive, endogamous groups is called Jati. Though there were several kinds of variations across the breadth of India, the Jati was the effective community within which one married and spent most of one's personal life. Often it was the community (Jati) which one turned to for support, for resolution of disputes and it was also the community which one sought to promote.

The Untouchables - Pariahs or Antyajas, were at the bottom of the social scale and even now perform the jobs nobody else wants such as disposal of corpses, night soil handling or execution of criminals. They lived in peripheries of the towns and villages and were not allowed to read holy books. It is, however, rather interesting that people of all Jatis across the spectrum, from the so-called upper castes to the lowest of castes, including the Untouchables, tended to avoid inter-marriage, sharing of food and drinks, or even close social interaction with a Jati other than their own. Indeed, for some of them, for example, the Tharu Boxas, even Brahmins were untouchable. Most of the Jati/castes did not see themselves as socially inferior to the others in any way. If at all, it was the other way round and most of them had folk narratives, traditions, myths and legends to bolster their sense of identity and cultural uniqueness.

An interesting perspective on ancient North Indian society is provided by the Greek Megasthenes, who, in his Indika, described the society as being made up of "seven classes":

"The whole population of India is divided into seven classes, of which the first is formed by the collective body of the Philosophers, which in point of number is inferior to the other classes, but in point of dignity pre-eminent over all. For the philosophers, being exempted from all public duties, are neither the masters nor the servants of others. They are, however, engaged by private persons to offer the sacrifices due in life-time, and to celebrate the obsequies of the dead: for they are believed to be most dear to the gods, and to be the most conversant with matters pertaining to Hades. In requital of such services they receive valuable gifts and privileges. To the people of India at large they also render great benefits, when, gathered together at the beginning of the year, they forewarn the assembled multitudes about droughts and wet weather, and also about propitious winds, and diseases, and other topics capable of profiting-the hearers. Thus, the people and the sovereign, learning beforehand what is to happen, always make adequate provision against a coming deficiency, and never fail to prepare beforehand what will help in a time of need. The philosopher, who errs in his predictions, incurs no other penalty than humiliation, and he then observes silence for the rest of his life."

The other classes are also described by Arrian, in The Anabasis Alexandrae, Book VIII: Indica (2nd c. CE) relying on the account of Megasthenes:

"Then next to these come the farmers, these being the most numerous class of Indians; they have no use for war-like arms or war-like deeds, but they till the land; and they pay the taxes to the kings and to the cities, such as are self-governing; and if there is internal war among the Indians, they may not touch these workers, and not even devastate the land itself; but some are making war and slaying all comers, and others close by are peacefully ploughing or gathering the fruits or shaking down apples or harvesting.

The third classes of Indians are the herdsmen, pastures of sheep and cattle, and these dwell neither by cities nor in the villages. They are nomads and get their living on the hillsides, and they pay taxes from their animals; they hunt also birds and wild animals in the country.

The fourth class is of artisans and shopkeepers; these are workers, and pay tribute from their works, save such as make weapons of war; these are paid by the community. In this class are the shipwrights and sailors, who navigate the rivers.

The fifth class of Indians is the soldiers' class, next after the farmers in number; these have the greatest freedom and the most spirit. They practice military pursuits only. Their weapons others forge for them, and again others provide horses; others to serve in the camps, those who groom their horses and polish their weapons, guide the elephants, and keep in order and drive the chariots. They themselves, when there is need of war, go to war, but in time of peace they make merry; and they receive so much pay from the community that they can easily from their pay support others.

The sixth classes of Indians are those called overseers. They oversee everything that goes on in the country or in the cities; and this they report to the king, where the Indians are governed by kings, or to the authorities, where they are independent. To these it is illegal to make any false report; nor was any Indian ever accused of such falsification.

The seventh class is those who deliberate about the community together with the king, or, in such cities as are self-governing, with the authorities. In number this class is small, but in wisdom and uprightness it bears the palm from all others; from this class are selected their governors, district governors and deputies, custodians of the treasures, officers of army and navy, financial officers and overseers of agricultural works.

The same man may not practise two pursuits; nor change from one class into another, as to turn farmer from shepherd, or shepherd from artisan. It is only permitted to join the wise-men out of any class; for their business is not an easy one, but of almost labourious."

Origin of Caste System in India

Several social thinkers, philosophers and scholars have tried to find out the origin of the Caste System in India. Several researchers have also been made but so far no definite and concrete proof is available on the basis of which the date of the origin of the caste-system may be enumerated or pointed out. Indian Caste System is very complicated.

Its complexity is evident from the fact that after a century of pains taping and meticulous research in the history of functions of social system, we do not process yet a valid expiation of the circumstances that might have contributed to the formation and development of this unique system.

In order to lie down or point out the origin of the caste-system, several theories have been advanced. Some of the important theories that try to establish the origin of the caste system are:

(1) Traditional theory, (2) Political theory, (3) Religious theory, (4) Occupational theory, (5) Evolutional theory, (6) Racial theory, (7) Cultural integration theory, and (8) Manu theory or theory of Manu.

Let us take all the theories one by one and discuss them a bit in detail:

(1) Traditional Theory

According to this theory, members of different castes were born out of different parts of the body of the original man Brahma, the creator of the universe. According to this theory, Brahmins were born out of mouth, Kshatriya out of the hands, Vaishyas out of stomach or things while the Sudras out of feet. According to the different functions of the body these castes have to perform the function accordingly.

This theory receives a classical interpretation in the account of Manu. His accounts rest on this assumption that the self-existent created Brahman, Kshatriya, Vaishya and Sudra from his mouth, arms, thighs and feet. According to this theory, after these castes, different sub-castes were born as a result of different types of marriages permitted in ancient India. The sub-castes are the results of different systems of the marriages.

(2) Political Theory

According to this theory, the caste system is the result of the political conspiracy of the Brahmins to earn superiormost places in the society and also have control over the functions of the society. This theory was originally pro-pounded by French scholar Nibey Dubais. Amongst Indian thinkers, Dr. Ghurey has also said something in support of this theory.

(3) Religious Theory

According to this theory, the caste system has grown out of religious customs; traditions, sanskars etc. In ancient India, the king or the ruler was recognised as the representative of the god and religion. Since, he was the representative of the religion; those who were connected with the religion were given higher position. Different people had to discharge different functions for the administration of the ruler. Those functions later on were responsible for origin and creation of different castes.

Supporters of this theory also put forward the view that caste system has grown out of the restriction on food habits taking food with different people and groups of people. Originally, there was no restrictions on taking food or inter-dining. People worship different gods and those who worship common god thought themselves to be the sons of common ancestors. Later on, worship of different gods to treat but with people, who worship some other god. This laid foundation for the Caste System.

(4) Occupational Theory

This theory was originally propounded by Nesfield, who said that occupation is the main base of the theory of the caste-system. Some of the occupations are considered superior while others are considered inferior and so, on the basis of the superiority and infirmity of these occupations, the followers of these occupations were considered superior and inferior.

As a result of this, caste-system was born. He has, in support of this theory that ancient Indian Brahmins alone do not come as Purohits. Kshatriyas also take to this task. All those who carried out functions of the Purohits were considered superior. As a result of the complications of the religion customs and traditions, Purohits had to take to specialisations. Thus all those, who knew this specialised takes were considered Brahmins and superior to others.

As the time is past, they organise themselves into a group and called themselves Brahmins. Similarly follows of other occupations also organised them into a group or a class and so the system of Caste or Caste System developed. Nesfield recognised functions as slow basis of Caste System.

(5) Evolutionary Theory

According to this theory, the caste system like other social institution has originated as a result of the process of the evolution. Originally the people were engaged in different occupations and they had their own organisational set up. Men of one occupation could take to another occupation. Later soon with this mortality was stopped and these occupational groups become closed groups. The Caste System came into being.

Denzil Ibtson has further pointed out that originally man laid a nomadic life. Latter on agriculture and there after the industry came into being exist. This group about the development of the economic life and the rural in order to purpose his economic policy had to divide the society into the various groups based on occupation. These groups on order to maintain their prestige and status, clashed with one another.

As a result of these structure, the class of the Purohits become vitreous and they not only established their supremacy but also established the practice of the endogamy other groups also followed suit and so different castes came into being.

(6) Racial Theory

It was Sir Herbert Roselyn, who for the first time in his book--The people of India, "propounded this theory, in which he has recognised the importance of the racial element. He has said that two factors, (a) Racial deficiencies, and (b) Endogamous marriage have been responsible for the development of the Caste System.

Different castes were born out of the mixture of these groups anti-classes. As a result of the struggle of different racial groups endogamous groups were born. They tried to maintain their racial and cultural purity and also maintain their unity. As a result of this, divine occupations were fixed for these different classes and later on the caste system developed.

(7) Cultural Integration Theory

According to this theory, Caste System is the result of the mingling and interaction process of mingling of the cultural characteristics. This theory was propounded by Professor S.C. Rai, who said that every race his own characteristics. In this respect, he pointed out that Indo-Aryans had the characteristics. In this respect, he pointed out that Indo-Aryans had the characteristics of born system and the concept of curve while Dravidians had the born-system and the pre-Dravidians had the characteristics of the concepts of the self. All these characteristics got influenced as a result of coming together of these races and some institution of caste system developed.

(8) Manu Theory or Theory of Manu

It was professor Hutton, an authority on the study of caste system who propounded this theory. According to professor Hutton, the caste system was present in India even before the Aryans came. Aryans made it more clear in putting themselves over the above everybody. He has further said that even today in India. There certain places where every village is an independent unit and all the inhabitants of that village follow the same occupation. This clearly proves that the caste system was present even before the Aryans came to this land.

In order to clarify the restrictions regarding the eating he took recourse to the theory of Manu. According to him, Manu is a power which is to be found in every object and which enters another person or object because of the contact or touch. It gives good as well as bad results.

That is why we suffer from the fear of touching or coming in contact with strangers. This feeling is present amongst the Nagas even today. Thus, according to Hutton, the main origin and development of the caste system is the occupational division and the feeling of the people to put certain restrictions on certain things.

These theories give the view of different scholars and social-thinkers in regard to the development of the caste system. In fact, caste system is not the result of one factor or two factors. Several factors are responsible for its origin and development. It is neither solely social nor religious. Similarly, it is neither based on occupational division nor on racial factors. As Hutton has pointed out, it is based on several factors.

It is urged that the Indian caste system is the natural result of the inter-action of a number of geographical, social, political, religious and economic factors not elsewhere found in conjunction.

History of the Caste System in India

Hindu scriptures

The most ancient scriptures-the Shruti texts, or Vedas, place very little importance on the caste system, mentioning caste only sparingly and descriptively (i.e., not prescriptive). Indeed, the only verse in the Rigveda which mentions all four varnas is 10.90, the Purushaskta. A hymn from the Rig Veda seems to indicate that one's caste is not necessarily determined by that of one's family:

Rig Veda 9.112.3

-I am a bard, my father is a physician, and my mother's job is to grind the corn.

In the Vedic period, there also seems to have been no discrimination against the Shudras on the issue of hearing the sacred words of the Vedas and fully participating in all religious rituals, something which became progressively restricted in the later times.

Later scriptures such as Bhagavad Gita and Manusmriti state that the four varnas are created by God. However, at the same time, the Gita says that one's varna is to be understood from one's personal qualities and one's karma (work), not one's birth. The Indian society honoured people on their achievements irrespective of their caste. For instance, Valmiki, once a low-caste robber, became a great sage and author of the epic Ramayana, Veda Vyasa, another respected sage and author of the monumental epic – the Mahabharata, was the son of a fisherwoman.

Manusmriti, dated between 200 BCE and 100 CE, contains some laws that codified the caste system. The Manusmriti belongs to a class of books that are geared towards ethics, morals, and social conduct - not spirituality or religion. In this text, the sage Manu explains that society is like the human body, where all body parts are required to function optimally in order to ensure the optimal function of society as a whole. He divided this metaphoric body into four main constituent parts: Head, Arms,

Torso, Legs. The head of a body is required for thinking, planning, and decision-making. Thus, the metaphoric head of society (the Brahmins) were also responsible for these things. The arms of a body are responsible for protection of the body. Thus, the arms of society were the Kshatriyas, who were responsible for protection of the society. The torso of the body is responsible for consumption, production, and to hold society together as a whole. Thus, the Vaishya class was likened to the torso and constituted of the peasants, farmers, merchants, etc. Finally, the legs of a body are what carry the entire body altogether without which the body can make no movement or progress. These legs are the hardest physically working part of the body. The Shudra class of labourers was likened to the legs and was responsible for most physical labour jobs.

The earliest expressions of caste can be found in one of India's vast bodies of religious scripture known as the Vedas, which are though to have been compiled between 1500 and 1000 BC, although the time of their composition is under debate. They were transmitted orally for many generations before being written down. Therefore, centuries may have passed before they were ever committed to writing.

These works are considered the source of ancient Indian wisdom. The first of the four basic Vedic books is the Rig Veda; a collection of over 1,000 hymns containing the basic mythology of the Aryan gods. The Rig Veda contains one of the most famous sections in ancient Indian literature in which the first man created, Purusa, is sacrificed in order to give rise to the four varnas.

It can be argued that the composers of the Vedas, especially those sections within the Vedas called the Brahmanas, were concerned with the inter-connections that organised reality (Smith, 7). This way of looking at the varnas allows us to see how such a system can survive several millennia. It classifies people not only in terms of their different qualities but also with respect to their different privileges. Each class, thus, has a special role to play in society as well as a unique function: this structure is a means of creating and organising an effective society.

The Varna system is inter-linked with creation, lending itself a great deal of reverence and validity. If space, time the congregation of the gods and goddesses, the natural world, scripture and ritual, and the human body itself, if all these realms bear classification according to Varna, how could an organisation of society be regarded as anything other than the way things should be? (Smith)

An important thing to note is that the Vedas do not mention a concept such as Untouchability. It is a part of the system that has been created by society itself.

Varna, Caste, and Other Divisions

Although many other nations are characterised by social inequality, perhaps nowhere else in the world has inequality been so elaborately constructed as in the Indian institution of caste? Caste has long existed in India, but in the modern period it has been severely criticised by both Indian and foreign observers. Although some educated Indians tell non-Indians that caste has been abolished or that "no one pays attention to caste anymore," such statements do not reflect reality.

Caste has undergone significant change since independence, but it still involves hundreds of millions of people. In its preamble, India's Constitution forbids negative public discrimination on the basis of caste. However, caste ranking and caste-based interaction have occurred for centuries and will continue to do so well into the foreseeable future, more in the countryside than in urban settings and more in the realms of kinship and marriage than in less personal interactions.

Castes are ranked, named, endogamous (in-marrying) groups, membership in which is achieved by birth. There are thousands of castes and sub-castes in India, and these large kinship-based groups are fundamental to South Asian social structure. Each caste is part of a locally-based system of interdependence with other groups, involving occupational specialisation, and is linked in complex ways with networks that stretch across regions and throughout the nation.

The word caste derives from the Portuguese 'casta', meaning breed, race, or kind. Among the Indian terms that are sometimes translated as caste are Varna, Jati, Jat, Biradri, and Samaj. All of these terms refer to ranked groups of various sizes and breadth. Varna, or colour, actually refers to large divisions that include various castes; the other terms include castes and sub-divisions of castes sometimes called sub-castes.

Many castes are traditionally associated with an occupation, such as high-ranking Brahmans; middle-ranking farmer and artisan groups, such as potters, barbers, and carpenters; and very low-ranking "Untouchable" leatherworkers, butchers, launderers, and latrine cleaners. There is some correlation between ritual rank on the caste hierarchy and economic prosperity. Members of higher-ranking castes tend, on the whole, to be more prosperous than members of lower-ranking castes. Many lower-caste people live in conditions of great poverty and social disadvantage.

According to the Rig Veda, sacred texts that date back to oral traditions of more than 3,000 years ago, progenitors of the four ranked Varna groups sprang from various parts of the body of the primordial man, which Brahma created from clay. Each group had a function in sustaining the life of society – the social body. Brahmans, or priests, were created from the mouth. They were to provide for the intellectual and spiritual needs of the community. Kshatriyas, warriors and rulers, were derived from the arms. Their role was to rule and to protect others. Vaishyas-landowners and merchants--sprang from the thighs, and were entrusted with the care of commerce and agriculture. Shudras-artisans and servants–came from the feet. Their task was to perform all manual labour.

Later conceptualised was a fifth category, "Untouchable" menials, relegated to carrying out very menial and polluting work related to bodily decay and dirt. Since 1935, "Untouchables" have been known as Scheduled Castes, referring to their listing on government rosters, or schedules. They are also often called by Mohandas Karamchand (Mahatma) Gandhi's term Harijans, or "Children of God." Although the term Untouchable appears in literature produced by these low-ranking castes, in the 1990s, many politically conscious members of these groups prefer to refer to themselves as Dalit, a Hindi word meaning oppressed or downtrodden. According to the 1991 census, there were 138 million Scheduled Caste members in India, approximately 16 per cent of the total population.

The first four Varnas apparently existed in the ancient Aryan society of northern India. Some historians say that these categories were originally somewhat fluid functional groups, not castes. A greater degree of fixity gradually developed, resulting in the complex ranking systems of medieval India that essentially continue in the late twentieth century.

Although a Varna is not a caste, when directly asked for their caste affiliation, particularly when the questioner is a Westerner, many Indians will reply with a Varna name. Pressed further, they may respond with a much more specific name of a caste, or jati, which falls within that varna. For example, a Brahman may specify that he is a member of a named caste group, such as a Jijotiya Brahman, or a Smartha Brahman, and so on. Within such castes, people may further belong to smaller sub-caste categories and to specific clans and lineages. These finer designations are particularly relevant when marriages are being arranged and often appear in newspaper matrimonial advertisements.

Members of a caste are typically spread out over a region, with representatives living in hundreds of settlements. In any small village, there may be representatives of a few or even a score or more castes.

Numerous groups usually called tribes (often referred to as Scheduled Tribes) are also integrated into the caste system to varying degrees. Some tribes live separately from others– particularly in the far north-east and in the forested center of the country, where tribes are more like ethnic groups than castes. Some tribes are themselves divided into groups similar to sub-castes. In regions where members of tribes live in peasant villages with non-tribal peoples, they are usually considered members of separate castes ranking low on the hierarchical scale.

Inequalities among castes are considered by the Hindu faithful to be part of the divinely ordained natural order and are expressed in terms of purity and pollution. Within a village, relative rank is most graphically expressed at a wedding or death feast, when all residents of the village are invited. At the home of a high-ranking caste member, food is prepared by a member of a caste from whom all can accept cooked food (usually by a Brahman). Diners are seated in lines; members of a single caste sit next to each other in a row, and members of other castes sit in perpendicular or parallel rows at some distance. Members of Dalit castes, such as leather-workers and sweepers, may be seated far from the other diners – even out in an alley. Farther away, at the edge of the feeding area, a Sweeper may wait with a large basket to receive discarded leavings tossed in by other diners. Eating food contaminated by contact with the saliva of others not of the same family is considered far too polluting to be practiced by members of any other castes. Generally, feasts and ceremonies given by Dalits are not attended by higher-ranking castes.

Among Muslims, although status differences prevail, brotherhood may be stressed. A Muslim feast usually includes a cloth laid either on clean ground or on a table, with all Muslims, rich and poor, dining from plates placed on the same cloth. Muslims who wish to provide hospitality to observant Hindus, however, must make separate arrangements for a high-caste Hindu cook and ritually pure foods and dining area.

Castes that fall within the top four ranked Varnas are sometimes referred to as the "clean castes," with Dalits considered "unclean." Castes of the top three ranked Varnas are often designated "twice-born," in reference to the ritual initiation undergone by male members, in which investiture with the Hindu sacred thread constitutes a kind of ritual rebirth. Non-Hindu caste like groups generally falls outside these designations.

Each caste is believed by devout Hindus to have its own dharma, or divinely ordained code of proper conduct. Accordingly, there is often a high-degree of tolerance for divergent lifestyles among different castes. Brahmans are usually expected to be non-violent and spiritual, according to their traditional roles as vegetarian teetotaller priests. Kshatriyas are supposed to be strong, as fighters and rulers should be, with a taste for aggression, eating meat, and drinking alcohol. Vaishyas are stereotyped as adept businessmen, in accord with their traditional activities in commerce. Shudras are often described by others as tolerably pleasant but expectably somewhat base in behaviour, whereas Dalits–especially Sweepers–are often regarded by others as followers of vulgar life-styles. Conversely, lower-caste people often view people of high rank as haughty and unfeeling.

The chastity of women is strongly related to caste status. Generally, the higher ranking the caste, the more sexual control its women are expected to exhibit. Brahman brides should be virginal, faithful to one husband and celibate in widowhood. By contrast, a Sweeper bride may or may not be a virgin, extramarital affair may be tolerated, and, if widowed or divorced, the woman is encouraged to remarry. For the higher castes, such control of female sexuality helps ensure purity of lineage of crucial importance to maintenance of high status. Among Muslims, too, high status is strongly correlated with female chastity.

Within castes explicit standards are maintained. Transgressions may be dealt with by a caste council, meeting periodically to adjudicate issues relevant to the caste. Such councils are usually formed of groups of elders, almost always males. Punishments such as fines and outcasting, either temporary or permanent, can be enforced. In rare cases, a person is excommunicated from the caste for gross infractions of caste rules. An example of such an infraction might be marrying or openly cohabiting with a mate of a caste lower than one's own; such behaviour would usually result in the higher-caste person dropping to the status of the lower-caste person.

Activities such as farming or trading can be carried out by anyone, but usually only members of the appropriate castes act as priests, barbers, potters, weavers, and other skilled artisans, whose occupational skills are handed down in families from one generation to another. As with other key features of Indian social structure, occupational specialisation is believed to be in accord with the divinely ordained order of the universe.

The existence of rigid ranking is supernaturally validated through the idea of rebirth according to a person's karma, the sum of an individual's deeds in this life and in past lives. After death, a person's life is judged by divine forces, and rebirth is assigned in a high or a low place, depending upon what is deserved. This supernatural sanction can never be neglected, because it brings a person to his or her position in the caste hierarchy, relevant to every transaction involving food or drink, speaking, or touching.

In past decades, Dalits in certain areas (especially in parts of the south) had to display extreme deference to high-status people, physically keeping their distance – lest their touch or even their shadow pollute others – wearing neither shoes nor any upper body covering (even for women) in the presence of the upper castes. The lowest-ranking had to jingle a little bell in warning of their polluting approach. In much of India, Dalits were prohibited from entering temples, using wells from which the "clean" castes drew their water, or even attending schools. In past centuries, dire punishments were prescribed for Dalits, who read or even heard sacred texts.

Such degrading discrimination was made illegal under legislation passed during British rule and was protested against by pre-independence reform movements led by Mahatma Gandhi and Bhimrao Ramji (B.R.) Ambedkar, a Dalit leader. Dalits agitated for the right to enter Hindu temples and to use village wells and effectively pressed for the enactment of stronger laws opposing disabilities imposed on them. After independence, Ambedkar almost single-handedly wrote India's Constitution, including key provisions barring caste-based discrimination.

Nonetheless, discriminatory treatment of Dalits remains a factor in daily life, especially in villages, as the end of the twentieth century approaches.

In modern times, as in the past, it is virtually impossible for an individual to raise his own status by falsely claiming to be a member of a higher-ranked caste. Such a ruse might work for a time in a place where the person is unknown, but no one would dine with or inter-marry with such a person or his offspring until the claim was validated through kinship networks. Rising on the ritual hierarchy can only be achieved by a caste as a group, over a long period of time, principally by adopting behaviour patterns of higher-ranked groups. This process, known as Sanskritisation, has been described by M.N. Srinivas and others. An example of such behaviour is that of some Leather-worker castes adopting a policy of not eating beef, in the hope that abstaining from the defiling practice of consuming the flesh of sacred bovines would enhance their castes' status. Increased economic prosperity for much of a caste greatly aids in the process of improving rank.

Genetic Analysis

There have been several DNA studies examining caste and tribal populations of India. These seek to discover, in part, if there are racial origins to the caste system. These studies have so far failed to achieve a consensus, possibly because of the developing nature of geno-typing science and technologies.

Several reports published between 1995 and 2005 propose that Indian tribal and caste population samples they studied, have similar genetic origins and have received limited gene input from outside India. These studies imply that racial differences may not have influenced caste system in India. Other reports, also published between 1995 and 2007 find that there was gene flow from many migratory populations. These studies propose that people migrated into India through north-west as well as north-east. Prior to these waves of human migrations, India had a settled native population. People in north-west India, as well as upper castes in other parts of India, share more genetic material with Central Asia, West Asia, and parts of Europe. People in northeast India share more genetic material with South-east Asia and East Asia. These genetic marker studies also find admixing between people and across castes were frequent and endogamy along caste lines may have been far less than what would be expected in a rigid caste system over thousands of years.

A 2009 article published in Nature finds strong evidence for at least two ancient populations in India, genetically divergent, that are Ancestral to most Indians today. One, the Ancestral North Indians, who are genetically close to Middle Easterners, Central Asians, and Europeans, whereas the other, the Ancestral South Indians, who are genetically distinct from Ancestral North Indians and East Asians as they are from each other. The study observes that genetic markers suggest endogamy within population clusters was prevalent in various Indian kingdoms over time. The report includes a novel method to estimate ancestry without accurate ancestral populations. With this method, the scientists show that Ancestral North Indians ancestry ranges from 39-71 per cent in most Indian groups, and is higher in traditionally upper caste and Indo-European language speakers. Groups with only Ancestral South Indians ancestry may no longer exist in mainland India due to genetic pool mixing. However, the indigenous Andaman Islanders are unique in being Ancestral South Indians-related groups without Ancestral North Indians ancestry. This study suggests that caste system in India may have some relationship to historical migration of diverse people into Indian sub-continent.

A 2010 review claims that there are at least four population groups in diverse India. Other than Ancestral North Indians and Ancestral South Indians, the population consists of Tibeto-Burman, Austro-Asiatic and Andamanese genetic pools suggesting human beings migrated into India from Africa, Eurasia, Tibet and Southeast Asia. The caste system in India is possibly a complex intra-group and inter-group admix of interactions between various population groups. The review paper notes that studies so far were based on small sample sets for the diversity in India. With the availability of new geno-typing technologies, future diversity studies encompassing a large number of populations, both tribals and castes, at the genome-wide level may help understand patterns of micro-evolution of populations in India.

Changes in the Caste System

Despite many problems, the caste system has operated successfully for centuries, providing goods and services to India's many millions of citizens. The system continues to operate, but changes are occurring. India's Constitution guarantees basic rights to all its citizens, including the right to equality and equal protection before the law. The practice of untouchability, as well as discrimination on the basis of caste, race, sex, or religion, has been legally abolished. All citizens have the right to vote, and political competition is lively. Voters from every stratum of society have formed interest groups, overlapping and cross-cutting castes, creating an evolving new style of integrating Indian society.

Castes themselves, however, far from being abolished, have certain rights under Indian law. As described by anthropologist Owen M. Lynch and other scholars, in the expanding political arena caste groups are becoming more politicised and forced to compete with other interest groups for social and economic benefits. In the growing cities, traditional inter-caste inter-dependencies are negligible.

Independent India has built on earlier British efforts to remedy problems suffered by Dalits by granting them some benefits of protective discrimination. Scheduled Castes are entitled to reserved electoral offices, reserved jobs in the Central and the State governments, and special educational benefits. The Constitution mandates that one-seventh of state and national legislative seats be reserved for members of Scheduled Castes in order to guarantee their voice in government. Reserving seats has proven useful because few, if any, Scheduled Caste candidates have ever been elected in non-reserved constituencies.

Educationally, Dalit students have benefitted from scholarships, and Scheduled Caste literacy increased (from 10.3 per cent in 1961 to 21.4 per cent in 1981, the last year for which such figures are available), although not as rapidly as among the general population. Improved access to education has resulted in the emergence of a substantial group of educated Dalits able to take up white-collar occupations and fight for their rights.

There has been tremendous resistance among non-Dalits to this protective discrimination for the Scheduled Castes, who constitute some 16 per cent of the total population, and efforts have been made to provide similar advantages to the so-called Backward Classes, who constitute an estimated 52 per cent of the population. In August 1990, Prime Minister Vishwanath Pratap (V.P.) Singh announced his intention to enforce the recommendations of the Backward Classes Commission (Mandal Commission), issued in December 1980, and largely ignored for a decade. The report, which urged special advantages for obtaining civil service positions and admission to higher education for the Backward Classes, resulted in riots and self-immolations and contributed to the fall of the prime minister. The upper castes have been particularly adamant against these policies because unemployment is a major problem in India, and many feel that they are being unjustly excluded from posts for which they are better qualified than lower-caste applicants.

As an act of protest, many Dalits have rejected Hinduism with its rigid ranking system. Following the example of their revered leader, Dr. Ambedkar, who converted to Buddhism four years before his death in 1956, millions of Dalits have embraced the faith of the Buddha. Over the past few centuries, many Dalits have also converted to Christianity and have often by this means raised their socio-economic status. However, Christians of Dalit origin still often suffer from discrimination by Christians–and others–of higher caste backgrounds.

Despite improvements in some aspects of Dalit status, 90 per cent of them live in rural areas in the mid-1990s, where an increasing proportion--more than 50 per cent--work as landless agricultural labourers. State and national governments have attempted to secure more just distribution of land by creating land ceilings and abolishing absentee landlordism, but evasive tactics by landowners have successfully prevented more than minimal redistribution of land to tenant farmers and labourers. In contemporary India, field hands face increased competition from tractors and harvesting machines. Similarly, artisans are being challenged by expanding commercial markets in mass-produced factory goods, undercutting traditional mutual obligations between patrons and clients. The spread of the Green Revolution has tended to increase the gap between the prosperous and the poor--most of whom are low-caste.

The growth of urbanisation (an estimated 26 per cent of the population now lives in cities) is having a far-reaching effect on caste practices, not only in cities but in villages. Among anonymous crowds in urban public spaces and on public transportation, caste affiliations are unknown, and observance of purity and pollution rules is negligible. Distinctive caste costumes have all but vanished, and low-caste names have been modified, although castes remain endogamous, and access to employment often occurs through intra-caste connections. Restrictions on interactions with other castes are becoming more relaxed, and, at the same time, observance of other pollution rules is declining -- especially those concerning birth, death, and menstruation. Several growing Hindu sects draw members from many castes and regions, and communication between cities and villages is expanding dramatically. Kin in town and country visit one another frequently, and television programmes available to huge numbers of villagers vividly portray new lifestyles. As new occupations open up in urban areas, the correlation of caste with occupation is declining.

Caste associations have expanded their areas of concern beyond traditional elite emulation and local politics into the wider political arenas of state and national politics. Finding power in numbers within India's democratic system, caste groups are pulling together closely allied sub-castes in their quest for political influence. In efforts to solidify caste bonds, some caste associations have organised marriage fairs where families can make matches for their children. Traditional hierarchical concerns are being minimised in favour of strengthening horizontal unity. Thus, while pollution observances are declining, caste consciousness is not.

Education and election to political office have advanced the status of many Dalits, but the overall picture remains one of great inequity. In recent decades, Dalit anger has been expressed in writings, demonstrations, strikes, and the activities of such groups as the Dalit Panthers, a radical political party demanding revolutionary change. A wider Dalit movement, including political parties, educational activities, self-help centres, and labour organisations, has spread too many areas of the country.

In a 1982 Dalit publication, Dilip Hiro wrote, "It is one of the great modern Indian tragedies and dangers that even well-meaning Indians still find it so difficult to accept Untouchable mobility as being legitimate in fact as well as in theory. . . ." Still, against all odds, a small intelligentsia has worked for many years toward the goal of freeing India of caste consciousness.

Other Backward Classes (OBCs)

Backwardness is expressed in lack of adequate opportunity for group and individual self-development, especially in economic life and in matters of health, housing and education. It is measured in terms of low levels of income, the extent of illiteracy, and the low standard of life demonstrated by living conditions. In the Constitution, Other Backward Classes are described as "socially and educationally backward class".

The population of the Scheduled Castes in India is 498 lakhs. This figure does not include backward groups which are not mentioned in the schedule. Such groups are known as "other backward class" and their population, according to the Ministry of Education Scholarship Board, was 546 lakhs in 1951. Article 340 of the Constitution has empowered the President to appoint a commission to determine the conditions of backward groups not included in the schedule of castes, who could be considered to be socially, economically and educationally backward. This Commission is known as the Backward Class Commission and one of its functions was to prepare a schedule of Other Backward Classes for the approval of the President.

The first Backward Classes Commission was set up by a presidential order on January 29, 1953 under the chairmanship of Kaka Kalelkar. The commission submitted its report on March 30, 1955. It had prepared a list of 2,399 backward castes or communities for the entire country and of which 837 had been classified as the "most backward". There was considerable divergence of opinion among the members of the commission as to what should be the criteria of backwardness. The commission in its final report recommended "caste as the criteria" to determine backwardness. But, this report was not accepted by the government as it feared that the Backward Classes excluded from the caste and communities selected by the commission may not be considered and the really needy would be swamped by the multitude and would hardly receive special attention. Thus, there was a need of second Backward Classes Commission. The second Backward Classes Commission was set up by the President on January 1, 1979. The commission is popularly known as the Mandal Commission, its chairman being B.P. Mandal. It submitted the report in December 1980. The terms of reference for the commission were: to determine the criteria for defining the socially and educationally backward classes, to recommend the steps to be taken for their advancement, to examine the desirability or otherwise for making any provision for the reservation of appointments or posts in their favour; and to present a report setting out the facts found by the commission.

The Mandal Commission covered more than 3000 castes under Other Backward Class (OBC) Category, regardless of their affluence or economic status and stated that OBCs form around 52 per cent of the Indian population. However, the National Sample Survey puts the figure at 32 per cent. There is substantial debate over the exact number of OBCs in India; it is generally estimated to be sizeable, but many believe that it is lower than the figures quoted by either the Mandal Commission or the National Sample Survey.

The caste-based reservations in India have led to widespread protests, such as the 2006 Indian anti-reservation protests, with many complaining of reverse discrimination against the forward castes (the castes that do not qualify for the reservation).

In May of 2011, the government approved a caste census with the intention of verifying the claims and counter-claims by various sections of the society about their actual numbers. The census would also help the government to re-examine and possibly undo some of the policies which were formed in haste like Mandal Commission and bring more objectivity to the policies with respect to contemporary realities. Critics of the reservation system believe that there is actually no social stigma at all associated with belonging to a backward caste and that because of the huge constitutional incentives in the form of educational and job reservations, a large number of people will falsely identify with a backward caste to receive the benefits. This would not only result in a marked inflation of the backward castes' numbers, but also lead to enormous administrative and judicial resources being devoted to social unrest and litigation when such dubious caste declarations are challenged.

The Mandal Commission was established in 1979 to "identify the socially or educationally backward" and to consider the question of seat reservations and quotas for people to redress caste discrimination. In 1980, the commission's report affirmed the affirmative action practice under Indian law, whereby additional members of lower castes-the other backward classes-were given exclusive access to another 27 per cent of government jobs and slots in public universities, in addition to the 23 per cent already reserved for the Dalits and Tribals. When V.P. Singh's administration tried to implement the recommendations of the Mandal Commission in 1989, massive protests were held in the country. Many alleged that the politicians were trying to cash in on caste-based reservations for their vested interests and vote-bank politics.

Many political parties in India have indulged in caste-based vote bank politics. Parties such as Bahujan Samaj Party (BSP), the Samajwadi Party and the Janata Dal claim that they are representing the Backward Castes, and rely on OBC support, often in alliance with Dalit and Muslim support, to win elections. Remarkably, in what is called a landmark election in the history of India's most populated state of Uttar Pradesh, the Bahujan Samaj Party was able to garner a majority in the State Assembly elections with the support of the high caste Brahmin community.

Kaka Kalelkar Commission

It was in the pathogenic environment of Indian State trying to consolidate its political legitimacy through pragmatic coalition on the one hand, and project its ideological credential on the other that the first Backward Classes Commission was set-up in 1953 under provision of Article 340 of the Constitution of India with Kaka Kalelkar as its Chairman, comprised the following members:

1.	Kakasaheb Kalelkar, M.P.	Chairman
2.	N.S. Kajrolkar	M.P.
3.	Bheekha Bhai	M.P.
4.	Shivdayal Singh Chaurasia	
5.	Rajeshwar Patel	M.P.
6.	Abdul Qaiyum Ansari, (Bihar)	M.L.A.
7.	T. Mariappa, (Mysore)	M.L.A.
8.	Atma Singh Namdhari	M.P.
9.	Lala Jagannath	
10.	N.R.M. Swamy	M.P.
11.	Arunangshu De	Member-Secretary

The terms of reference of the Commission as laid down in the notification announced by the Ministry of Home Affairs on 29th January 1953 were as follows:

(a) Determine the criteria to be adopted to considering whether any sections of the people in territory of India (in addition to the Scheduled Castes and Scheduled Tribes specified by notifications issued under Articles 341 and 342 of the Constitution), should be treated as socially and educationally backward classes; and, in accordance with such criteria, prepare a list of such classes setting down also their approximate numbers and their territorial distribution.

(b) Investigate the conditions of all such socially and educationally Backward Classes and the difficulties under which they labour; and make recommendations: (i) as to the steps that should be taken by the union or any state to remove such difficulties or to improve their condition; and (ii) as to the grants that should be made for the purpose by the Union or any State and the conditions subject to which, such grants should be made.

(c) Investigate such other matters as the President may hereafter refer to them; and

(d) Present to the President a report setting out the facts as found by them and making such recommendations as they think proper.

On 18th March 1953, the President of India inaugurated the Commission. Speaking on the occasion both the President and the Prime Minister expressed the hope that the labours of the Commission would pave the way for a classless society in the country. The Prime Minister disliked the term 'backward classes' and remarked that it was basically wrong to label any section of the people as backward even if they were so, particularly when 90 per cent of the people in the country were poor and backward. (1st BCC, 1955, p. 3).

The first Backward Classes Commission formulated the following criteria for identifying socially and educationally backward classes: (1) Low social position in the traditional caste hierarchy of Hindu society, (2) Lack of general educational advancement among the major section of a caste or community, (3) Inadequate or no representation in government service, (4) Inadequate representation in the field of trade, commerce and industry.

The Commission worked for about two years and submitted a three volumes report to the President of India on 30th March 1955. It prepared a list of 2399 backward castes or communities for the entire country and 837 of these were classified as most backward. The Registrar General and Census Commissioner of India assigned the commission in making population projections of 930 backward castes and communities. The Census Commissioner provided two sets of figures. One was that of the communities included in the list, who were not published. They constituted 19.9 per cent of the total population in 1951. There were several castes and communities listed by Kalelkar Commission which were not enumerated in 1951, but for which information was available in the earlier censuses. The Census Commissioner also made an estimation of each such caste based on the data available in 1911, 1921 and 1931 censuses. The aggregate of such estimated population came up to 20.5 per cent of the total population of the country. Kalelkar Commission however got an estimation done on its own by taking into consideration names of castes which did not find mention even in earlier censuses. According to the estimate the socially and educationally Backward Classes constituted 31.8 per cent of the total population if the Ezavas of Travancore were not included and 32.28 per cent if the latter were also included.

The estimation made by Kalelkar Commission is however questionable, as the report does not give any indication of how in the absence of any data they could estimate the numerical strength of various castes and communities. A careful examination of the list shows that many of them are surnames, sub-caste names of castes and communities, some of which are related to many castes. For instance in West Bengal the surname Ghosh is found among many castes including the non-Brahman higher castes, but Kalelkar Commission has treated them as SEBC.

The recommendations of the Kalelkar commission for the uplift of the Backward Classes are extremely wide-ranging and comprehensive. They cover such diverse fields as: Extensive land reforms, Reorganisation of village economy, Bhoodan Movement, Development of livestock, Dairy farming, Cattle insurance, Bee-keeping, Piggery, Fisheries, Development of rural and cottage industries, Rural housing, Public health and rural water supply, Adult literacy, University education, Representation of Backward Classes in government services, etc.

Kalelkar Commission recommended reservation of 70 per cent seats in all technical and professional institutions for qualified students of Backward Classes and also minimum reservation of vacancies in all government services and local bodies for others, Backward Classes on the following scale: Class I-25 per cent, Class-II 33.5 per cent, Class-III and IV-40 per cent.

Apart from all this, the Commission's work was marked by utter confusion and dissent. On almost every crucial issue, its members spoke in different voices. For example, three of them Dr. Anup Singh, Arunangshu De and P.G. Shah did not agree that caste should determine the backwardness of the people and opposed the reservation of posts on its basis. On the other hand, one member S.D.S. Chaurasia made a forceful argument, in his 67-page note, for including the caste criterion for both these things. Yet, another member T. Mariappa was concerned only with the inclusion of a couple of castes in the list of other backward classes. Kaka Kalelkar, took rather equivocal stand on the issue though he did not give a formal minute of dissent. While forwarding the report, he expressed his reservations regarding several recommendations and opposed caste as a basis of backwardness.

Critically speaking, the Commission's identification of the OBCs was faulty. It no doubt modified the Education Ministry's original lists of the 'OBCs' in the light of the facts collected by it. But the fact remains that it broadly adopted the lists of Other Educationally Backward Classes prepared by another agency for an entirely different objective passed it on as the list socially and educationally Backward Classes of India. This was done without undertaking any field survey to check their validity for the purpose of the Commission. Nor were they examined against the criteria evolved by the Commission for identifying socially and educationally backward classes. Thus, there was a need of second Backward Classes of Commission.

Mandal Commission

The Congress Party ruled the country for more than twenty five years after the Constitution of India came into existence on 26th January, 1950. During this period the Congress government at Centre appointed the First Commission for Backward Classes, the report of which was not accepted by them having absolute majority in both Houses of the Parliament. Both Prime Minister Jawahar Lal Nehru and Indira Gandhi were powerful leaders but they realised and felt pulse and heat of the public and kept the report in cold storage. After emergency era was over the Janata Party, first non-Congress government came into power at centre. During the Janata Party rule, on 20th December, 1978, the then Prime Minister, Morarji Desai in Parliament announced the decision to appoint a commission for the Backward Classes under the chairmanship of B.P. Mandal. Accordingly, in exercise of the powers conferred by Article 340 of the Constitution, the President of India appointed a Commission for the Backward Classes to investigate the conditions of socially and educationally Backward Classes within the territory of India. The composition of the Commission was as follows:

1.	B.P. Mandal (Ex-M.P.)	Chairman
2.	R.R. Bhole, M.P.	Member
3.	L.R. Naik (Ex-M.P.)	Member
4.	Dewan Mohan Lal	Member
5.	K. Subramanium	Members, and
6.	S. S. Gill	Secretary

The Chairman and the members were appointed on part-time basis and worked in an honourary capacity. The terms of reference of the Commission were:

• to determine the criteria for defining the socially and educationally backward classes;

• to recommend steps to be taken for the advancement of the socially and educationally Backward Classes of citizens so identified;

• to examine the desirability or otherwise of making provisions for the reservation of appointments or posts in favour of such Backward Classes of citizens which are not adequately represented in public services and posts in connection with the affairs of the Union or of any State; and

• present to the President a report setting out the facts as found by them and making such recommendations as they think proper.

In this connection, the Commission was also to examine the recommendations of the Backward Classes Commission appointed earlier under the Chairmanship of Kaka Kalelkar and the considerations which stood in the way of the acceptance of its recommendations by Government.

Criteria for Social and Educational Backwardness

The Commission evolved eleven indicators or criteria for determining social and educational backwardness. These eleven indicators were grouped under three broad heads, i.e., social, educational, and economical. These are as follows:

(A) Social

(i) Castes/Classes considered as socially backward by others.

(ii) Castes/Classes which mainly depend on manual labour for their livelihood.

(iii) Castes/Classes where at least 25 per cent females and 10 per cent males above the State average got married at an age below 17 years in rural areas and at least 10 per cent females and five per cent males do so in urban areas.

(iv) Castes/Classes where participation of females in work is at least 25 per cent above the State average.

(B) Education

(v) Castes/Classes where the number of children in the age group of 5-25 years, who never attended school is at least 25 per cent above the State average.

(vi) Castes/Classes where the rate of student dropout in the age group of 5-15 years is at least 25 per cent above the state average.

(vii) Castes/Classes amongst whom the proportion of matriculates is at least 25 per cent below the State average.

(C) Economic

(viii) Castes/Classes where the average value of family assets is at least 25 per cent below the State average.

(ix) Castes/Classes where the number of families living in Kutcha house is at least 25 per cent above the State average.

(x) Castes/Classes where the source of drinking water is beyond half a kilometre for more than 50 per cent of the households.

(xi) Castes/Classes where the number of households having taken consumption loan is at least 25 per cent above the State average.

As the three groups are not of equal importance for the purpose separate weightage was given to indicators in each group. As the social indicators were given a weightage of three points each, educational indicators a weightage of two points each and economic indicators a weightage of one point each. Economic, in addition to social and educational indicators, were considered important as they directly flowed from social and educational backwardness. This also helped to highlights the fact that socially and educationally Backward Classes are economically backward also. It will be seen that from the values given to each indicators, the total score adds up to 22. All these eleven indicators were applied to all castes covered by the survey for a particular State.

As a result of this application all castes which had a score of 50 per cent (11 points) for above were listed as socially and educationally backward and the rest were treated as advanced. Further, in case the numbers of households covered by the survey for any particular caste were below 20, it was left out of consideration, as the sample was considered too small for any dependable inference.

The above system of listing castes as socially and educationally backward on the basis of their score may appear somewhat arbitrary. On the face of it, this is a tangible viewpoint. On the other hand, the points scored by a particular caste under the above system actually reflect the number of indicators of backwardness which it satisfies. Secondly, this method has the great merit of objectivity as point systems allow no subjective assessment. Thirdly, this method was found to be highly dependable in practice. For instance, as a result of its application, most of the well-known socially and educationally backward castes were identified as backward.

B.K. Roy Burman (1992), was associated as an expert social science member in the Second Backward Classes Commission headed by B.P. Mandal. He critically reviewed the report. He found many deficiencies in the report. Some of which are listed here:

(i) The Mandal Commission did not make any analysis of the social and political process in the Indian Society and the Indian state, which stood in the way of acceptance of Kalelkar Commission's recommendations by the Central Government in the matter of recognition of SEBC's on the basis of caste.

(ii) He found that the commission compared facts with incomparable facts. For example, the practice of recording the caste in service had been discontinued by 1951. Then, level of education achieved by father or grandfather of the respondent was not recorded. Then how was it possible for the commission to arrive at the conclusion that the particular employee in service belonged to socially and educationally backward and included in the category of OBCs.

(iii) The commission's claim of scrutiny of village monographs have been reputed by Kalla (1990), of Department of Anthropology, University of Delhi, Delhi on the ground that there was no such monograph as mentioned in the Report.

Without any doubt, acceptance of the Mandal Commission recommendation of 27 per cent reservation of jobs in the Central Government and public undertakings for the backward castes is impossible to give peace to any government at the Centre. Job reservation is bound to create a host of problems continually. Some of them would be: (1) To qualify for the 'backward caste' concessions, the government may require a certificate, which is not very difficult to obtain. (2) The Mandal Commission has categorised as many as 3,743 castes as backward in contrast to 2,399 identified by the Kalelkar Commission (1953). Despite this dose of extravagant generosity, more and more castes would clamour for inclusion in the beneficiaries' list, and this would generate unending clash in society. (3) As the backward castes themselves are not homogeneous socially, economically and educationally, most jobs would inevitably be hogged by a few castes – more accurately the elite among the better placed. A demand for fixation of sub-quotas for each caste or cluster of backward castes is likely to be made under the name of true social justice.

Obviously, it is not respect for the sanctity of law, but undaunted rush on the part of the capitalist farmers, (the core of which is constituted by the intermediate castes in many parts of the country) to seize the administrative power in the political amphitheatre, where, as analysed earlier, state-orientation and society-orientation in political orders were at loggerheads for quite some time, and where observations in the functioning of the statist apparatus had brought about a coalition of forces under the cover of anarcho-syndicalist neo-Gandhian ideology. Mandal Commission was constituted when this coalition gained the upper hand, but before it could complete its task, the statist platform led by Indira Gandhi came back to power. Mandal Commission submitted its report in December 1980, and after its formal presentation to the Parliament in 1982, was shelved.

National Commission of Other Backward Classes

The government is enjoined to ensure social and educational development of Backward Classes. Until 1985, the affairs of Backward Classes were looked after by the Backward Classes Cell (BCC) in the Ministry of Home Affairs. With the creation of separate Ministry of Welfare in 1985 renamed as Ministry of Social Justice and Empowerment on 25th May, 1998, the matters relating to Scheduled Castes, Scheduled Tribes, Other Backward Classes and Minorities were transferred to the new Ministry. The Backward Classes Division in the Ministry looks after the policy, planning and implementation of programmes relating to social and economic empowerment of OBCs. It also looks after matters relating to two institutions set up for the welfare of OBCs: National Backward Classes Finance, and Development Corporation and the National Commission for Backward Classes. The National Commission for Backward Classes is an Indian statutory body established on 14th August 1993, under the provisions of National Commission for Backward Classes Act, 1993 (Act No. 27 of 1993). The Commission was the outcome of the direction of the Supreme Court in the Mandal case judgment. The commission has five members: a chairperson who is or has been a judge of the Supreme Court or of a High Court; a social scientist; two persons, who have special knowledge in matters relating to backward classes; and a Member-Secretary, who is or has been an officer of the Central Government in the rank of a Secretary to the Government of India. Their term is of three years. The main function of the Commission is to include in and exclude from the lists of communities notified as backward for the purpose of job reservations and tenders the needful advice to the Central Government. The National Commission for Other Backward Classes, after studying the criteria/indicators framed by the Mandal Commission and the commissions set up in the past by different state Governments and other relevant materials, formulated the following guidelines for considering requests for inclusion in the list of Other Backward Classes:

(A) SOCIAL

1. Castes and communities generally considered as socially backward.

(a) Castes and communities, which mainly depend on agricultural and/or other manual labour for their livelihood and are lacking any significant resource base.

(b) Castes and communities, which, for their livelihood, mainly depend on agricultural and/or other manual labour for wage and are lacking any significant base.

(c) Castes and communities, the women of which, as a general practice, are for their family's livelihood, engaged in agricultural and/or other manual labour, for wage.

(d) Castes and communities, the children of which, as a general practice, are, for family's livelihood or for supplementing family's low income, mainly engaged in agricultural and/or manual labour.

(e) Castes and communities, which in terms of caste system, are identified with traditional crafts or traditional or hereditary occupations considered to be lowly or undinified.

(f) Castes and communities, which in terms of the caste system, are identified with traditional or hereditary occupations considered to be 'unclean' or stigmatised.

(g) Nomadic and semi-nomadic castes and communities.

(h) Denotified or Vimukta Jati castes and communities.

Explanation: The term refers to castes/communities which had been categorised as Criminal Tribes under the Criminal Tribes Act, 1924, Act No. VI of 1924 passed by the Indian Legislature and repealed by the Criminal Tribes (Repeal) Act, 1952, Act No. XXIV of 1952, and subsequently refered to as Denotified or Vimukta Jatis.

2. Castes and communities, having no representation or poor representation in the State Legislative Assembly and/or district-level Panchayati Raj institutions during the ten years preceding the date of the application

Explanation: This is only intended to measure, as an indicator, the presence of a caste or community in these bodies.

The term "poor representation" may be taken to refer to a caste or community whose presence in the body is less than 25 per cent of its proportion in the population.

(B) EDUCATIONAL

1. Castes and communities, whose literacy rate is at least eight per cent less than the State or district average.

2. Castes and communities of which the proportion of matriculates is at least 20 per cent less than the State or district average.

3. Castes and communities, of which the proportion of graduates is at least 20 per cent less than the State or district average.

(C) ECONOMIC

1. Castes and communities in a significant proportion of whose members reside only in *Kachha* houses.

2. Castes and communities, the share of whose members in number of cases and in extent of agricultural lands surrendered under the Agricultural Land Ceiling Act of the State, is nil or significantly low.

3. Castes and communities, the share of whose members in State Government posts and services of Group A and B/Classes I and II, is not equal to the population-equivalent proportion of the caste/community.

References

Ambedkar, B.R. (1935). "The Untouchables, Who were they and why they become Untouchables?" http://www.ambedkar.org/.

"Annual Report, 2007-2008". National Commission for Backward Classes, Government of India. 2009. http://www.ncbc.nic.in/Pdf/annual.pdf.

Ambedkar, B.R. (1946). The Untouchables: Who were they and why they became Untouchables? As reprinted in Volume 7 of Dr Babasaheb Ambedkar Writings and Speeches, published by Government of Maharashtra 1990; Complete Writings.

Ambedkar, B.R. (1946), who were the *Shudras*.

Atal, Yogesh (1968), "The Changing Frontiers of Caste" Delhi, National Publishing House, 1968.

Atal, Yogesh, "Changing Indian Society" Chapter on *Varna* and *Jati*. Jaipur, Rawat Publications, 2006.

Austin, Granville, the Indian Constitution: Corner Stone of a Nation, Oxford, 1966, p. 50.

Baines, Jervoise Athelstane (1893). General report on the Census of India, 1891, London, Her Majesty's Stationery Office.

Blunt, E.A.H. (1931). The Caste System of Northern India, republished 1964, S. Chand & Co., Delhi.

Bayly, Susan. Caste, Society and Politics in India from the Eighteenth Century to the Modern Age. Cambridge University Press, 1999.

Burman, B.K. Roy, Beyond Mandal and After – Backward Classes in Perspective, Mittal Publications, New Delhi, 1992.

Baldev Upadhyaya, *Kashi Ki Panditya Parampara,* Sharda Sansthan, Varanasi, 1985.

Constituent Assembly Debates, Vol. VII, Government of India (New Delhi), 1947, pp. 696-97.

"Constitution of India". Ministry of Law, Government of India. http://lawmin.nic.in/olwing/coi/coi-english/coi-indexenglish.htm. Retrieved 2012.

Dumont, Louis. Homo Hierarchicus: The Caste System and Its Implications. Complete English edition, revised. 540 p. 1970, 1980 Series: (Nature of Human Society).

E.A.H. Blunt, The Caste System of North India, first edition in 1931 by Oxford University Press, new edition by S. Chand Publishers, 1969.

"Early Evidence for Caste in South India," pp. 467-492 in Dimensions of Social Life: Essays in Honour of David G. Mandelbaum, Edited by Paul Hockings and Mouton de Gruyter, Berlin, New York, Amsterdam, 1987.

Genetic Evidence on the Origins of Indian Caste Populations — Bamshad *et al.* 11 (6): 994. Genome Research.

Ghurye, G.S., Caste and Race in India, Popular Prakashan, Mumbai, 1969 (1932).

Galanter, Marc, Competing Equalities: Law and Backward Classes in India, Oxford (New Delhi), 1984, p. 159.

Galanter, Marc. "Who are the OBCs? An introduction to a Constitutional Puzzle", EPW, 1978.

Ghosh, Partha S. "Positive discrimination in India: A Political Analysis", Ethnic Studies Report, Vol. XV No. 2, July 1997.

Jogendra Nath Bhattacharya, Hindu Castes and Sects, Munshiram Manoharlal, Delhi, first edition 1896, new edition 1995.

Kamble, J.R., Rise and Awakenning of Depressed Classes in India, National Publisher, New Delhi, 1979, pp. 67-68.

Kane, Pandurang Vaman: History of Dharmasastra: (ancient and mediaeval, religious and civil law) — Poona: Bhandarkar Oriental Research Institute, 1962–1975.

Lal, K.S. Growth of Scheduled Tribes and Castes in Medieval India (1995).

Lata Sinha, origin of caste system of India, Just another worldpress.com.

Mathur, M.L., Encyclopaedia of Backward Castes (In 4 Volumes), Reservation (Volume 1), Kalpaz Publications, Delhi, 2004.

Mathur, M.L., Encyclopaedia of Backward Castes (In 4 Volumes) (Judgments: Before and After Mandal Judgment, Volume 4), Kalpaz Publications, Delhi, 2004.

Mathur, M.L., Encyclopaedia of Backward Castes (In 4 Volumes), Commissions (Vol. 2), Kalpaz Publications, Delhi, 2004.

Murray Milner, Jr., Status and Sacredness: A General Theory of Status Relations and an Analysis of Indian Culture, New York: Oxford University Press, 1994.

Mathur, M.L., Encyclopaedia of Backward Castes (In 4 Volumes), Reservation (Volume 1), Kalpaz Publications, New Delhi, 2004.

Michaels, Axel, Hinduism: Past and Present 188-97 (Princeton 2004) ISBN 0-691-08953-1.

M.N. Srinivas, Social Change in Modern India, Orient Longman, Delhi, 1995.

Mookherjee, Dulal, the Essence of Bhagavad Gita. Academic Publishers, 2002, p. 472. ISBN 978-81-87504-40-5.

Mishra, R.G. and Kaur, Gurvinder, Reservation Policy and Personnel Selection, Uppal Publishing House, New Delhi, 1990, p. 14.

National Front: Lok Sabha Election Manifesto, 1989, p. 36.

OBC Quota Law held valid, News Panorama of India and World (pages no. 18-19), Vol. 20, No. 8, June, 2008.

Padhy, K.S. and Mahapatra, Jayashree, "Reservation Policy in India", Ashish Publishing House, New Delhi, 1985.

Panandiker, V.A. Pai, (ed.), The Politics of Backwardness, Reservation Policy in India, Konark Publishers Pvt. Ltd., Delhi.

Prasad, A., Reservational Justice to OBCs, Theoretical and Practical Issues", Deep and Deep Publications, New Delhi, 1997.

Padhy, K. S. and Mahapatra, Jayashree, Reservation Policy in India, Ashish Publishing House, New Delhi, 1988, p. 17.

"Profile: Mayawati Kumari". BBC News. 16th July 2009. http://news.bbc.co.uk/2/hi/1958378.stm.

Radha Krishnan, P., Job Quotas in the Private Sectors", *EPW*, Oct. 2, 2004.

Sharma, Dr Shish Ram, Protective Discrimination – Other Backward Classes in India, Raj Publications, Delhi, 2002.

Srinivas, M.N., Religion and Society among the Coorgs of South India, p. 32 (Oxford, 1952).

Susan Bayly - Saints, Goddesses and Kings: Muslims and Christians in South Indian Society, pp. 243-253, Cambridge University Press, 2004, ISBN 0-521-89103-5 [2].

Singer and Cohn, Structure and Change in Indian Society. Aldine Publishing Co., 2007, ISBN 978-0-202-36138-3.

Swami Sahajanand Saraswati Rachnawali (Selected works of Swami Sahajanand Saraswati), Prakashan Sansthan, Delhi, 2003.

Second Backward Classes Commission, 1980, p. 2.

The Constitution of India, Ministry of Law and Justice, Delhi Controller of Publications, New Delhi, 1986, p. 14.

Vidyasagar, R. and Suresh V., "Backward Classes and Reservation", *EPW*, Vol. 25, No. 16, April 21. 1990.

2

Other Backward Classes in India

Reservation: Historical Background

The history of 'reservation' as a means of promoting equality of opportunity will be useful in providing an insight regarding the debate over the intended beneficiaries of the protective discrimination, and the conflicting pulls and pressures both social and political necessitating preferential policies. Such an analysis will also help us in the evaluation of the judicial treatment of the governmental schemes giving preferences to the backward groups.

The policy of reservation in India was quite firmly established during the closing decades of the British rule but such a policy was designed more to redress communal inequalities in the representation in public service rather than as a social engineering device to redress the rooted socio-economic inequalities of the disadvantaged sections of the society because of past societal discrimination. The British India government had introduced special provisions and concessions for the educational advancement of Backward Classes which was later converted into caste-based reservations for jobs. The people of these classes had obtained entry into the four walls of literate learning consequent to the social reform movements which were to certain extent supported by the liberal attitude of the

Englishmen during 19th century. The entry of a non-forward caste/*shudra* into an educational institution in the country was recorded in year 1856. In June, 1856, a Scheduled Caste boy applied for admission into a government school in Dharwal, Bombay Presidency. The incident had created furor in the administration which ultimately attracted the attention of the rulers. The board of directors was then forced to formulate an educational policy where it was stated that those schools run by government, would give admission to all students without any distinction of caste, religion and race. This policy was further strengthened with the enactment of the Caste Disability Act of 1872. This Act was a severe blow to the social and legal inequalities suffered by weaker sections. This was how a small beginning was made in the field of educational development of weaker sections in India which was later supported by legislations. The demand for entry into educational institutions and for equality of opportunity was first started in the south. The Southern States including parts of Maharashtra witnessed movements of the weaker sections for equality because of the pioneering work done by Brahma Naidu, Narayana Guru, and Jyothirao Phule among others.

Reservation policy for Backward Classes (Scheduled Castes, Scheduled Tribes and Other Backward Classes) was introduced by two southern Provincial Governments — Madras and Mysore and one in western India, Bombay Presidency. All these developments took place before Independence.

Madras Provincial Governments

Provincial governments in India have been implemented special programmes for the welfare of depressed or deprived sections of society about more than hundred years ago. The first step was taken by Madras Government with the framing of Grant-in-Aid code in 1885 to regulate financial aid to educational institutions providing special facilities for students of depressed classes. Madras Presidency continued its efforts to ameliorate the conditions of depressed classes. After 36 years of implementation of Grant-in-Aid Code in 1885, the Government in 1921, acting on a resolution passed by the state legislative council, took steps for higher representation of non-*brahmins* in Government Services. The scheme was reviewed in 1927, and the scope of reservation was exchanged further, dividing all the communities in the state into five broad categories and earmarking separate quota for each categories.

Mysore Provincial Governments

After ten years of introduction of Grant-in-Aid code in 1885 by Madras Government, Mysore Government issued circular making provision of reservation of certain posts in favour of backward castes in June 19-21, 1895. On the basis of representations received from the Depressed Communities in 1918, the Maharaja of Mysore appointed a Miller Committee to suggest measures for adequate representation of non-*brahmins* in the service of the state. The Government of Mysore, on the basis of the Miller Committee report, extended special benefits to these classes, in education and recruitment in the state services.

Bombay Presidency

Bombay presidency was the third government which introduced reservation policy for Backward Classes after almost four decades of Madras and Mysore Provincial Governments. It was in 1928 that the Government of Bombay set-up a committee under the Chairmanship of O.A.B. started to identify Backward Classes and recommend special provisions for their improvement. In its report submitted in 1930, this Committee divided Backward Classes into three categories, i.e., "Depressed Classes, Aboriginals and Hill Tribes and Other Backward Classes."

Reservation Policy: At National Level

Political representation as a means to emancipate the backward sections of Indian society from the age-old bondage was not accorded due recognition during the 19th century. Thus, the Government of India Act of 1858, and the Indian Council Acts of 1861, and 1892 did not recognise the special claims of the depressed classes. The dawn of 20th century also did not herald their recognition as a political entry. In the Government of India Act, 1909 certain privileges were provided to Muslims, but no representation for the depressed classes was provided.

The Montford Report (1918), recognised the claims only of Sikhs. However, the Franchise Committee (1918-19) while recognising the claims of depressed classes, favoured the system of nomination in place of election as more reliable and practical method of political representation for them. The committee recommended for each Provincial Council the nomination from depressed classes in the following way:

Madras—2, Bombay—1, Bengal—1, United Province—1, Punjab—Nil, Bihar and Orissa—1, Central Provinces and Berar—1, Assam—Nil.

The Government of India Act, 1919, for the first time in the India history gave recognition to the existence of depressed classes and recognised their claim for political representation. The Government of India Act, 1919 provided for communal representations for Muslims, Sikhs, Anglo-Indians, Indian Christians, Depressed Classes, Aborigines etc. Among the 14 non-official members nominated by the Governor General to the Central Legislative Assembly, one representative was of the depressed classes. In the Provincial Legislature, the depressed classes were represented through four nominations in the Central Provinces, two in Bombay, two in Bihar and one each in Bengal and the United Provinces. In Madras ten members got nomination as representatives of nine specified depressed classes.

Ambedkar, Gandhi and Depressed Classes: Rights of Representation in Legislatives

The next constitutional advancement included the existence of the principle of responsible self-government in the provinces. B.R. Ambedkar submitted a classic memorandum to the Simon Commission for the safeguards and protection of the Depressed Classes. He did this on behalf of the *Behishkrit Hitkarini* Sabha. The memorandum stated that those in charge of nation's affairs always did injustice to the dumb millions and complained that under the Act of 1919 grave injustice was done to the depressed classes, who constitute one-fifth of the population of British India. It demanded 22 out of 140 seats in Bombay Legislative Council, vehemently opposed the principal of nomination, and insisted upon the extension of the principle of election to the depressed classes. It said that they were in need of political education and as ministership was an important privilege, they must find a place in the Cabinet.

The Simon Commission (1930) noted that "our object is to make a beginning which will bring the depressed classes within the circle of elected representation." It did not accept the system of separate electorate as it would mean "a precise definition of all, who are covered by the team and the boundary, would be in some cases difficult to draw. It means stigmatising each individual voter in the list and militated against the process which is already beginning, and which needs to be in every way encouraged that of helping those who are depressed to rise in the social and economic scale." It recommended that there should be reservation of seats for depressed classes with a cap of three quarters of the depressed class population to the total population of the electorate area of the province. The convening of a Round Table Conference in London in 1930 was a very significant event in the history of India. It was for the first time in history that their claims were being considered along with other Indians including the right to be consulted in the framing of the Constitution for India. It marked the beginning of the claims of the untouchables in the arena of the devolution of the political power from the British rulers to the Indian natives. The Second Round Table Conference is needed very historic as the Congress also agreed to take part in the conference and secondly, there began a historic and long-drawn controversy between Mahatma Gandhi and B.R. Ambedkar regarding the position of the depressed classes in India. Mahatma Gandhi wanted to change the society with the willing consent of the orthodox, but Ambedkar was not willing for any pretences. He was forthright in first demanding adequate share for the most dehumanised people, the untouchables followed by fight for the backwards and other weaker sections of society. His priorities included breaking the shackles of social bondage of the untouchables from the *Brahminical* order followed by political independence. Mahatma Gandhi refused to consider both the separate electorates for the depressed classes as well as any form of special representation including reserved seats. After the Third Round Table Conference in 1932, the Communal Award of Ramsay Macdonald was declared. According to this award the Mohammedan, Sikh and depressed classes would elect their candidate by voting in separate communal electorates. The most important part of the Award namely, the one relating to the depressed classes ran as follows: "Members of the depressed classes qualified to vote will vote in a general constituency. In view of the fact that for a considerable period these classes would be unlikely, by the means alone to secure adequate representation in the legislature, a number of special seats will be assigned to them. These seats will be filled by election from special constituencies in which only members of the depressed classes, electorally qualified, will be entitled to vote. Any person voting in such a special constituency will, as stated above, be also entitled to vote in a general constituency. It is intended that those constituencies should be formed in selected areas where the depressed classes are most numerous, and that, except in Madras, they should not cover the whole area of the province."

Gandhi's Fast: Mahatma Gandhi was against of Communal Award for which he undertook a fast unto death. Ambedkar had to compromise to save Gandhiji's life and Poona Pact was thus born. The deprived got right to enter Parliament and occupy positions of authority. The five thousand years old rock like walls of *Brahmanism* were pierced. Fresh air went in equal place in political life, but in ultimate analysis Mahatma Gandhi succeeded in securing a promise from Ambedkar and a new lease of life for Hindus, at the same time making the caste Hindus realise that there shall be seats reserved for depressed classes out of the general electorate seats in the Provincial Legislatures as follows: Madras 30; Bombay and Sind 15; Punjab 8; Bihar and Orissa 18; Central Provinces 20; Assam 7; Bengal 30; United Provinces 20; Total 148. Whereas there were only 71 seats in the Communal Award for these depressed classes. In the Central Legislative 18 per cent of the seats were to be reserved for the depressed classes. The voting was to be on the principle of joint electorate system. The Poona Pact had given birth to two principal concepts:

1. that depressed castes will remain within the Hindu fold. 2. that they will enjoy rights to rule themselves jointly with others.

The Government of India Act, 1935 took care of the development arising from Round Table Conference as well as the Poona Pact. The new chapter in our social and constitutional history bade good-bye to Manu and adopted the code of Modern Manu Ambedkar. The excluded became included. The expression Scheduled Caste, which was first coined by Simon Commission was used in the Government of India Act, 1935. Under it the Scheduled Castes replaced Depressed Classes and separate list of Scheduled Castes was notified for various provinces in 1936. The First Scheduled Part I Section 26 of Government of India Act, 1935, defined the term Scheduled Caste, Scheduled Castes means such castes, races or tribes or parts or groups within castes, races or tribes being castes, races, tribes, parts or groups which appear to His Majesty-in-Council to correspond the classes of persons formerly known as the "Depressed Class" as His Majesty-in-Council may specify. Under the Government of India Act, 1935 the proportion of seats was given as: Council of State, British India; Total membership-156 and Scheduled Castes-7; Central Assembly: Total membership – 250 and Scheduled Castes – 19. Ever since 1925, the scheme of reservation applied to Indian Civil Service, Class I, Class II and Subordinate Services under the administrative control of the Government of India with the exception of certain services for which high technical qualifications were essential. The Government of India issued instructions on July 4, 1934 for reserving posts for depressed classes. The Government, however, did not consider it necessary as that stage to reserve a fixed percentage of vacancies for the depressed classes in view of their educational backwardness. In 1942, the Government of India for the first time decided to fix a certain percentage of jobs for the Depressed Classes in order to give them necessary stimulus to equip themselves with better qualification in order to become eligible for posts and services. Several steps like age concession, reduction in examination fee etc., were taken. In 1943, 8.5 per cent of job-reservation was provided for the Depressed Classes and it was decided to consider the question of raising this percentage as soon as sufficient numbers of qualified candidates were found available. However, the percentage of the Scheduled Castes population according to 1931 census was 12.75 per cent. This reservation was applicable only in case of recruitment and not for promotion. In 1946, however, the percentage of reservation was raised from 8.5 to 12.5 per cent corresponding to their population.

Era of Emancipation

The era of emancipation of these depressed castes from the legacy of the past began with the advent of the British rule and leading of the stature of Ambedkar and Mahatma Gandhi took keen interest in their affairs. But the real constitutional provisions on it came after 1950, with special justice as the fundamental constitutional end. The Constitution-makers were fully aware of their fact and hence resolved to constitute India into sovereign, socialist, secular, Democratic and Republic and *inter-alia* secure justice, social, economic and political as enshrined in the preamble. The Constitution as an instrument for social, economic and political transformations of the nation. It has therefore, provided in Article 37(1), under directive principles that "the state shall strive to promote the welfare of the people by effectively securing and protecting a social order in which justice, economic and political shall inform all the institutions of the national life". Article 37(2): The state shall in particular strive to minimise the inequalities in income, and endeavour to eliminate inequalities in status, facilities and opportunities not only among individuals but also amongst groups of people residing in different areas or engaged in different vocations." It has further been provided in Article 39, that the state shall direct its policy towards securing that (a) the citizens, men and women equally have the right to an adequate means of livelihood; (b) that the ownership and control of the material resources of the community are so distributed as to best subserve the common good; (c) that the operation of the economic system does not result in the concentration of wealth and means of production to the common detriment.

The area of employment, offices and appointments under the state is governed by Article 16 alone and preferences within this area must be within the scope of Article 16(4). This includes judicial offices as well as administrative posts, but not elective offices. Article 16(4) covers not only preferences in initial recruitment into government services but also preferences in promotions within the services. The legal provisions are embodied in Part XVI of the Constitution of India, which is entitled: "Special provisions relating to certain classes." From this provision it is clear that in 1950 Constitution maker's visualised need to make special provisions only for the classes like Scheduled Castes and Scheduled Tribes; Anglo-Indian Community; and Socially and Educationally backward classes. At the State level there are similar reservations for Scheduled Castes and Scheduled Tribes. The scheme of reservation is applicable to Public Sector Undertakings also. Voluntary agencies which receive grant-in-aid from the government are also required to adopt certain specific features of the reservation scheme in their establishment. But they have not done so.

As regards the socially and educationally backward classes, popularly known as "OBC" the only special provision for them is under Article 340 of Part XVI of the Constitution. In consonance with the provisions of Directive Principles of State Policy, under Article 340 of the Constitution, provision has been made for the appointment of a permanent body. The Government of India has implemented National Commission for Backward Classes Act, 1993 in pursuance of Supreme Court's Judgment in the Mandal Case (1992). Under this Act the Government of India appoints members of the Commission for a period of three years. The function of the Commission is to examine requests of Individual/Class to include the caste/sub-caste/communities in the CLBC Commission to investigate the conditions of Backward Classes and tender advice to the Central Government to include a caste in the Central List of Backward Classes. The provision under Article 340 is supplemented by clause (4) of Article 15 which says that nothing in this Article (Article 15 relates to prohibition of discrimination on ground of religion, race, caste, sex and place of birth) or in clause (2) of Article 29 (Article 29 relates to protection and interest of minorities), shall prevent the State from making any special provision for the advancement of any socially and educationally Backward Classes of citizens or for the Scheduled Castes and Scheduled Tribes.

The Mandate in the Constitution

In accordance with the mandate contained in the preamble of the Constitution and the Directive Principles of State Policy, the Government of India appointed the First Backward Classes Commission under Article 340 on January 29, 1953 with Kakasaheb Kalelkar as its Chairman. The Commission submitted its reports on March 30, 1955. On the basis of criteria evolved by it the Commission listed 2,399 castes as socially and educationally backward. It recommended various welfare measures for OBCs which included reservation in government services and educational institutions. The Central Government however did not accept the recommendations of the Commission on the ground that it had not applied any objective tests for identifying backward classes. While rejecting the main recommendations of this Commission the Central Government informed the State Governments that they were free to draw their respective lists of Backward Classes on the basis of criteria worked out by them and take whatever further action they deemed necessary in the matter. Consequently, a number of State Governments set-up their own Commissions or Committees for defining criteria for backwardness and recommending measures for its removal. Immediately, ten state Governments set-up fifteen Commissions and committees in this behalf. These states were: Andhra Pradesh, Bihar, Gujarat, Jammu and Kashmir, Karnataka, Kerala, Maharashtra, Punjab, Uttar Pradesh and Tamil Nadu. Further eight other states and Union Territories had notified lists of other Backward Classes for the grant of various educational, employment and other benefits. These are: Assam, Delhi, Haryana, Himachal Pradesh, Meghalaya, Orissa, Pondicherry and Rajasthan. These State Governments and UTs mostly relied on the lists of OBCs maintained by them for the grant of post-Matric scholarships, etc., under the Education Ministry's scheme formulated in 1944, and another list prepared by the Commission for SCs and STs at the time of drafting of first Five Year Plan.

More than two decades the Government of India did not take any action plan for giving reservation benefit to Other Backward Classes. With the change of government at the Centre in 1977, the backward classes' problems received the attention of the Janata Party government, and subsequently the Second Backward Classes Commission was appointed in December 1978 under the Chairmanship of B.P. Mandal. The Commission presented its report to President on December 31, 1980. Various welfare measures for the castes listed as socially and educationally backward were recommended in this report. The Janata Party Government did not implement the recommendations of the Second Backward Classes. As a result, this report also met the same fate into cold storage as the first one for a decade. After the fall of Janata Party Government, Congress Party Government did not act upon the report realising heart and pulse of people of the country. National Front Government came into power at the Centre in December 1989. The manifesto of National Front included the implementation of Mandal Commission recommendation as one of its promises. Hence, the government declared its decision on the implementation of some recommendations of Mandal Commission Report regarding reservations in employment. The Government of India issued a Office Memorandum dated 13th August, 1990 declaring 27 per cent reservation for Other Backward Classes in Government Services, etc. After declaration of the decision of the government there was a spate of reactions by people belonging to different walks of life. The decision of the government to implement some of its recommendations in a precipitated manner agitated the minds of the Indian public, particularly in the Hindi heartland. This led to unprecedented loss of young lives and valuable property which caused extreme distress, but the government showed unpardonable insensitivity towards the feelings of young people. After about a year the Government of India issued another Office Memorandum, dated 25th September, 1991 on this subject.

However, the new government of Congress (I) at the Centre gave a new twist to whole of the issue by providing ten per cent reservation to the poor among forward castes, and also by introducing an economical criterion to the OBCs. This policy of the government was stated in the affidavit submitted to the Supreme Court. The court referred the case to nine-judge Bench and the Supreme Court in a majority judgment upheld job reservations for Backward Classes in the Central Government and declared valid the V.P. Singh government's order on 27 per cent job quotas but struck down the economic criterion that was later inducted by the Narasimha Rao government. To exclude economically well off persons belonging to OBCs the Government of India appointed an Expert Committee for specifying the criteria for identification of socially advanced persons among the socially and educationally Backward Classes under the Chairmanship of Justice Ram Nandan Prasad. The Expert submitted its report to the Government of India on the 10th March, 1993 which was accepted by the Government. As per directions in the Mandal Judgment (1992), the Government of India set-up a National Commission for Backward Classes under the National Commission for Backward Classes Act, 1993. Similar action was also taken by State Governments.

Reservational Justice to Backward Castes: Some Issues

The reservation benefits are available at present to Backward Classes that includes Scheduled Castes, Scheduled Tribes and Other Backward Classes (OBCs). The first two categories of people have been granted Constitutional benefits while Other Backward Classes have been granted benefits under executive order. The Constitution specifically mentions Scheduled Castes and Scheduled Tribes under Articles 15(4), 46, 334, 338, 341 and 342. Article 335 mentions their claims to services and posts. It reads, "The claims of the members of the Scheduled Castes and the Scheduled Tribes shall be taken into consideration, consistently with the maintenance of efficiency of administration, in making of appointments to services and posts in connection with the affairs of the Union and of a State." It is only they for whom reservation of seats is provided in the House of the People and in the Legislative Assemblies of the States. They belong to weaker sections with special mention. Article 46 provides that "the State shall promote with special care the educational and economic interests of the weaker sections of the people, and, in particular, of the Scheduled Castes and the Scheduled Tribes, and shall protect them from social injustice and all kind of exploitations." If any provision deals with backward class of citizens without specific mention of SCs and STs their claim is first charged in respect of backwardness. To make it more specific 'backward' used in Article 16(4) is wider than 'Socially and educationally backward' used in Article 15(4) and 'weaker sections' used in Article 46. SCs and STs are covered in all the expressions.

The expression 'Backward Class' in Article 16(4) takes in Other Backward Classes, Scheduled Castes and Scheduled Tribes. The accent in Article 16(4) is upon social backwardness. Social backwardness leads to educational backwardness and economic backwardness. They are mutually contributory to each other and are inter-twined with low occupations in the Indian society. The Constitution of India has commitment to ensure justice to all sections of the people. But it does not incorporate the use of expression Other Backward Classes (OBCs). The Constitution uses the expression Socially and Educationally Backward Classes (SEBCs). Thus, the category of Backward Classes other than SCs and STs belongs to SEBCs also. Article 15(4) speaks of making special provisions for advancement of SEBCs and Article 340 speaks of appointment of a Commission by the President to investigate into conditions of the SEBCs. Under this Article, Kaka Kalelkar Commission in 1953 and Mandal Commission in 1978 were appointed for investigating conditions of backward classes. The Notification regarding implementation of Mandal Commission's recommendations has been upheld by the Supreme Court of India, in Indira Sawhney and others versus Union of India and others on 16.11.1992. Parliament enacted National Commission for Backward Classes Act, 1993 in order to constitute a permanent statutory body National Commission for Backward Classes. The Commission shall examine requests of any individual of any backward caste in the Central List of Backward Classes.

Caste as Basis of Backwardness: Legal Position

The Constitution of India intends to wipe out discrimination on the ground of caste. But the real problem which the country is confronting within: can caste be eliminated from the criterion of identification of backward classes? In pre-Constitution period the expressions, 'class' and 'caste' were used interchangeably. As a matter of fact, Ambedkar declared in his speech in the Parliament at the time of the First Amendment to the Constitution that "Backward Classes are nothing else but a collection of certain castes." A caste is an enclosed class, issuing clarification of the use of the word class in Article 16(4) Kania, C.J. and Venkatachaliah, Ahmadi Jeevan Reddy, JJ. pointed out in Mandal Case (1992), Vol. I, that the obvious reason of using the expression 'Class' in Article 16(4) was that otherwise non-Hindus would have got excluded from its purview as they do not use 'caste'. Therefore, from the use of the word 'class' in Article 16(4), it cannot be deducted either that 'class' is anti-thetical to "caste" or that a caste cannot be a class or that a caste as such can never be taken as a backward class of citizens.

Caste is the only criterion for awarding benefits to SCs and STs. About OBCs 'class' is used and it has caused serious concern whether class should be equated to caste. Whether such classes are castes? Absence of a categorical value measure of a casteless society has been strongly condemned by Ghurye, who says, "We are marching towards caste pluralism instead of a casteless society." Many castes in India are bound together by common faith and organisation. The question then arises can a caste be taken as basis for determining backwardness? Let us discuss the position analytically from legal point of view.

Neither Sole nor Dominant Criteria During 1960s the Supreme Court of India attempted to dilute the domineering role of caste in identification of backwardness. In *Balaji* versus *State of Mysore,* P.B. Gajendragadkar, J. speaking for the unanimous Constitution Bench conceding the harsh reality of caste factor among Hindus pointed out that, "though castes in relation to Hindus may be a relevant factor to consider in determining the social backwardness of groups or class of citizens it cannot be made the sole or the dominant test in that behalf." Subba Rao, J, further secularised it in his majority decision in *R. Chitralekha* versus *State of Mysore*. He stressed that under no circumstances a 'class' could be equated to a 'caste', though the caste of an individual or a group of individuals may be regarded along with other relevant factors in putting him in a particular class. He also stressed that if caste is excluded in ascertaining backwardness of class in a particular situation it would not be bad. In his dissenting judgment Mudholkar, J. declared that taking into account the 'caste' of a person to identify backwardness of a class would be against Article 15 or 29(2). In his view, non-abstante clause of Article 15(4) does not justify the inference that "castes have any relevance in ascertaining what socially and educationally backward communities are."

Some Shift Started—Caste not to be Ignored Altogether. A somewhat different tone started in judicial verdicts by the end of 1960s. In *P. Rajendran* versus *State of Madras*, Wanchoo, C.J. speaking for the Constitution Bench conceding that determination of backwardness based solely on caste without taking into consideration the social and educational backwardness would be violative of Article 15(1), clarified the point: "But it must not be forgotten that a caste is also a class of citizens and if the caste as a whole is socially and educationally backward, reservation can be made in favour of such a caste on the ground that it is a socially and educationally backward class of citizens within the meaning of Article 15(4). In *State of Andhra Pradesh* versus *P. Sagar*, the Supreme Court spoke in similar tone avoiding caste as sole criterion but granting that "the expression 'class' means a homogeneous section of the people grouped together due to certain likeness or common traits and who are identifiable by some common attributes such as status, rank, occupation, residence in a locality, race, religion and the like. In determining whether a particular section forms a class, caste cannot be excluded altogether."

Caste as a Class. Hegde J. asserted in *A. Peeriakaruppan* versus *State of TN*, that "a caste has always been recognised as a Class." So was the tone of Vadialingam J. in *State of A.P.* versus *U.S.V. Balaram*, wherein various test of backwardness were pointed out but the list of Backward Classes was to be accepted even though the said list was "exclusively based on caste".

Extremism for a while: Chief Justice A.N. Ray said in *K.S. Jayashree* versus *State of Kerala* that 'in determining social backwardness of a class of citizens it may not be irrelevant to consider the caste of the group of citizens; Caste cannot however, be made only or dominant test.

1980s scenario—caste reality by birth: In *K.C. Vasantha Kumar* versus *State of Karnataka* barring Chief Justice Chandrachud, all other four learned judges of the Constitution Bench thoroughly discussed the issue of caste backwardness relationship. After analysing the role of caste in the Indian social structure O. Chinnappa Reddy, J. spoke: "Social hierarchy and economic position exhibit an indisputable mutuality. The lower the caste, the poorer its members, the poorer the members of a caste, the lower the caste and economic situation, reflecting each other as they do are the *deus examchina* of the social status occupied and the economic poor wielded by an individual or class in the rural society". D.A. Desai, J. also accepted the reality of the role of caste in the Indian Society, but in order to get rid of pernicious effect of caste-system he wanted economic and poverty criterion of the identification of backwardness. A.P. Sen J. wished poverty as criterion but acknowledged caste for identification of acute backwardness.

Kania, C.J. and Venkatachaliah, Ahmadi and Jeevan Reddy, JJ. forming the leading majority verdict made it clear that a caste is nothing but a social class – a socially homogeneous class. It is also an occupational group with the difference that its membership is hereditary. One is born into it. Its membership is involuntary. Even if one stops to follow that occupation still he remains and continues to be a member of that group. Caste is a socially and occupationally homogenous class. Endogamy is its main feature. The conclusion of leading majority verdict is that a caste can be and generally is a social class in India. If it is backward socially, it would be backward class for the purposes of Article 16(4). Class under Article 16(4) is neither anti-thetical to caste nor can it be said that it cannot be a class or that caste as such can never be taken as a backward class of citizens. Pandian, J. in his concurring judgement expressed the opinion that a caste is also a class of citizens and that if that caste satisfies the requisite tests of backwardness, the classification of that caste as a backward class is not opposed to Article 16(4).

Swant J. in his concurring judgement pointed out that casteism has been the bane of entire Indian society. Every individual is born in a particular caste which he cannot change. A caste by itself may constitute a class. However, Sawant, J. observed that in order to constitute a backward class, the caste concerned must be socially backward and its educational and economic backwardness must be due to its social backwardness. In their dissent, Thommen and Kuldip Singh, JJ ruled out caste as criteria for determination of backward classes. Thommen, J. expressed the opinion that the grounds prohibited in Article 15(1) including caste cannot be the only or dominant criterion. Instead along with them there should be criterion of illiteracy, poverty, demeaning occupation, malnutrition, etc. Kuldip Singh, J. expressed the opinion that 'classes under Article 16(4) cannot be read as 'caste' and castes cannot be adopted as collectivities for the purpose of identifying backward class under Article 16(4). In his view, caste-collectivity is unconstitutional and as such not permitted. Similar opinion was expressed by Sahai, J. in his dissent. From the above analysis two viewpoints emerge. First, caste by itself may constitute class and can be the basis of backwardness, Second, caste cannot be read as class and therefore as such be basis for determination of backwardness.

Backwardness of Other Backward Classes *vis-à-vis* Backwardness of Scheduled Castes and Scheduled Tribes

Scheduled Castes, Scheduled Tribes and Other Backward Castes (OBCs) are three different social classes or groups having different level of social and educational backwardness. There is difference in degree of backwardness between the two and this attracts different treatment. But there have been some stray observations both judicial and extra-judicial which have shown the similarity between the two. In *Balaji* versus *State of Mysore* while dealing with the issue of division of backwards into backward and more backward, the Supreme Court made certain remarks which give the impression that the backwardness of the Backward Class under Article 16(4) being social and educational must be similar to the backwardness from which the Scheduled Castes and Scheduled Tribes suffer. The Supreme Court of India observed: "It seems fairly clear that the Backward Classes of citizens for whom special provision is authorised to be made are, by Article 15(4) itself, treated as being similar to the Scheduled Castes and Scheduled Tribes. Scheduled Castes and Scheduled Tribes which have been defined were known to be backward and the Constitution makers felt no doubt that special provision had to be made for their advancement. It was realised that in the Indian society there were other classes of citizens who were equally, or may be somewhat less backward than the Scheduled Castes and Tribes and it was thought that some special provision ought to be made even for them.

The Balaji test was elaborated by the Supreme Court in *Janki Prasad Parimoo* versus *State of J and K* to mean that backwardness for whose improvement special provision was contemplated by Article 15(4) must be comparable to Scheduled Castes and Scheduled Tribes who are standing examples of backwardness socially and educationally. Similar opinion was expressed in *K.S. Jayshree* versus *State of Kerala*. Chief Justice Chandrachud in his separate judgment spoke of comparability of backwardness of Backward Classes to Scheduled Castes and Scheduled Tribes. These opinions represent one side of the coin which does not properly appreciate the use of alternate expressions and separate provisions in the Constitution. The other side of the issue attracting Constitutional dimension is represented in various set of opinions finally getting approval of majority opinions in *Indira Sawhney and Others* versus *Union of India and Others*. In *State of A.P.* versus *U.S.V. Balaram,* the earlier opinion was explained by pointing out that Balaji ruling does not lay down that backwardness of the Other Backward Classes must be exactly in all respects to that of the Scheduled Castes and Scheduled Tribes.

Another explanation was attached by Justice Sawant in his concurring opinion view in Mandal Case. The learned judge ruled that the test of comparable backwardness laid down in Balaji has not been and is not to be understood to mean that backwardness of the Other Backward Classes has to be of the same degree as or similar in all respects to that of the Scheduled Castes and the Scheduled Tribes. The learned judge placed main reliance upon the constitutional provisions and gave two convincing arguments for his conclusions.

1. That it is necessary that the social, educational and economic backwardness of the other Backward Classes should be exactly of the same kind and degree as that of the Scheduled Castes and the Scheduled Tribes is recognised by the different provisions of the Constitution itself since they make difference between the Scheduled Castes and the Scheduled Tribes on the one hand, and other "socially and educationally backward classes" or "Backward Classes of citizens" on the other.

2. What is further, if the other Backward Classes are backward exactly in all respects as the Scheduled Castes and Scheduled Tribes, the President has power to notify them as Scheduled Castes and Scheduled Tribes, and then they would not remain the other backward classes?

Does the Backward Class of Citizens mean both Socially and Educationally Backward Class?

One of the significant issues in relation to 'backward class of citizens' under Article 16(4) is whether backwardness under that clause is both social and educational or not. So far as clause (4) of 15 is concerned it was ruled in *Balaji* versus *State of Mysore* that backwardness contemplated under that Article was both social and educational. It is not either only social or only educational but it is both social and educational. In *Janki Prasad Parimoo* versus *State of J and K,* the Court read expression, backward class of citizens used in Article 16(4) to mean "socially and educationally backward class of citizens". Mr. Justice Palekar, who pronounced the judgment proceeded to equate the two terms on assumption that "it was well-settled that the expression 'Backward Class' in Article 16(4) implies the same thing as the expression, any socially and educationally Backward Classes of citizens in Article 15(4). It is submitted that the conclusion was based on assumptions and none of the decisions had tried to equate the two terms. Similarly in *K.C. Vasanth Kumar* versus *State of Karnataka,* Mr. Justice Chinnappa Reddy, Justice D.A. Desai, Justice Sen and Justice Venkataramaiah proceeded on the footing that Backward Class of citizens' was synonymous with the expression 'socially and educationally backward class'. But the leading majority judgment in Mandal Case delivered by B.P. Jeevan Reddy, J. (for himself Kania, C.J. Venkatachaliah and Ahmadi, JJ) did not approve of the above logic. It found no basis of the assumption that the expression Backward Class of citizens in Article 16(4) implies the same thing as the expression, any socially and educationally 'Backward Class of citizens' in Article 15(4). It was made clear that clause (4) of Article 16 does not contain the qualifying words 'socially and educationally' as does clause (4) of Article 15. The majority decision pointed out the width of Article 16(4). It is wider than as contemplated by Articles 15(4) and Article 340. Thus, the expression 'Backward Class of citizens' in Article 16(4) includes SCs/STs and all Other Backward Classes of citizens including the socially and educationally backward classes. And, therefore, certain classes which may not qualify for Article 15(4) may qualify for Article 16(4) as backward class of citizens. The backwardness contemplated under Article 16(4) is chiefly social backwardness, and therefore it would not be right to say that the backwardness under Article 16(4) should be both social and educational. Backwardness under Article 16(4) is much wider. The accent in Article 16(4) is more on social backwardness. Of course, social, educational and economic backwardness are closely intertwined in the Indian context. Likewise Pandian, J. in his concurring judgment made it clear that the primary consideration in identifying a class and in ascertaining the insufficient representation of that class in the services under the State under Article 16(4) is social backwardness which results in educational backwardness, both of which end up in economic backwardness.

Justice Sawant also put main stress on social backwardness. He made it clear that the only 'backward class' for which reservations are provided and Article 16(4) is the 'socially backward class' whose educational and economic backwardness is on account of the social backwardness. He stressed that 'a class which is not socially and educationally backward though economically or even educationally backward is not a backward class for the purposes of the said clause [Article 16(4)]. Sawant, J. very clearly pointed out the actual purpose behind Article 16(4): "the purpose of keeping reservations even in favour of socially and educationally Backward Classes under Clause (4) is not to alleviate poverty but to give it an adequate share in power." In their dissenting judgments Thommen, J. Kuldip Singh, J. and Sahai, J. expressed different opinions. Thommen, J. expressed the view that 'backward class' used in Article 16(4) is synonym for the classes mentioned in Article 15(4). Kuldip Singh, J. did not agree with proposition that social backwardness is an essential feature of the 'backward classes under Article 16(4) and R.M. Sahai J. considered both social and educational backwardness necessary for the purpose of Article 16(4).

Identification of OBCs

Article 16(4) speaks of reservations in public employments for 'backward class of citizens'. This expression was not originally suggested by the Ad hoc Committee whose recommendation read: "Nothing herein contained shall prevent the State from making provision for reservation of appointments or posts in favour of any of citizens who in the opinion of the State are not adequately represented in the services under the State".

It was the drafting committee under the chairmanship of Dr. B.R. Ambedkar that inserted the word "backward" in between the words "in favour of any" and "class of citizens". The discussion on draft Article 10 took place on November 30, 1948. Several members including Damodar Swaroop Seth, Pt. Hirdya Nath Kunzru and R.M. Nalavade complained that the expressions 'backward' and 'backward classes' are quite vague and are likely to lead to complications in future. They suggested that the appointments in public services should be made purely on the basis of merit. Some others suggested that such reservations should be available only for a period of first ten years of the Constitution. To this criticism the Vice-President of the Assembly

(Dr H.C. Mookherjee) replied at length. Mookherjee also received support of Chandrika Ram (Bihar-General) and P. Kakkan (Madras-General) on expression 'backward classes'. It is mentioned that draft Article 10 corresponds to Article 16. The debate in the Constituent Assembly on draft Article 10, and particularly clause (3), thereof (corresponding to clause (4) of Article 16 helps us to appreciate the background and understand the objective underlying Article 16, and in particular, clause (4) thereof.

In Mandal case, the leading majority decision for four learned judges made it clear that the Government of India and the State Governments have power to, and ought to, create a permanent mechanism in nature of Commission or Tribunal for examination of requests of inclusion and complaints of over-inclusion or non-inclusion in the list of OBCs and to advise the Government and in the case of the non-acceptance of the advice by the Government, it must record its reasons thereof. Similar views were shared by Pandian, J. who favoured permanent Commission/Committee, Thommen, J. who wished periodic administrative review by a permanent expert body and Sawant, J. who agreed in principle. The Commission/Committee may be constituted either under clause (4) of Article 16 itself or under Article 16 (4) read with Article 340.

Parliament/Legislatures as Authorities for Reservation to OBCs

In *Balaji* versus *State of Mysore* provision under clause (4) of Article 16 was allowed to be made by the executive wing of the government. The same was done by the Supreme Court in *Comptroller and Auditor-General of India* versus *Mohan Lal Mehrotra*. An unsuccessful attempt was made in Mandal Case to challenge the validity of Government Memorandum on the plea that since the provisions of Article 16(4) affects fundamental rights of other citizens such a provision can be made only by the Parliament/Legislature. It was pleaded that exercise of power by the executive was attuning to misuse of power because of political and electoral conclusions. On the other hand, legislature will offer proper forum for deliberation and balanced decision. The leading majority decision delivered by Jeevan Reddy, J. ruled out the apprehension about misuse of powers by executive in the light of the objectivity stipulated in determination of backwardness. The Court put emphasis on definition, of law given under Article 13(3)(a) which includes order, 'bye-law', 'rule' and 'regulation' and definition of 'State' under Article 12 of the Constitution. Keeping in view these provisions, the Court ruled that: "it becomes clear that a measure of the nature contemplated by Article 16(4) can be provided not only by the Parliament/ Legislature but also by the executive in respect of Central/State services and by local bodies and 'other authorities' contemplated by Article 12, in respect of their respective services." Thus, in Mandal Case Kania, C.J. and Venkatachaliah, Ahmadi, Jeevan Reddy, Pandian, Kuldip Singh and Sawant, JJ. upheld the Memorandum as it need not necessarily be made by the Parliament. Sahai, J. pointed out that reservation by executive order may not be valid but since it was being made for the first time in services under the Union the propriety demanded that it should have been laid before Parliament because of two reasons: (i) to lay down a healthy convention, and (ii) to take into account the change in social, economic and political conditions of the country as nearly ten years had elapsed from the date of the submission of Mandal Commission Report which was a period considered sufficient for re-evaluation if the reservation may be continued or not.

As to the efficacy of the Memorandum Kania C.J. and Venkatachaliah, Ahmadi and Kuldip Singh, JJ. held the view that any provision made under Article 16(4) becomes effective and enforceable by itself. They fall under Article 73 read with Article 16(4). Sawant, J. also took the similar view. Kuldip Singh, J. expressed the opinion that executive instructions under Articles 16(4), 73 and 162 providing reservation contrary to rules under Article 309 shall not be operative so far as it is contrary to statutory provisions/rules. Sahai, J. thought it proper to be laid before Parliament.

Division of OBCs into Backward and Most Backward Classes

It is not that the backwardness of all Backward Classes will be of the same magnitude. Whether Backward Classes may be divided into Backward Classes and most Backward Classes came to be decided in *Balaji* versus *State of Mysore*. It had two main features: (i) it related to Article 15(4), and (ii) it was meant for giving reservations separately to the two classes and thereby raising percentage of reservation. This aspect was noted by Gajendragadkar, J. (as he then was) who delivered the judgment. The learned judge pointed out that sub-classification made by the Order between Backward Classes and More Backward Classes and did not seem to be justified under Article 15(4) because that authorise special provision being made for the really backward classes. Gajendragadkar, J. said: "In introducing two categories of Backward Classes, what the impugned order, in substance, purports to do is to devise measures for benefit of all the classes of citizens, who are less advanced compared to the most advanced classes in the State and that in our opinion is not the scope of Article 15(4)." Gajendragadkar, J. observed that the results of method adopted by impugned order was that nearly 90 per cent of the population of the State was considered as backward and that illustrated how the order in fact divided the population of the State into the most advanced and the rest and put latter into two categories of Backward Classes and most backward. In his view that was not warranted under Article 15(4). In *K.C. Vasantah Kumar* versus *State of Karnataka,* Chinnappa Reddy, J. conceded that the propriety of such a course may be open to question on the facts of each case, but he found no justification "why on principle there cannot be classification into Backward Classes and More Backward Classes, if both classes are not merely a little behind, but far behind the most advanced classes". Chinnappa Reddy, J. pointed out that "all that we can say is that sub-classification may be permissible if there are classes of people, who are definitely far behind the advanced classes but ahead of the very backward classes." The difference between Articles 15(4) and 16(4) is that the former deals with the issue of the extent of the special provision to be made there under and latter is invoked with regard to so-called meritarian principle which argues that large reservation would inevitably affect efficiency. In his Report of Third Karnataka Backward Classes Commission Chinnappa Reddy, J. identified three factors inter-relatively contributing towards backwardness. Such factors are Caste, Economic and Educational. Lack of economic development, educational unawareness and caste humiliation all contribute backwardness.

Earlier Bihar Government appointed a Backward Classes Commission under the Chairmanship of Mungeri Lal in June 1971 and it submitted its report in February 1976. The Commission identified 128 communities as 'backward' and 94 of them as 'most backward'. It recommended 20 per cent reservation for them in all Government Departments, local bodies, and state Government Undertakings for the candidates of OBCs and 30 per cent each for women and economically weaker sections (only those candidates should be given this benefit whose family income was below the minimum income-tax limit) and 24 per cent seats in engineering, medical and other professional institutions for students of OBCs and grant of various other benefits like allotment of house sites, grant of scholarships, reimbursement of tuition fees, etc., to OBCs. The State Government accepted the recommendations of Mungeri Lal Commission in October 1978, and this gave rise to a lot of agitation as both forward and backward communities were unsatisfied with Government's order. Based on that Report on November 18, 1978 Karpoori Thakur Government issued a G.O. providing for reservation. The G.O. provoked widespread backlash on the part of the forward castes. The universities and colleges were closed. Trains and buses were attacked and the government property was damaged. Subsequently, the government of Bihar corrected this misconception in July, 1979 and classified that the reservation quota indicated the minimum and not the maximum quota for backward class candidates. It was also clarified that the percentage of backward class candidates selected on merit should be adjusted against their reserved quota.

So far the identification of Backward Classes and most Backward Classes was done in an order to give separate percentage of reservations among them so as to ensure justice intra-backward classes. Second point to be noted is that the issue of reservation to Backward Classes related to reservation in state services and not national services wherein no scheme of reservation was applicable for OBCs.

Mandal Commission was confronted with the issue of dividing backwards among backwards and most backwards on the plea of anti-reservationists that the benefit of reservation will be cornered by forwards among the backwards. Mandal clarified it on different counts.

(a) Such arguments were given by the ruling elite which was keep on preserving its privileges. Thus, reasoning was partisan one.

(b) The objective of Mandal Report was not to provide job to BCs and convert them into forward, but to provide psychological 'spin off' and moral booster.

Report Reads

"It is not at all our contention that by offering a few thousand jobs to OBC candidates we shall be able to make 52 per cent of the Indian population as forward. But we must recognise that an essential part of the battle against social backwardness is to be fought in the minds of the backward people. In India, Government service has always been looked upon as a symbol of prestige and power. By increasing the representation of OBCs in Government services, we give them an immediate feeling of participation in the governance of this country.... (para 13.4, p. 57)".

The report narrates the effect of reservation services to OBCs "when a backward class candidate becomes a collector or a Superintendent of Police, the material benefits accruing from its position are restricted to the members of his family only. But the psychological spin off of this phenomenon is tremendous; the entire community of that backward class candidate feels socially uplifted. Even when no tangible benefits flow to the community at large, the feeling that now it has its "Own man" in the "Corridors of power" works as a moral booster (para 13.4, p. 57).

The Mandal Commission's refusal to divide backward among backward and more backward depended on the class character of reservation intended under Article 16(4) – for the above described reason. Even in his Minute of dissent Mr. L.R. Naik, ex-M.P. divided backwards into two categories, (i) the intermediate backward classes, and (ii) depressed classes. Treating latter nearer to SC/STs, he suggested separate treatment for them. Mr. Naik preferred division among backwards on ancient adage, "if a big fish and a small fish are put together, the former will swallow the latter." His division of Backward Classes was for separate treatment and not for denial to any segment.

The issue of division of Backward Classes again came up in the Mandal Case. The majority was of view that there is no constitutional bar to classify the Backward Classes of citizens into backward and more backward categories. It did not recommend that it needs to be done. It only said that if the Government chose to do that that would not be invalid. Such a division was approved on two grounds:

(a) On Mandal criteria itself the division is approved, as any caste, group or class which scored eleven or more points was constituted as a backward class. It is not as if all the many thousands of castes/groups/classes scored identical points. There may have been some castes/groups/classes which have score points in between 20 to 22, and there may have been some who have scored points in between 11 to 13. It cannot reasonably be denied that there is no difference between these two sets of castes/groups/classes.

(b) Article 16(4) recognises only one class *viz.*, "Backward Class of citizens" and does not speak of SCs/STs separately as does Article 15(4). Even then SCs/STs are included in "Backward Class of citizens" and separate reservation is made for them. The logic behind it is that if SCs/STs and OBCs are grouped together, OBCs will take away all the vacancies leaving SCs and STs high and dry. The same logic also warrants categorisation as between more backward and less backward classes.

Backward Caste's Right to Reservation

The nature of reservational right as fundamental right or otherwise is very much linked to the nature of the provision of Article 16(4). During the first two decades of the functioning of the Constitution there had been some controversy on the point. Dealing with clause (4) of Article 15 in *Balaji* versus *State of Mysore,* Gajandragadkar, J. ruled that "there is no doubt that Article 15(4) has to be read as a provision or an exception to Articles 15(1) and 29(2). Following Balaji ruling the majority in *T. Devadasan* versus *Union of India* said that "clause (4) of Article 16 is by way of a proviso or an exception to clause (1)." However, Subba Rao, J. expressed the opinion in his dissent that Article 16(4) is not an exception to Article 16(1). The dissenting opinion of Subba Rao, J. took some time to take the shape of rule. Meanwhile, in a series of cases Article 16(4) was conceded as an exception to the general rule of equality enshrined in clause (1). The dissent of Subba Rao, J. in Devadasan case received majority support in *State of Kerala* versus *N.M. Thomas* wherein Ray, C.J. and Mathew, Krishna Iyer and Fuzl Ali, JJ., expressed the opinion that Article 16(4) is not an exception to Article 16(1). It is an emphatic way of stating a principle implicit in Article 16(1). Thomas ruling held that Article 16(1) being a facet of equality enshrined in Article 14 permits reasonable classification just as Article 14 does. This view of Thomas case was considered as correct one by Chief Justice Kania and Venkatachaliah, Ahmadi and Jeevan Reddy, JJ, in *Indira Sawhney* versus *Union of India.* It was explained: "Article 16(1) does permit reasonable classification for ensuring attainment of the equality of opportunity assured by it. For assuring equality of opportunity it may well be necessary in certain situations to treat unequally situated persons unequally. Not doing so, would perpetuate and accentuate inequality." It was further made clear that: "Article 16(4) is an instance of such classification, put into place the matter beyond controversy. The "backward class of citizens are classified as a separate category deserving a special treatment in the nature of reservation of appointments/posts in the services of the State...It is an instance of classification implicit and permitted by clause (1)."

Parmanand Singh finds it illogical, unsound as well as unbalanced and even undesirable in the light of DMK leadership's claim of 69 per cent reservation in Tamil Nadu despite Mandal case and Kerala's unwillingness to implement creamy layer. His main stress is on the following grounds:

• Articles 15(4) and 16(4) are subject to many limitations like: (a) firm evidence of clear and legitimate identification of backward classes; (b) impermissibility of reservation in promotions; (c) no reservation in specialties and super specialties like Medicine and Engineering, University Professorship, Defence, Space Science and Nuclear Research.

• If they are recognised as guaranteed right each individual claim to secure enforcement of such right will be subject to judicial determination.

• Even until Mandal Case courts are not responsive to such claims as a matter of enforceable right. Even Mandal case has recognised Articles 15(4) and 16(4) as enabling provision.

• A distinction has to be made between equality as a matter of policy and equality as a matter of right. Articles 15(4) and 16(4) present the matter of policy. According to him a policy stipulates a collective goal which a community seeks to achieve. A right is an individual claim which seeks to protect individual interest. Thus, Article 15(4) and 16(4) may be considered as authorising norms in Kelsenian sense, justifying encroachment of the individual's right to equality for achieving real equality for the members of the disadvantaged groups.

• Professor Dworkin's thesis of right as 'trump' advanced for the defence of affirmative action may help M.P. Singh's claim of preferential discrimination but not for justifying a fundamental right to reservation. In the opinion of Parmanand Singh, the justification of debate that takes place in America is of little relevance in India in view of a clear constitutional policy of compensatory discrimination as mentioned in Articles 15(4) and 16(4).

• Main thesis of fundamental right of reservation based on judicial verdicts as to the nature of Articles 15(4) and 16(4) not as an exception to 15(1), 16(1) and (2) but as a separate provision as part of equality also looses force in view of: (i) non-abstante clause attached with Article 15(4) which is wider and Article 16(4) is restricted to reservation and exceptional nature is not disturbed even by Mandal case. Even Thomas supports extent of reservation and does not acknowledge a fundamental right to affirmative action.

• Article 16(4) exhausts all power of backward class preferences and in this sense is recognised as an exception to clause (1) of Article 16 in relation to backward classes.

• The analogy of right to education in view of directive principle and Article 21 is also disputable. Such positive claims can only be promoted and are not capable of being 'enforced' by affirmative litigation. It can be further justified in light of reluctance of court to recognise right to work and means of livelihood as enforceable right and restricting of right to education upto primary education in Unnikrishnan's case.

Accepting the weakening thread of Hohfeldian right-duty correlativity, Parmanand Singh arrived at conclusion that "the claims advanced in guise of right to reservation should be accepted as a social or collective goal or as a matter of policy rather than acknowledged as fundamental rights."

Articles 15(4) and 16(4) as Fundamental Rights

The move towards recognition of Article 16(4) as fundamental right gained strength after Thomas case though the seeds were sown by Justice Subba Rao in Devadasan through his dissent that Article 16(4) has not really carved out an exception, but has preserved a power untrammeled by the other provisions of the Article. Thomas began a new constitutional vista and a foreigner eminent scholar on competing equalities in India foresaw a number of contingencies during the starting year of 1980s.

"First, do the litigants and their lawyers have the legal imagination to devise these claims?

Second, do they have the capacity to organise to sustain such litigation and press for the implementation of favourable rulings? (Of Course, the capacity for organisation might be enhanced by creative deployment of legal services).

Third, are the judges like to be responsive to such claims, claims that ask them to depart from deeply held notion about judicial role? They would not only have to innovate original standards of what is appropriate movement towards equality, they would have to undertake a sustained activist monitoring of government that they may find both ideologically uncongenial and institutionally discomfiting.

Fourth, even if claimants come forward and courts are responsive, do the realities of litigation in India, the delay and manoeuver and cost, make it possible for groups to improve their position through litigation against powerful adversaries?

Fifth, are the real barriers to improvement of the conditions of these groups reachable by even most well-disposed and capable judiciary?"

Some illusion and dilemma is observed in judicial outlook. In *Kumari Usha Rani* versus *M. D. University, Rohtak*, the power of the University to reduce seats for admission, to the Medical College from 150 to 115 and reservation for Backward Classes from ten per cent to two per cent was challenged. Taking unconsciously recourse to Hohfeldian concept of right strict sense M.M. Punchi, J. ruled that "Article 16(4) does not confer any right to a citizen to have created reservations in favour of any backward class of citizens. Correspondingly, there is no constitutional duty imposed on the Government to make reservations in favour of Scheduled Castes/Scheduled Tribes and Backward Classes. Treating Articles 16(4) and 15(4) as enabling provisions giving only discretionary power on State, the learned judge ruled that "no one can claim reservation as a matter of right". More surprising was the decision of Bombay High Court in *Anil* versus *The Dean, Government Medical College, Nagpur*, wherein a backward class student challenged Rule 5-A(d) which provided ten per cent reservation for backward classes. The clarification issued to the Rule provided that "ten per cent is not an overall ceiling for the OBC candidates. It is open to the OBC candidates to secure more than ten per cent seats on the basis of merit. However, if the admissions they secure on merit are less than ten per cent there should be reservation for them to the extent of the shortfall below ten per cent." The contention of Backward Classes was ten per cent seats must be reserved in addition merit seats occupied by BCs too. And this was the right content. But it did not appeal to the High Court. Rejecting the argument Ginwala, J. ruled that provision made in Clause (4) of Article 15 is only by way of exception to the fundamental right guaranteed under Clause (1) of Article 15, and Clause (2) of Article 29 and that it is only enabling provision." Ginwala, J. emphatically ruled that "Clause (4) of Article 15 of Constitution does not confer any right, much less a fundamental right in the classes, castes or tribes specified in that clause to have seats reserved for them in services or educational institutions." It need not be described here that logic in both the cases was misplaced and so unconvincing and against the basic philosophy of reservational justice that it has lost its force in light of later decisions of Supreme Court and specific rules made by the government explaining application of the reservational rule.

In *P and T SC/ST Employees Welfare Association* versus *Union of India,* the Supreme Court directed the Government of India to pursue the same policy of reservation for SCs and STs in the Post and Telegraph department as it pursued in other departments. Thus, if the government does something to discriminate among the various departments of the government services, the Supreme Court has chosen to interfere. In the above referred case by an agreement in 1983 between the Ministry of Communication and certain Associations a consistent policy of promotion to higher cadre was fixed after 16 years irrespective of being SC/ST general category members. Earlier SC/ST candidates were getting promotion after completion of 12 to 13 years. Delivering the judgment of the Court Venkataramiah, J. made it clear that: "Deprivation violated the equality clause of the Constitution. Similar advantage was being enjoyed by persons belonging to the Scheduled Castes and Scheduled Tribes in other Departments and only the employees of P and T Department had been deprived of it. While it may be true that no writ can be issued ordinarily compelling the Government to make reservation under Article 16(4) which is only an enabling clause, the circumstances in which the members belonging to the Scheduled Castes and Scheduled Tribes in the Posts and Telegraphs Department are deprived of indirectly the advantage of such reservation which they were enjoying earlier while others who are similarly situated in the other departments are allowed to enjoy it make the action of Government discriminatory and invite intervention by the Court." In this case, the court did not take recourse to Article 16(4) but granted relief under equality clause. It could have very well said that once the government creates right in favour of certain classes it could not deprive them of that benefit and to do so would violate Article 16(4). In *Joy Kanta Hira* versus *State of Assam,* the High Court did the same thing. It granted relief to a member of SC which he was entitled under a government notification but was denied by administration. The High Court supported its decision by reference to Articles 39 and 46 of the Constitution. The same analogy would apply to OBCs.

Article 16 (4) and the Concept of Reservation in Favour of OBCs

The question of providing reservation to OBCs under Article 16(4) has been debated at length in various cases. The Mandal Judgement also threw light on it and decided the case. Kania C. J. and Venkatachaliah, Ahmadi and Jeevan Reddy, JJ took the view in Mandal case that clause (4) of Article 16 is exhaustive of the provisions that can be made in favour of the Backward Classes in the matter of employment. Pandian, J. in his concurring view made it clear that Article 16(4) is exhaustive of all the reservations that can be made in favour of any Backward Classes of citizens. He further made it clear that no reservation can be made under Article 16(4) for classes other than backward classes. Sawant, J. in his concurring judgment made it clear that so far as Backward Classes are concerned, the reservation for them can only be made under clause (4) as they have been taken out from classes intended under Article 16(1). The implicit message of Article 16(4) is that it is exhaustive for Backward Classes and therefore no reservation can be made under Article 16(4) for any class other than "backward classes". That is to say it would not be open to make provision for reservation in services in favour of physically handicapped, army personnel and freedom fighters and their dependents, project affected persons, etc., under Article 16(4). Thommen, J. too considered Article 16(4) as exhaustive for backward classes. Kuldip Singh, J. allowed its exhaustiveness in light of permissible classification of the equality of opportunity. Clause (4) of Article 16 was treated as another facet of Article 16(1), and it exclusively provides for reservation which is one of the forms of the classification Sahai, J. too expressed the similar opinion.

Kania, C.J. and Venkatachaliah, Ahmadi and Jeevan Reddy, JJ. in their judgment made it clear that: "Clause (4) is not, and cannot be held to be, exhaustive of the concept of reservations – it is exhaustive of reservations in favour of Backward Classes alone. Merely because one form of the classification is stated as a specific clause, it does not follow that the very concept and power of classification implicit in clause (1) is exhausted thereby. To say so would not be correct in principle". And a note of caution was issued: "But at the same time, one thing is clear. It is in very exceptional situation – and not for all and sundry reasons — that any further reservations, of whatever kind, should be provided under clause (1). In such cases, the State has to satisfy, if called upon that making such a provision was necessary (in public interest) to redress a specific situation. The very presence of clause (4) should act as a damper upon the propensity to create further classes deserving special treatment. For, if reservations are made both under clause (4) as well as clause (1), the vacancies available for the free competition as well as reserved categories would be correspondingly whittled down and that is not a reasonable thing to do."

Pandian, J. in his concurring judgment expressed the opinion that clause (4) of Article 16 is exhaustive for backward classes. For other classes Article 16(1) is to be invoked. Pandian, J. ruled that under clause (1) of Article 16 reservation for appointments or posts can be made to other sections of the society such as physically handicapped, etc.

Sawant, J. in his concurring view expressed the opinion that classification can be made in favour of physically handicapped, army personnel and freedom fighters and their dependents, project- affected persons. Such classification would not be hit by Article 16(2). Sawant, J. clarified it, "Apart from the fact that they cut across all classes, the reservations in their favour are made on considerations other than that of backwardness within the meaning of clause (4)."

Kuldip Singh, J. and R.M. Sahai, J. ruled out the possibility of any reservation in addition to reservation of Backward Classes under Article 16(4). R.M. Sahai, J. ruled that Article 16(4) being part of the scheme of equality doctrine is exhaustive of reservation, therefore, no reservation can be made under Article 16(1). The learned judge gave many reasons for his conclusion:

Firstly, extension of reservation to new categories under Articles 15(4) and 16(4) beyond the 50 per cent rule laid down in Balaji and Devadasan, as such to government nominees, political sufferers, defence personnel, sportsmen, children of MISA and DISIR detenus, etc., under the cover of reasonable classification is a constitutional distortion and therefore cannot be legitimately and legally accepted as valid.

Secondly, reservation cannot be linked with population. On plain construction inadequacy of representation cannot be the measure of reservation. Proportionate representation cannot be read into Article 16(4).

Thirdly, since the Constitution considers all citizens equal for purposes of employment except those who fall under Article 16(4) any further classification or grouping for reservation would be constitutionally invalid.

On the above reasons, the conclusion of Sahai, J. is that no reservation can be made for any class other than backward class either under Article 16(1) or 16(4). Kuldip Singh, J. fully endorsed it.

Unlike Kania, C.J. and, Venkatachaliah, Ahmadi, Jeevan Reddy, Pandian and Sawant, JJ. Thommen, Kuldip Singh and Sahai, JJ., were not agreeable to give reservation to classes other than Backward Classes under Article 16(1). Thommen, J. was willing to grant preferences without reservation like prescribing longer period for passing a test or by awarding additional marks or granting other advantages such as relaxation of age or other minimum requirements to all disadvantaged classes of citizens. Thus, he observed that disadvantaged citizens like blind, deaf, dumb and maimed and like may be beneficiaries of preferences short of reservation. Kuldip Singh, J. held that protective discrimination, short of reservations, which satisfy the test of reasonableness, is permitted under Article 16(1). R.M. Sahai, J. at length discussed the preferential treatment which can be allowed under Article 16. He maintained distinction between the reservation and preferential treatment: "In one a group of class or collectivity is separately provided for and the competition are amongst them only. Whereas in preferential treatment, the collectivity is part of the same group but it is permitted with some weightage due to social, economic or any justifiable reasons."

So long as only preferential treatment is allowed to disadvantaged sections other than backwards, as conceded by Thommen, Kuldip Singh and Sahai, JJ. there is no problem of adjustment. But if reservation is conceded to them as recognised by majority the problem of adjustment may come up. In cases of reservations made under Article 16(1) it has to be adjusted and implemented as not to exceed the level of representation fixed for the Backward Classes of citizens. The adjustment is to be done within 50 per cent limit and the case of handicapped, political sufferer's dependents, etc., is adjusted in quota meant for his castes' other men, i.e., if he belongs to upper caste his case would be adjusted against open posts, if OBCs, then within 27 per cent and SCs/STs then within 23 per cent.

As to the exhaustiveness of reservation under Article 16(4) Kania, C.J. and Venkatachaliah, Ahmadi and Jeevan Reddy, JJ. interpreted reservation in view of its use. The words "any provision for the reservation of appointments or posts," were taken into consideration and the question to be put was whether the said words contemplate only one form of provision namely, reservation simpliciter, or do they take in other forms of special provisions such as preferences, concessions and exemptions. The conclusion drawn was: "reservation is the highest form of special provision, while preference, concession and exemption are lesser forms. The constitutional scheme and context of Article 16(4) induces us to take the view that larger concept of reservations take within its sweep all supplemental and ancillary provisions as also lesser types of special provisions like exemptions, concessions, relaxations, consistent no doubt with the requirement of maintenance of efficiency of administration – the admonition of Article 335."

Sawant, J. in his concurring judgment too recognised different forms of reservations including preferences, concessions, exemptions, extra facilities, etc., or often exclusive quota in appointments. Sawant, J. made it clear, "when measures other than an exclusive quota for appointments are adopted, they form part of the reservation measures or are ancillary to or necessary for availing of the reservations. Whatever the form of reservation, the Backward Classes have to look for them to Article 16(4) and the other classes to Article 16(1)".

Real Aims of Affirmative Action and Protective Discrimination for OBCs

The Constitution of India provided protection for Backward Classes to help them overcome their social disabilities. A certain proportion of seats in the Parliament, and in the state legislatures were reserved for SCs and STs as were jobs in the Government and seats in educational institutions. The Constitution abolished untouchability through the Untouchability Act, 1955. Protection of Civil Rights Act of 1976, and Prevention of Atrocities Act 1989 also were passed. These radical measures were a right beginning to eliminate caste like discrimination and to help the Backward Classes overcome their social disabilities. Backward Classes other than SCs and STs were also brought under the protective discrimination policy with the decision of the Government of India in 1990 to implement the recommendations of the Mandal Commission report and recommendations regarding the benefits to be extended to the socially and educationally backward classes. Accordingly, orders were issued for 27 per cent of the vacancies in civil posts and services under the government of India to be reserved for socially and educationally Backward Classes in case of direct recruitment. After this decision of implementation of recommendations of the Mandal Commission there was wide spread protest against it. Writ petitions were filed in the Supreme Court challenging this decision of the government. The judgment in the Writ Petition (civil) No. 930 of 1990, *Indira Sawhney and others* versus *Union of India and others,* was delivered on 16-11-1992 by the Supreme Court of India. In this judgement, the Supreme Court went into several basic questions including those relating to reservation. By following the decision of the Supreme Court, the Government of India has decided that the benefit of reservations intended for the OBCs will not be extended to persons/sections falling under the category of the Creamy Layer.

By now it is well-accepted principle of equalitarian justice that it has to be made effective by equalising measures. Article 15(4) speaks of making special provisions and Article 16(4) speaks of 'reservation'. One invites positive action programmes and the other positive discrimination programmes. Does it make any difference?

In Mandal case, the leading majority decision of Kania, C.J. Venkatachaliah, Ahmadi and Jeevan Reddy, JJ. discounted the possibility of compartmentalisation of the constitutional scheme into positive action and positive discrimination. It was elaborated: "By now, it is well-settled that reservation in educational institutions and other walks of life can be provided under Article 15(4) just as reservations can be provided in services under Article 16(4). If so, it would not be correct to confine Article 15(4) to programmes of positive action alone. Article 15(4) is wider than Article 16(4) in as much as several kinds of positive action programmes can also be evolved and implemented thereunder (in addition to reservation) to improve the conditions of SEBCs, Scheduled Castes and Scheduled Tribes, whereas Article 16(4) speaks of only one type of remedial measure, namely, reservation of appointment/posts." Minority clarified that "it may not be entirely right to say that Article 15(4) is a provision envisaging programmes of positive action. Indeed, even programmes of positive action may sometimes involve a degree of discrimination."

Articles 15(4) and 16(4) presents two sides of the same coin. Some differences shown between the two are not very convincing. For instance, Thommen, J. pointed out in Mandal case that "reservation is a remedy for historical discrimination and its continuing ill-effects, other affirmative action programmes are intended to redress discrimination of all kinds, whether current or historical." With due respect, it is submitted that conceptualisation and generalisation on the basis of theoretical formulations do not reveal the clear picture. The cases narrated in the beginning may indicate that everything is not right with non-reserved posts. The less meritorious may get job through unwritten reservations and meritorious OBCs may be ousted. Thus, in some cases reservation may be necessary for protection of merit, and resisting and eradicating the ill-effect of current-hostile discrimination.

The real difference between the positive action under Article 15(4) and positive discrimination under Article 16(4), what one may prefer to say, is that the main aim behind the positive action in the form of preferential treatment through special provisions is the amelioration of the status of Backward Classes for the purpose of the redressal of backwardness. It may be part of compensatory justice appropriately compensating the victims of past discrimination. It may be needed to qualify the test of distributive justice seeking to ensure that community resources are more equitably and justly shared among all classes of citizens, as Thommen, J. observed in Mandal case. On the other hand, "the provision for reservation in appointments under Article 16(4) is not aimed at economic betterment or alleviation of poverty. Article 16(4) is specially designed "to give a due share in the State power to those who have remained out of it mainly on account of their social and therefore, educational and economic backwardness." Thus, the main objective of Article 16(4) is to give to Backward Classes their fair share in power. This debate throws a question "whether power structure in Indian Society is static or dynamic in nature? In caste-based society, where apparatus is like water-tight compartment caste status and position remain at the same level what has been ascribed, and goes on from generation to generation. This answers static nature of society. Educational and economic advancements of an individual person belonging to SC, ST and Backward Caste is an individual achievement and not of a caste as a whole. In that sense, this can be a case of dynamic nature of Indian society.

OBC Quota Law Held Valid

The Supreme Court, on April 9, upheld the law enacted by the Union Government providing 27 per cent quota for Other Backward Classes in Central educational institutions such as IITs/IIMs from the academic year 2008-2009. A five-judge Constitution Bench in a unanimous verdict running into over 500 pages also held that the 93rd Constitution Amendment inserting Article 15(5) in the Constitution to enable the Centre and the States to enact quota laws is valid. The Court disposed of a batch of petitions questioning the quota law and the 93rd Amendment. Earlier, in March 2007, the apex court had restrained the Centre from implementing the quota law on the ground that no data was furnished by the Government and the data relied on was only 1931 census. While deciding the issue in favour of the government, the court had struck a balance by directing exclusion of creamy layer among the Backward Classes.

From that time onwards continuous efforts have also been made to assess the success and failures of such protective discrimination. Many social scientists, political parties, caste/community organisations have participated in such debates and argued in many ways. Many social scientists claim that such efforts have benefited only the creamy layer of the caste/communities so protected. Other says that reservation should not be made a permanent phenomenon as it appears today because it is neither in the interest of the OBCs nor the nation. Similarly, other issues raised, like the caste has lost its traditional sanctions and functions but caste continues to occupy the central place in regard to the policy of reservation. The provisions made under the protective discrimination policy attract criticism as no scientific criterion is evolved to assess the backwardness of castes/communities and thus the genuine OBCs are not benefitted from the existing reservation policy. As protective discrimination has taken a political turn and become very complex and lost its relevance. The reservation has now become a politically sensitive issue. Political parties and caste/community organisations are utilising the reservation issue for their vested interest up to a great extent. They are engaged in extending reservations to more and more castes which is building resentment among the castes. Representatives of the castes/communities complain that the more educated and socially advantaged castes in the reserved categories have monopolised the privileges of reservation and a new trend to demand separate quotas for each of the castes within the reserved categories has started. This trend is sharpening the identity of castes and of even sub-castes within castes.

Constitutional Provisions

The Constitution provides benefits to weaker section of society under Articles 15(4) and 16(4) mainly related to educational development and employment opportunities in Government services. It is the responsibility of the State to provide educational opportunities and employment opportunities to all including weaker sections of the society on the principle of equality. It was the enormity of inequality that gave rise to various low caste movements, particularly in the south, right from the beginning of this century. As a result of sustained agitations, specific quotas of seats had been ear-marked in medical and engineering colleges in the state. In post-independence India, the first important step to remedy this situation was taken with the incorporation of clause 4 under Article 16 of the Constitution, which empowered the states to reserve posts in favour of Backward Classes of citizens. After Independence, Scheduled Castes and Scheduled Tribes have been constitutionally recognised as groups under the category of weaker sections. They have started getting benefits in educational institutions and employment. Other Backward Castes (OBCs) got recognition in 1993. The present section focusses on Constitutional provisions related to various benefits available to these groups.

Social justice is a means to achieve the aim of establishing an egalitarian society and eradicating distribution of power in its several social sections. To achieve the goals of distribution of political, administrative and economic power, the Constitution of India was amended 85 times during the last 50 years. The democratic, secular and liberal Constitution of India is doing well under the ethos of social milieu and it is playing a major role in shaping its policies and competing to gain and control political power. The Indian constitutional law is a unique social document which accepts social pluralism and makes provisions for safeguarding the interests of different social sections. It has been aimed at bringing social equality, social justice and distribution of power along with protection of right to equality. However, in the last few years, it has become imperative for the defenders of the exploitative social order and monopolisers of social, economic and political power to take to the streets and approach the judiciary to create hindrances in the way of social legislation for distribution of power. On the other hand, the leaders of the deprived and disadvantaged social sections have been trying to get benefit of the special provisions made for bringing social justice to the poor and deprived social sections, in order to have a share in the distribution of state power.

The expression 'Backward Classes' has not been defined anywhere in the Indian Constitution. Backward Classes include

Scheduled Castes (SCs) and Scheduled Tribes (STs) and Other Backward Classes (OBCs). The OBCs are other than SCs and STs, and who are also socially and educationally backward in comparison to the other advanced sections of the society.

Articles 15(4) and 340 use the words 'socially and educationally backward classes'. It may be mentioned that whereas Article 16(4) refers to "any backward class citizen", in clause (4) of Article 15, the reference is "any socially and educationally backward classes". As Pt. Nehru explained before the select committee, this departure was made to bring the language of Article 15(4) in line with that of Article 340, which provides that Backward Classes Commission may be set-up for "socially and educationally backward class citizens". Perusal of the Parliament debate on this amendment clearly shows that irrespective of the criteria for the classification of Backward Classes there had to be a list of castes and communities. Pt. Nehru observed, "We want to put an end to ...... all those infinite divisions that have grown up in our social life. We may call them by any name you like, the caste system or religious divisions, etc...." (B.P. Mandal, 1980, p. 24, Vol. I).

Article 16(4) speaks of just 'Backward Classes', and Article mentions the 'weaker sections of the people'. Even now, the term 'Backward Classes' is defined differently in the reports of the different Backward Classes commissions and the judgments of various High Courts and the Supreme Court of India. As leader of the Congress Party in Constituent Assembly of India, Jawaharlal Nehru moved a historic resolution on the aims and objectives of the Constitution. It was regarding provisions for adequate safeguards to the minorities, backward and depressed sections of society. The resolution stated that: "Wherein shall be guaranteed and secured to all the people of India, justice, social, economic and political, equality of status and opportunity before the law, freedom of thought, expression, belief faith, worship, vocation, association and action, subject to law and public morality, and wherein adequate safeguards shall be made available to minorities, backward and tribal areas, and depressed and other Backward Classes.

The problems of Backward Classes including the issue of distribution of political and administrative power through policy of reservation and other benefits enjoyed by them till the attainment of independence and the future of these policies were thoroughly debated before appropriate Articles and provisions were incorporated in the Indian Constitution. Despite the divergent views expressed as to the meaning of the term 'Backward Classes' there was a consensus that the term would include not just the Scheduled Castes and Scheduled Tribes, but also others who were economically, educationally and socially backward. In India, there are some communities, apart from the Scheduled Castes and Scheduled Tribes, which give a definite impression of social and educational backwardness and inferiority and powerlessness in comparison to the monopoly of social, economic and political power by the traditional upper castes. The sub-committee on Fundamental Rights had discussed the question of other Backward Classes in detail. It, however, did not provide reservation and any other special measures to them. It was left it for the State Governments to identify the Backward Classes in their respective territories and to assist them. Thus, the chance of OBCs to share power in the Central services became futile but they became important power brokers at the state level.

The Constitution of India made certain provisions for the welfare of deprived social section, known as affirmative action, reservation policy and positive discrimination. The aims and objectives of the Constitution, the general agreement and the compromises reached in the Constituent Assembly are reflected in the different Articles and provisions relating to backward classes, e.g., the Preamble, Articles 38 and 46 of the Directive Principles of State Policy, Articles 14, 15 and 16 of the Fundamental Rights and Articles 338 and 340 of the Constitution of India. The Preamble to the Constitution expresses the determination and aspirations of the people of India in the following terms: "...Justice, Social, Economic and Political, Liberty of thought, expression, belief, faith and worship: Equality of status and of opportunity; and to promote fraternity among them all assuring the dignity of the individual and the unity and integrity of the Nation." The two objectives: justice – social, economic and political; and equality of status and opportunity of the Preamble are especially relevant and linked to the advancement of the weaker sections and Backward Classes. In short, the Constitution of India promises not only political democracy, but also social democracy as described by Ambedkar in his speech in Constitution Assembly: "It means a way of life which recognises liberty, equality and fraternity which are not treated as separate items in a trinity. They form a union of trinity in the sense that to divorce one from the other is to defeat the very purpose of democracy. Liberty cannot be divorced from equality and cannot be divorced from liberty, nor can liberty and equality be divorced from fraternity".

The Constitution of India includes a number of Articles which deal with compensatory preference for the Backward Classes. The most important among them are Articles 15(4) and 16(4). Articles 46, 325, 338, 340, 341, 342, 366(24) and 366(25) also have an influence on the subject.

Along with the Right to Equality, the Constitution of India provides separate and special provisions for the advancement of Backward Classes. It is often called compensatory discrimination, protective discrimination and discrimination in reverse. These provisions permit the government to undertake special steps for the betterment of the Backward Classes. Article 15(4), which was incorporated into the Indian Constitution under the Constitution (First Amendment) Act, 1951 declares: "Nothing in Article 15 or in Clause (2) of Article 29 shall prevent the State from making any special provision for the advancement of any socially and educationally Backward Classes of citizens or for the Scheduled Castes and the Scheduled Tribes." Article 15(4) provides the ground to the State to make special provisions for the Backward Classes in all the areas within its jurisdiction. The expression 'class' in Article 15(4) means a homogeneous section of the people ground together on account of certain common traits and by being identifiable by some common attributes such as status, rank, occupation, residence in a locality, race and religion. In defining whether a particular section forms a class, caste cannot be totally excluded. At the same time, a test based upon only caste or community cannot be accepted. Article 16(4) which is relevant to government jobs, says: "Nothing in this Article shall prevent the State from making any provision for the reservation of appointments or posts in favour of any backward class of citizens which in the opinion of the State is not adequately represented in the services under the State."

Article 340 is connected with the appointment of commissions for the investigation of the socio-economic considerations of SCs, STs and OBCs. It makes it obligatory for the appointment of commissions by the President, (i) to look into and report on the administration of the scheduled areas and the welfare of the Scheduled Tribes, and (ii) to investigate the conditions of socially and educationally Backward Classes and to make recommendations as to the step that should be taken by the Union or State Government to ameliorate those conditions. So far two such commissions have been appointed by the President of India under the Article 340 of the Constitution.

Backward Classes and Directive Principles of State Policy

The Directive Principles of State Policy enshrined in the Articles 38 and 46 of the Indian Constitution make it the duty of the State to strive to promote the welfare of the people in general and weaker sections, including the Backward Classes, in particular. Article 38 of the Indian Constitution reads thus:

1. The State shall strive to promote the welfare of the people by securing and protecting as effectively as it may a social order in which justice, social, economic and political, shall inform all the institutions of national life.

2. The State shall, in particular, strive to minimise the inequalities in income, and endeavour to eliminate inequalities in status, facilities and opportunities, not only amongst individuals but also amongst groups of people residing in different areas or engaged in different vocations. Thus, the Directive Principles along with the Preamble embody the socio-economic ideals which the nation had set before itself during the freedom

movement. It points out to the political mind of the makers of the Constitution who visualised the creation of a new social order in India on the basis of social, economic and political justice, eliminating the evils of the existing socio-economic system. Though the nature of the 'social order' is not defined in the Constitution, but is interpreted to mean a 'welfare state' and 'socialistic pattern of society'. As a part of this objective, the State is directed to remove the existing inequalities of income, status, facilities and opportunities among the individuals and groups in India. Further, Article 46 directs that: "The State shall promote with special care the educational and economic interests of weaker sections of the people, and, in particular, of the Scheduled Castes and Scheduled Tribes, and shall protect them from social injustice and all forms of exploitation."

As can be seen, Article 46 makes the State duty-bound to take action to ameliorate the conditions of the weaker sections including the Backward Classes. They are two-fold: (i) to promote with special care the educational and economic interests by taking 'positive measures'; and (ii) to prevent social injustice and all forms of exploitation by taking 'preventive measures'.

Analysis of Supreme Court and High Court Decisions

The Constitution accords to weaker sections of society protective discrimination in various Articles including Article 15(4). This clause empowers the State, notwithstanding anything to the contrary in Articles 15(1) and 29(2) to take special reservation for the advancement of any socially and educationally Backward Classes of citizens or for the Scheduled Castes and Scheduled Tribes. But the Constitution neither numerates the class of citizens who are backward nor provides the State with criteria for classifying Backward Classes of citizens. The task of the policy-makers, be it at the Central or State level, becomes complex as they have to keep in the definite prohibitions enumerated in Articles 15(1) and 29(2). The identification of Backward Classes in the Indian Society is not an easy task. Caste-wise enumeration was last done in Census 1931. Again an endeavour was made at the time of census 2001, but a final decision could not be taken. In 2012, there was caste census but till date data is not published. However, according to an estimate given in the Mandal Report based on Census of India 1931, population of other Backward Classes was approximately 52 per cent. The influence of "caste" on the social, educational and economic backwardness of classes of people in the Indian Society has been the subject of debate and research by sociologists. Is the factor of "caste" alone significant in the making of social and educational backwardness or are there other factors? What is the correlation between caste and such other factor and the importance to be given to all these factors, (including caste), with reference to different communities and regions? The question of other determinant like class, or religious group or social group cannot be taken as a base for consideration of social and educational backwardness because these groups have emerged out of many social, economic and political factors. Whether a caste is a class has been debated by many social scientists and in particular sociologists. This point always remained unsettled. Therefore, a number of variables are relevant in the determination of these questions.

The wide language of Article 15(4) "indicates that the Constitution makers relied primarily on the discretion of the politicians and administrators of the future rather than on the courts to keep the principle of preference within boundaries consistent with the Constitution's overall scheme of eliminating caste, religious and other discrimination. These provisions are an expedient hopefully a temporary one – giving the executive and legislatures based discretion in their application. However, this discretion is not so broad as to exclude entirely judicial review of determination of backwardness". The main areas of concretisation of legislative and executive discretion are education, welfare and economic activities such as housing, grant of land etc., and public services.

Who are Backward Classes?

The first decision of the Supreme Court on the scope of Article 15(4) was *Balaji* v. *State of Mysore*. Since 1958, the state of Karnataka (then Mysore) had been attempting to make special provisions for the advancement of its socially and educationally

Backward Classes of citizens under Article 15(4) and whenever any order was passed, its validity was challenged in the High Court which quashed them. The petitions in this case were filed under Article 32 to challenge the validity of the order of the Mysore Government in 1962. The effect of the order was to divide Backward Classes into two categories (i) Backward Classes, and (ii) More Backward Classes. Out of the 50 per cent as the quota for the Backward Classes 28 per cent of seats in technical and professional institutions were reserved for Backward Classes and 22 per cent for more Backward Classes, 15 per cent for Scheduled Castes and three per cent for Scheduled Tribes. Thus, we find that the total quantum of reservation was 68 per cent. Only 32 per cent of the seats were available to the merit pool. This order of the Mysore Government was a sequal to the recommendation of an expert committee set-up by the state government known as the Nagan Gowda Committee, which had investigated the problem of identifying criteria for classifying Backward Classes in the state. The Committee felt that in India a higher social status was generally accorded on the basis of caste and the low social position of any class or community was, therefore, merely on account of the caste system. Whatever the committee observed the social status on the basis of caste is ascribed and not achieved. Those persons who do not fall under four-fold classification *dwija* castes automatically fall in the category of non-Scheduled Castes, non-Scheduled Tribes, i.e., under a separate category of backward castes by virtue of no place in caste apparatus. Social backwardness was considered to be mainly based on racial, tribal and caste differences even though economic backwardness might have also contributed. The Committee had felt that in the prevalent circumstances, the only practicable method of classifying the Backward Classes in the state was on the basis of caste and communities. According to the Committee, the entire Lingayat Community was socially forward and that all sections of Vokkaligas excuding Bhunts were socially backward. With regard to Muslims, majority of the committee felt that they should be classified as backward. The committee further felt that the Backward Classes should be sub-divided into two categories – backward and the more backward.

In case of Muslims (though they do not consider caste system) all castes/communities cannot be socially and educationally backward. For example, Sheikh, Syyed, Pathan, Moghul, Mallik and Mirza are considered to be forward while rest of castes are considered backward or lower class. Even in other religious groups like Sikhs and Christians, caste system exists but that may not be strictly in accordance with the system. However, classification does exist in this regard.

The Supreme Court in a unanimous opinion delivered by Justice Gajendragadkar held the order of the state government unconstitutional. In deciding on the validity of classification of Backward Classes, the Court had to determine the factor for social backwardness educational backwardness. On the question of social backwardness, the court said that in the Hindu Social structure, caste unfortunately played an important role in determining the status of citizens; yet, the special provisions were contemplated for classes of citizens and not for individual citizens as such. It may not be irrelevant to consider the caste of the group, but its primacy should not be over emphasised. The caste system had been the greatest obstacle to the achievement of an egalitarian society and the recognition of specific castes as backward might maintain and perpetuate the existing distinctions on the basis of castes. In addition, the sole test of "caste" would break down in relation to many sections of Indian societies, as for instance, Muslims and Christians, who do not recognise castes in the Hindus conventional sense. "Social backwardness is in the ultimate analysis the result of poverty to a very large extent. The classes of citizens, who are deplorably poor automatically, become socially backward." The court also referred to occupation and place of habitation as contributing to social backwardness. The Backward Classes can, in the matter of their backwardness, be compared with the Scheduled Castes and Scheduled Tribes. The concept of backwardness is not relative in the sense that classes which are backward in relation to the most advanced classes should be included in it. In such relative tests are applied by reason of the most advanced classes, there will be several layers of Backward Classes and each of them may claim to be included under exception clauses. It is significant that the Court referred to the Report of the Backward Classes Commission 1955 (appointed by the Central government in 1953 and known as Kaka Kalelkar Commission), the Memorandum of the Government thereon, the Report of the Commissioner for Scheduled Castes and Scheduled Tribes, 1959, and also the method adopted in Maharashtra Government had defined Backward Classes on the basis of annual income of the family. Monetary grants were given to students pursuing higher education, where it was shown that the annual income of their families was below a prescribed minimum. Though the Court did not express any final opinion, it seemed to view with approval such a scheme coupled with the establishment of more technical and vocational institutions and reservation of seats therein.

The Supreme Court made it clear that backwardness must be social and educational and not either social or educational. If that were the case then common criteria should be evolved for determining social backwardness and educational backwardness. If different standards are applied for both, it is possible that the classes listed as educationally backward may not be so socially and *vice versa*. In fact, the Supreme Court in Balaji's case actually considered the two separately in discussing different criteria for determining social and educational backwardness.

The Supreme Court considered again whether caste was also a class of citizens and whether caste as a whole could be classified as backward. Justice Subha Rao on behalf of the majority observed: Article 15(4) does not speak of castes but only speaks of classes. If the makers of the Constitution intended to take caste also as units of social and educational backwardness, they would have said so as they have said in the case of the Scheduled Castes, and the Scheduled Tribes. Though, it may be suggested that the wider expression "class" is used in clause (4) of Article 15 as there are communities without caste, if the intention was to equate classes with castes, nothing prevented the makers of the Constitution to use the expression "Backward Classes or castes". The juxtaposition of the expression "Backward Classes", "Scheduled Castes" in Article 15(4) also leads to a reasonable inference that the expression classes are not synonymous with castes.

In tune with the conspectus of constitutional provisions, "castes" and "classes" cannot be considered synonymously. The judge said: if we interpret the expression "classes" as "castes" the objective of the Constitution will be defeated and the people who do not deserve any adventitious aid may get it to the exclusion of those who really deserve.

This anomaly would not arise, if without equating caste with class, caste is taken as only one of the factors to determine whether a person belongs to a Backward Class or not. The majority held that under no circumstance a "class" could be equated to a "caste" though the caste of an individual or a group of individuals might be considered along with other relevant factors in placing him in a particular class. Accordingly, Mysore Government's Order of July 1963 was upheld. Justice Mudholkar, who constituted the minority on other aspects of the Chitralekha case felt that "Castes have no relevance in determining what are socially and educationally backward communities" as that would go against clause (1) of Article 15 or clause (2) of Article 29. This is so despite the non-obstante clause in clause 4 of Article 15. In Balaji and Chitralekha case, the Court did not approve of classification of a caste as a whole as backward. Justice Subba Rao in Chitralekha had suggested that if any sub-caste was wholly backward, it might be included in the Scheduled Castes by following the procedure laid down in Article 341(2) of the Constitution.

The Chitralekha approach was departed from in the subsequent decision of the Supreme Court in *P. Rajendran* v. *State of Madras*. The Court had to consider the validity of rules made by the State of Madras for the selection of candidates for admission to the first year integrated MBBS course. Rule 5 classified as socially and educationally backward and reserved seat for the classes specified in group III of the revised appendix 17-A to the Madras Educational Rules. In this case, the petitioners challenged, among other things, the validity of Rule 5 reserving the seats for Backward Classes as violative of Article 15(1), because the list prepared by the state was exclusively on the basis of caste. It was contended on behalf of the state that the list of Backward Classes was made starting from 1906 and was kept updated and that the main criteria for inclusion in the list was the social and educational backwardness of the caste based on occupations pursued by these castes. As the members of the caste as a whole were found to be socially and educationally backward they were placed in the list. The Court also found that the classes of persons referred to in Rule 5 as socially and educationally backward were only castes. The Court further held that: caste is also a class of citizens and if the caste as a whole is socially and educationally backward reservation can be made in favour of such a caste on the ground that it is a socially and educationally backward class of citizens within the meaning of Article 15(4).

Another Supreme Court decision of recent vintage was *K.S. Jayasree* v. *State of Kerala*, an off-shoot of the acceptance of the recommendations of the Kerala Backward Classes Commission (Kumara Pillai Commission) by the Kerala Government. This Commission was set-up in 1964, and it submitted its report in 1965. The Commission adopted a means-cum-caste/community test (application of income test within the backward classes) and recommended that people in Kerala, who are members of families which have an aggregate income of less than Rs 4,200 per annum from all sources and which belong to caste or communities. Kerala Government agreed with the Commission's recommendations but raised the financial ceiling initially to Rs 6,000 and subsequently to Rs 10,000. Those government orders were challenged in the Kerala High Court. In *Shameem* v. *Medical College,* Trivandram, the single Judge quashed the government order holding that irrespective of their economic status all families from the Backward Classes were entitled to protective discrimination as "the test of poverty cannot be the determining factor of social backwardness". The ceiling of Rs 6,000 was also held to be arbitrary. However, on appeal, the Division Bench of the same High Court in *State of Kerala* v. *Krishna Kumari,* reversed the decision of the Single Bench and upheld the government's order. The High Court held that economic backwardness plays a part in social and educational backwardness. So poverty or economic standard is a relevant factor.

The Court felt that the Commission had material before it to conclude that those among the castes who were economically better off were not socially backward. The Court also felt that it was not for it to weigh the quantum of evidence before the Commission or substitute its own view for that of the Commission in this matter.

The Supreme Court in *Jayasree* vs *State of Kerala* upheld the decision of the Kerala High Court, Chief Justice Ray held that neither caste nor poverty would be the sole determining factor of social backwardness. He upheld the validity of the impugned order on the basis that the classification made by it was based not on income but on social and educational backwardness. He also declared that a classification based only on poverty was not logical. In reality, the classification in the instant case was made on the ground of poverty. The test of poverty was based on the income. The purpose of classification was to group the backward castes listed by the Commission into more affluent and less affluent on the basis of certain income limit and to deny protective discrimination to the former group.

Quantum of Reservation

The Supreme Court in Balaji's case while striking down 68 per cent total reservation in favour of Backward Classes, Scheduled Castes and Scheduled Tribes aptly reserved that a special provision envisaged by Article 15(4) must be within reasonable limits. The interests of weaker sections of society which are to be protected by the state have to be adjusted with the interest of the community as a whole. The adjustment of those competing claims is a complex task but, if under the guise of making special provision, a state reserved practically all the seats available....that clearly would be subverting the object of Article 15(4). In this matter again, we are reluctant to say definitely what would be a proper provision to make speaking generally and in a broad way a special provision, should be less than 50 per cent, how much less than 50 per cent would depend upon the relevant prevailing circumstances in each case. Accordingly, the Court held that reservation of 68 per cent made by the impugned order of the Mysore Government was violative of Article 15(4) and as such was "a fraud on the Constitutional power conferred on the State".

A scheme providing for excessive reservation in favour of Harijans, Adivasis and Backward Classes in the disposal of reverbed lands was challenged in *Dahyabhai Chaturbhais* v. *State*. A Government circular had regulated the disposal of reverbed lands to certain groups of people to the exclusion of others after cancellation of the existing order regarding the disposal of such lands by public auction. The priorities for disposal of such lands were: (i) bona fide agriculturalists of the village holding not less than five acres, preference will be given to Harijans, Adivasis and Backward Classes people, (ii) holders of land adjoining Bet Bhatha lands holding land less than 16 acres and who in the Collector's opinion have a genuine need of additional lands for maintenance of their families *inter se* preference in this case also will be as per the above lines, mentioned in (i), (iii) co-operative farming societies of Harijans, Adivasis and Backward Class persons, (iv) co-operative farming society consisting of landless labourers or small holders and (v) any of the priority holders under the Water Land Rules.

The Gujarat High Court held that the effect of those clauses was not to make a special provision for small landholders or landless people who need the land for their maintenance and who could not bid at the public auction as against rich people. The whole classification was based on two essential principles – that the individual would be excluded both by co-operative society and by an individual member of Harijans, Adivasis and Backward class people. The state did not produce any list even though the State had been given proper opportunity to file an additional affidavit of persons, who were regarded as Backward Class people and for whose benefit this reservation was sought to be made. There was, therefore, no material whatever to indicate the category of "backward class people" as understood in the relevant Government Resolution. Besides, the reservation was so excessive as in cases of Harijans, Adivasis and Backward Class people that they would completely exclude bona fide agriculturalists having no land or having landless than five acres, who would have fallen otherwise under the first category of priority holders. Almost all the hundred per cent land would go to those Harijans, Adivasis and Backward persons and the reservation would cease to be a reservation within the meaning of Article 15(4). The Government order was held to be unconstitutional.

No Degrees of Backwardness among the Backward Classes

The question whether it is constitutionally permissible to sub-classify the Backward Classes on the basis of relative backwardness came up for decision in Balaji's case. In that case, the Mysore Government's order of 1962 had divided the Backward Classes into two categories, namely, (i) Backward Classes and (ii) More Backward Classes. Out of 50 per cent fixed as the quota for Backward Classes, 28 per cent was fixed for Backward Classes and 22 per cent for More Backward Classes. The Supreme Court held that such sub-classification of the Backward Classes was unconstitutional under Article 15(4). In effect Article 15(4) makes special provision for the really Backward Classes in making two categories of Backward Classes, the Order in substance had devised measures for the benefit of all the classes who were less advanced compared to the most advanced classes in the State. The up-shot of the method adopted by the Order was that nearly 90 per cent of the population was treated as backward. This case is authority for the proposition that the concept of backwardness is not relative in the sense that classes which are backward in relation to the most advanced classes should be included in it.

The Mysore High Court in *Ramakrishna Singh* vs *State of Mysore*, (pre-Balaji decision) held that the list of Backward Classes including 95 per cent of the population of the State was a "fraud" on the Constitution because it excluded communities who represented five per cent of the population. This was more a discrimination against the excluded class of population than a provision for the Backward Classes. Besides it was a provision not for socially and educationally backward classes, but for the classes who were comparatively backward to the most advanced classes. This was not warranted under Article 15(4).

No Prohibition on Backward Classes to Compete with Others

In *V. Raguramulu* vs *State of Andhra Pradesh,* (a pre-Balaji decision) the applicants belonging to Backward Classes applied for admission to Medical Colleges. They were interviewed but were not selected on the basis that a maximum of 15 per cent of the total number of seats allotted for the Backward Classes was exhausted by the other applicants from Backward Classes who secured higher marks than the petitioners, though in fact they got higher marks than the two candidates, who were selected for the seats thrown open for general competition. The two candidates challenged the selection as violative of Article 15 and 29(2).

Chief Justice K. Subba Rao invalidated the reservation on a maximum percentage basis for the Backward Classes on the ground that such a provision would not be for the advancement of the Backward Classes. On the other hand, if a maximum is fixed, instead of providing for the advancement of those classes in the contingency visualised above, it would retard their progress; for students of those classes who secure more marks than students who compete for the general seats and get less marks than students belonging to their classes, would not get seats. To this extent, the order of the government would be in excess of the power conferred on it under clause (4) and, therefore, could not affect the fundamental rights of the citizens whether they belonged to the Backward Classes or not.

The Court suggested that the rule may be modified but substituting the words "minimum of 15 per cent" for the words "maximum of 15 per cent".

In *Ramakrishna Singh* vs. *State of Mysore,* two orders of Mysore Government dated 14th May, 1959 and 22nd July, 1959 listing Backward Classes and their reservation for admission to professional colleges were challenged. The list of Backward Classes included 95 per cent of the population of the State and all communities and castes of the Hindus other than *Brahmins, Banias, Kayasthas* and all the communities in the State except Anglo-Indians and Parsis had been included in the list. The two orders had fixed 20 per cent for Scheduled Castes and Scheduled Tribes and 45 per cent for the socially and educationally Backward Classes and the remaining 35 per cent was to be filled up on the basis of merit.

The order of 22nd July, 1959 had further sub-divided the listed Backward Classes into several categories and fixed different percentages for the reservation of seats. The net effect was that the person belonging to each sub-group could only compete for the seats reserved for them and were not eligible for the remaining seats reserved for the Backward Classes. In other words, they were debarred from competing for the remaining seats in open competition amongst the members of the Backward Classes listed in the orders.

The Mysore High Court (now Karnataka High Court) through Justice S.R. Das Gupta held that socially and educationally Backward Classes of citizens could be determined on the basis of castes. Other criterion such as geographical or occupational is employed to determine the socially and educationally backward classes.

The Court also held that it was to the extent as provided in Article 15(4) that the fundamental rights conferred upon the citizens of the State by Articles 15(1) and Article 29(2) could be abridged. If the reservation in question could not be justified by the provisions of Article 15(4), then the same had to be struck down as violative of the fundamental right of the citizens. The court cited with approval the decisions of the Andhra Pradesh High Court in *Raghuramulu* vs. *State of Andhra Pradesh* and *Sudarsan* vs. *State of Andhra Pradesh*.

The court disapproved of the principles applied by the Government in classifying the socially and educationally Backward Classes in the instant case. In fact, the 1941 census report was relied upon to determine Backward Classes in 1959.

This was not justifiable in the view of the court, taking into account the considerable changes that had taken place since 1941. On the classification of educational backwardness, the English literacy test adopted by the State for the area covered by the old Mysore State was not approved by the court as an intelligible test for the whole of the new Mysore State. Further, no indication was given by the State on which the social backwardness of the communities had been determined. The classes grouped under the orders must be both socially and educationally backward. Further, the decision of the listed Backward Classes into various sub-groups on the basis of the population of the community and the specification of the percentage of reservation of seats in respect of each group was held to be unconstitutional because the persons of each sub-group could only compete for the seats reserved for that group and were not eligible for the remaining seats reserved for the Backward Class. Hence, the notification, instead of benefitting the Backward Classes abridged their fundamental rights and could not be sustained under Article 15(4).

As regards the legality of transferring unfilled seats out of the reservation made for Scheduled Castes and Scheduled Tribes to benefit other Backward Classes, the court said that it had to be examined in the light of the fundamental rights in Articles 15(1) and 29(2) of the Constitution. Regarding the transfer of unfilled seats of Scheduled Castes and Scheduled Tribes to Other Backward Classes, the court said that those three groups were three different categories whose classification was based on different indicia and the classification of other Backward Classes might vary from time to time and with reference to the nature of their backwardness. Consequently, it was held that the allotment of seats under the provisions of the impugned orders in favour of other Backward Classes in excess of the 22 per cent reserved for them in a manner otherwise than by open competition is an unreasonable restraint on the fundamental right of other citizens and, therefore, opposed to the Constitution.

Backward Classes Commissions in Various States

The different commissions have been taken different approaches in fixing up the criteria for identification of OBCs which reflect the absence of uniform basis backwardness. The two Central Commissions like Kaka Kalelkar and Mandal Commissions had different outlooks. The State Governments' Commissions had different considerations. Wide differences between these Commissions on various issues, in some cases irrational, have not only expressed absence of uniform policy, but it has also become a source of constant bitterness between the two groups of people. Some people though better off are enjoying privileges of backwardness in various States and the Central Government services. Others, who really deserve privileges, suffer because they belong to castes outside the jurisdiction of backwards. In this situation, calls for an analysis of different Commissions constituted by the State Governments, in brief, the existing situation and approaches towards the reservation policy for OBCs.

State Backward Classes Commissions

Andhra Pradesh

Before the organisation of Andhra Pradesh, the OBCs were getting preferential treatment in the State of Madras. In 1966, the Government of Andhra Pradesh notified a list of 112 communities belonging to OBCs and ordered for reservation of seats for them in government services and professional colleges, etc. Several writ petitions were filed against this order. This order was struck down by the High Court of Andhra Pradesh on the ground that the State could not produce evidence regarding the social and educational backwardness of the listed communities. This decision was upheld by the Supreme Court.

Manohar Pershad Commission, 1968: On 12th April, 1968, the State Government appointed a Backward Classes Commission, chaired by Manohar Pershad, for preparing a list of all the Backward Classes which were not adequately represented in the services of the State and to make suggestions in regard to (a) the reservation of government posts in favour of such backward classes; and (b) the percentage of proportion of such reservation and the fixed time during which such reservation might be made. In its report of 20th June, 1970, the Commission listed 92 classes as other Backward Classes. Further, it recommended reservation of 30 per cent of the vacancies in government service and educational institutions for candidates belonging to the Backward Classes. This would be in addition to the seats the backward class candidates might avail in the open competition. The Commission distributed the reserved vacancies among four categories of OBCs: (i) Aboriginal tribes, vimukta jatis, nomadic and semi-nomadic tribes (seven per cent), (ii) Vocational groups (13 per cent), (iii) Harijan converts (one per cent) and (iv) other classes (nine per cent). Finally, it approved the view that caste was also a class and that reservation in favour of a caste was acceptable if the whole caste was socially and educationally backward.

Veerapa Committee, 1975: Vidhan Sabha of the fifth general election in Andhra Pradesh appointed a Committee of the legislature headed by Agisam Veerappa in 1975 to recommend welfare measures for the benefit of the Backward Classes. The committee, which submitted its report in 1977, suggested the following measures along with 25 per cent reservation: (a) sanction of scholarships from class I onwards instead of VI standard as was the practice; (b) an increase in the amount of the scholarship; and (c) a lowering of the minimum marks required for students belonging to OBCs for admission from 40 per cent to 35 per cent.

Muralidhar Rao Commission, 1982: The third State Commission, constituted in February, 1982, was headed by Muralidhar Rao. The Commission, in its report in September 1982, suggested 44 per cent reservation of seats and posts for 52 per cent state population of OBCs. The Commission included 10 more castes and sub-castes in the list of OBCs and the total rose to 102. The recommendations could not be implemented by the Congress Party. It was defeated in the elections of state assembly elections in 1983. The ruling Telugu Desham Party (TDP) implemented it only in July 1986. The High Court of Andhra Pradesh struck it down on 5th September, 1986. The government decision witnessed public protest against reserving 71 per cent of seats and posts.

Bihar

In 1951, the Government of Bihar had prepared a list of 109 Backward Classes for awarding post-matric scholarships, etc., under a scheme launched by the Ministry of Education, Government of India advised the State Government to draw their own list as they did not accept the recommendations given by Kaka Kalelkar Commission. In 1964, Patna High Court (AIR 1965, Patna 372), in view of Supreme Court's judgment in Balaji's case, declared Bihar government's list of Backward Classes as invalid as it had relied on caste as the criterion of Backward Classes. In view of this, the State Government decided that the current educational benefits should be given only to such students of other Backward Classes mentioned in the 1951 order whose family income was below Rs 500 per month. For admission to medical colleges, the income limit was fixed at Rs 250 per month.

Mungerilal Commission, 1971: Bihar government appointed a Backward Classes Commission under the chairmanship of Mungerilal in June 1971, and it submitted its report in February 1976. The Commission took note of representation in government and private services, membership and elected bodies, occupation and share in trade, commerce, industry, etc. It began with a list prepared in 1951 for the grant of scholarship to students of the backward and the most backward castes in Bihar. Its enquiry was based on the Other Backward Classes lists prepared by Kalelkar Commission. The Commission then prepared its own list of socially and educationally Backward Classes on caste and economic basis. This list contains 128 backward castes, including 94 castes known as 'most backward classes'. In Bihar, it estimated 38.1 per cent population as OBCs. It favoured rebate of 10 per cent marks for getting admission in educational institutions. The most important measures of the commission was the recommendation about reservation of 24 per cent of the seats in medical and other professional institutions and 26 per cent posts in government and semi-government jobs for the Other Backward Classes. The Jagannath Mishra Government did not take any action on these recommendations obviously in view of its support base of forward castes.

Karpoori Thakur, 1978: In 1978, the Janata Party government chaired by Karpoori Thakur implemented the recommendations of Mungerilal Commission. The State government accepted the recommendations in October, 1978 and this gave rise to a lot of agitation. Both the forward and the backward communities were dissatisfied with the government. The implementation of Commissions' recommendations also raised lot of controversy. Subsequently, the Government of Bihar corrected this misconception in July, 1979 and clarified that the reservation quota indicated the minimum and not the maximum quota for Backward Class candidates. It was also clarified that the percentage of Backward Class candidates selected on merit should not be adjusted against their reserved quotas.

U.N. Sinha, 1994: The second Backward Classes Commission was appointed in 1994 headed by U.N. Sinha. On the basis of recommendations of Sinha Committee even a few OBCs of Bihar do not came under the exclusion of advanced sections as rarely OBCs have annual income of Rs 10 lakh per year or urban property of Rs 20 lakh. It even recommended inclusion of any well-off sections or individuals availing the benefit of reservation within the recommendations of the Mandal Commission. It is a politically motivated report on the suggestions of the Chief Minister of Bihar to get political benefit out of it. It was planned to checkmate the Samata Dal leader Nitish Kumar's support among the economically advanced sections of OBCs such as Kurmi and Koiri.

Gujarat

In Gujarat, State government appointed four Backward Classes Commission for identifying SEBCs or OBCs in the State.

Bakshi Commission, 1972: This Commission was appointed to prepare a list of OBCs and recommended measures for their amelioration in August 1972 under the chairmanship of A.R. Bakshi, a retired High Court Judge and Chairman of the Law Commission. The Commission submitted its report to Gujarat Government in February 1976. It listed 82 castes and communities as socially and educationally backward and recommended the following steps for their advancement:

(a) reservation of 10 per cent of seats in medical, engineering and other professional institutions; (b) reservation of 10 per cent of the Class III and Class IV posts in all government services; (c) reservation of five per cent of all Class I and Class II vacancies in all government services, local bodies, or public undertaking, etc.; (d) reservation of 10 per cent of the seats in training-cum-production centres; and (e) granting of scholarships and other educational facilities, provided the parental income did not exceed Rs 4,800 per year. This income limit was increased to Rs 7,200 in the case of nomadic and denotified tribes.

The government run by Janata Party accepted all the recommendations of the Commission in April 1978, and implemented them. Some castes, which the Commission did not accept socially and educationally backward, made representations to the government requesting reconsideration of their castes. Representations were also made by members of those castes which had due to some reasons failed to make representations to the Bakshi Commission.

Rane Commission, 1981: After that, Government appointed the second Backward Classes Commission in April 1981, headed by C.V. Rane, a retired Judge of the High Court of Gujarat, to consider whether there were any other castes/communities/classes which could be included in the category of socially and educationally backward classes. The terms of reference of this commission were the same as those of the Bakshi commission. The Commission undertook an extensive tour of all the districts (except the district of Dangs) in the State for gathering information from various sources and recording evidence. It's submitted its report to the government in October, 1983.

The Rane Commission was the first Backward Classes Commission to reject the caste yardstick for deciding social backwardness. The Commission also held that the identification of socially and educationally Backward Classes in terms of caste was not feasible in the caste of non-Hindu communities. In reality, only the lower income groups were socially and educationally backward. The Commission took occupation as a parameter in place of caste for identifying Backward Classes. It identified 63 occupations as socially and educationally backward which included agricultural labourers, small farmers, marginal farmers, share-croppers, etc., as well as rural and urban artisans. It suggested that only those employed in 63 occupations and receiving less than Rs 1,000 yearly be treated as backward.

Justice Mankad Report

Amar Singh Chaudhary became the Chief Minister of Gujarat in place of Madhav Singh Solanki when the agitation in Gujarat was on. He immediately withdrew the increase of 18 per cent reservation for the OBCs. He also agreed to agitationists to appoint another commission headed by a High Court Judge. Justice R.C. Mankad was appointed in June 1987, and asked to submit its report by December, 1987. He could not do so and finally the existing system under Bakshi Commission continued.

Haryana

Haryana was earlier part of the Punjab State till 1966. Two committees were appointed in 1951 and 1961 by the erstwhile Punjab state government to recommend measures for welfare of OBCs. The last committee is known Brish Bhan Committee. During the year 1969, the Government of Haryana published a list of Backward Classes without a formal inquiry into their economic backwardness and social status. It declared 10 per cent reservation in government services and two per cent in professional and technical institutions. The facilities and concessions awarded were: (a) All members of the Backward Classes are eligible for the reserved posts at the time of initial appointment, whatever their income is; (b) Reservations included promotions as well in the case of Class III and Class IV posts; (c) Income limit for students of the Backward Classes to be eligible for scholarships has been raised from Rs 1,800 to Rs 4,200 a year.

Gurman Singh Commission, 1991; In the year 1990, when anti-Mandal agitation was very strong in all parts of Haryana, Jats, the dominant caste of Haryana were asking for inclusion of 'Jat' in the list of OBCs. In early 1991, the first Backward Classes Commission was constituted under the chairmanship of

Gurman Singh. The Commission gave its report in 1991, itself in which the most numerous and dominant castes were included in OBCs. These castes are *Jat, Ahir, Bishnoi, Gujar, Saini, Rajput, Meo* and others. Now, 27 per cent posts are kept reserved for OBCs in Haryana besides 19 per cent to SCs. There is no separate reservation for STs in Haryana. The report has many weaknesses and lack objectivity.

Himachal Pradesh

Like in Haryana, the Government of Himachal Pradesh also followed the list of OBCs declared by the erstwhile State of Punjab for the areas merged in the state of Himachal Pradesh. Official of State government had prepared a list on the basis of economic backwardness and social status. They identified the following sections of people as backward: (a) All the residents of Himachal Pradesh whose annual income is less than Rs 6,000 are backward whatever their caste or community and whatever their professions or occupation; (b) Members of certain communities are backward if their annual family income is not more than Rs 6,000.

Jammu and Kashmir

Reservation Policy in Jammu and Kashmir has been a controversial issue between the government and the judiciary. Judicial intervention forced the State Government to appoint three Backward Classes Commissions. In 1956, the State Government passed Civil Services Rules which provided for reservation for the Backward Classes in government services without making any special class of people as backward.

Gajendragadkar Commission, 1967: On 6th November, 1967, this Commission was appointed for the purpose of making an assessment of the development programmes apportioned to the various regions of the State and to recommend steps necessary to give assurance that the resources available to the State Government are being shared equitably and also to convey a sense of equal participation in the integrated development of the State; and to examine the existing recruitment policies of government and recommend measures for giving an equitable share to the various regions and Backward Classes in government employment.

In its report, the Gajendragadkar Commission (1968), recommended that a high-power committee should be appointed to make a list of Backward Classes on the grounds of the following criteria: (a) economic backwardness (based on a suitable ad hoc figure of annual income); (b) the occupation or occupations pursued; (c) area of permanent residence; (d) number of students per thousand of the population; and (e) caste in the case of the Hindus.

Wazir Committee, 1969: Acting on the suggestion of Gajendragadkar Commission, the State Government appointed a committee headed by J.N. Wazir in February 1969. On the recommendation of the Wazir Committee, submitted in November 1969, the government passed the Jammu and Kashmir Scheduled Castes and Backward Classes (Reservation) Rules, 1970 and reserved vacancies for the Scheduled Castes and Backward Classes in each jobs, class category and grade in the State services in accordance with the following ratios: (a) Scheduled Castes eight per cent, and (b) Backward Classes 42 per cent (including two per cent for the permanent residents of Ladakh). It was challenged in the High Court and the Supreme Court which found fault in the rules. In its report, the Committee had classified Backward Classes into six broad categories as follows: (a) traditional occupations, (b) social castes, (c) cultivators, (d) pensioners, (e) areas adjourning the ceasefire line, and (f) bad pockets.

Anand Committee, 1976: The State Government appointed a Backward Classes Committee in the month of August, 1976, headed by Justice Adarsh Sein Anand to advice on the removal of the various anomalies in the Act of 1970 as ordered by the Supreme Court. It asked the Committee to make recommendations with regard to the following issues: (a) to determine the criteria to be followed in deciding backwardness; (b) to identify and prepare a list of Backward Classes; (c) to categorise Backward Classes and suggest safeguards for giving benefits to the real deserving only; and (d) to examine the question of reservation in government posts at every stage. Having undergone a detailed discussion with the cross-section of the people at various levels and of various areas, the Committee found the 22 groups of population classified as backward. The Committee regards them weak and underprivileged classes. It prepared a list of two categories of Backward Classes: (a) weak and underprivileged sections, and (b) residents of backward areas, i.e., of (i) bad pockets; and (ii) regions within eight kilometers of the Line of Actual Control (LoC). Based on the above recommendations, 42 per cent government jobs and seats in professional and technical institutions and in other institutions of higher learning were reserved for the Backward Classes. This policy remained in practice till 1993. Now, nine per cent seats and posts are reserved for SCs, 13 per cent for STs, and 27 per cent for OBCs. All the inhabitants of Ladakh region are considered STs.

Karnataka

Miller Committee, 1918: In August, 1918, the Maharaja of Mysore appointed a Committee under the chairmanship of Sir L.C. Miller then Chief Justice of Mysore to recommend steps for adequate representation for non-*Brahmins* in the services of the state. The committee was asked to examine the following questions also: (a) changes required in the then rules of recruitment to the public services; (b) special facilities needed to encourage higher and professional education among the members of the Backward Classes; and (c) any other special steps needed to increase the representation of the backward communities in the public service without materially affecting the efficiency, due regard being paid also to the general well-being accruing to the state by a wider diffusion of education and a feeling of increased status which would thereby be produced in the backward communities. After almost a year in July 1919, the Committee submitted its report. The State Government accepted its recommendation that the term 'backward communities' should be taken to include all communities in the state other than *Brahmins*, Anglo-Indians, and Christians.

Nagan Gowda Committee, 1961: The State Government, under the chief ministership of S. Nijalingappa, formed a committee under the chairmanship of Naganna Gowda, in January 1960, the terms of reference being to suggest: (a) the criteria to be adopted in determining which sections of people in the State should be treated as socially and educationally backward, and (b) the right manner in which the criteria thus indicated should be followed to enable the State Government to determine the persons, who should secure such preference, as may be determined by government; regarding admissions to technical institutions and appointment to government services. The Committee suggested 36 per cent reservation for 35.34 per cent. The final report was given to the government in May 1961, in which some 214 castes under Article 15(4) and 185 castes under Article 16(4) were recommended and the communities were divided as backward and more backward, the former assumed to be 50 per cent for the purpose of Article 15(4) and the latter 45 per cent for the purpose of Article 16(4).

Havanur Commission, 1975: Being a member of the small community of Ursus, in 1969, D. Devaraj Urs was the first non-Lingayat and non-Vokkaliga legislator to become the Chief Minister of Mysore State. He remained the Chief Minister till 1980. During his tenure, he sedulously cultivated the faith of minority backward communities without rousing the opposition of the dominant communities. In 1972, Devaraj Urs constituted the first Backward Classes Commission under the chairmanship of L.G. Havanur in response to the regular demand of the people as the existing occupation-cum-income test of backwardness was most unsatisfactory. The Commission presented its voluminous report in 1975, listing the Backward Classes under three categories, viz., backward communities, backward castes and backward tribes, and suggested compartmental reservations for each of these groups.

The Chief Minister, Devaraj Urs, while accepting the recommendations of the Havanur Commission, thought it fit to include the Muslims as a whole in the first category of backward castes. Same way, he included the Scheduled Caste converts to

Christianity up to the second generation in the second category of backward castes. The order on the Havanur report was passed after considerable deliberation on 22nd February, 1977. One more change, made in the order passed on 4th March, 1977, was that only such citizens of these Backward Classes, whose family income from all sources is Rs 8,000 (subsequently raised to Rs 10,000) and less shall be entitled to special treatment under the said Articles.

Venkataswamy Commission, 1985: The Supreme Court, in the judgement of *K.C. Vasanth Kumar* versus *State of Karnataka* (1985), asked the Karnataka government to redetermine the whole reservation of seats and posts. After that, in 1985, the Karnataka government constituted the second Backward Classes Commission chaired by a retired Judge, T. Venkataswamy to find out the OBCs in Karnataka and suggest measures for their betterment. It went into the problem in depth and undertook extensive survey of secondary school leaving certificate students for identifying educational backwardness. It identified 33 per cent of the State population as OBCs, derecognising many castes and suggested 27 per cent reservation for them in place of then 49 per cent. It divided OBCs in four groups like backward communities, backward castes, backward tribes and backward special group. But Vokkaligas caste and 35 other castes were excluded from the list of OBCs by the Commission. The Janata legislators belonging to Vokkaliga caste threatened to leave the party if the report was implemented. Ultimately, the Karnataka government rejected the report on 7th October, 1986, and in its place started a new policy which benefitted five categories of OBCs covering 73.5 per cent of the State Population by reservation of 50 per cent of jobs for them.

Chinnappa Reddy Commission, 1990: This Backward Classes Commission chaired by Chinnappa Reddy, dealt with the question of economic criterion for reservation at some length. Due to the recommendations of Chinnappa Reddy Commission report in 1994, the reservation policy in Karnataka remained in controversy. On 25th July 1994, the Karnataka government raised reservation for OBCs in the state to 57 per cent which was further raised to 80 per cent. The matter again went to judiciary and the Apex Court withheld the government order on 1st August, 1994. In October 1994, the State Government got the Karnataka Reservation Law for 73 per cent reservation passed by the State Legislative Assembly. The President of India gave his approval to this Act on 23rd October, 1994. Now, the Karnataka reservation policy got constitutional protection under Article 31(B) and free from judicial intervention.

Kerala

Vishwanathan Committee, 1961: The Evaluation Committee on Backward Classes was appointed in June 1961, under the chairmanship of V.K. Vishwanathan. The Committee submitted its report in October 1963. Its prominent recommendations were as follows: (a) 40 per cent of the seats in technical and professional colleges should be reserved for students of the Other Backward Classes and 10 per cent of seats for students belonging to the SCs and STs; (b) the above reservation should be made applicable to all fresh appointment to posts under the State Government also; (c) appointment of an Expert Committee to go into the question of reclassification of backward communities. The Government of Kerala accepted the recommendations of the committee but restricted reservation at the level of 25 per cent seats for the Backward Classes.

Pillai Commission, 1965: The State government appointed a commission under the chairmanship of G. Kumara Pillai in July 1964, and the commission submitted its report in December, 1965. Its main recommendations were: (i) It classified 91 communities as backward and stipulated that the benefits recommended in the report should be extended only to those members of the Backward Classes whose aggregate family income was below Rs 4,200 per year; and (ii) In technical and professional institutions 25 per cent of the seats should be reserved for OBCs. The state government accepted the recommendations with the modification that the income ceiling of Rs 4,200 was raised to Rs 6,000 per annum. It may be noted that the High Court had desired the State Government to institute an enquiry for granting educational benefits to OBCs under

Article 15(4) of the Constitution only. In view of this State Government kept reservation at 40 per cent level in government jobs.

Damodaran Commission, 1970: After two years, in 1967, the Kerala High Court suggested the appointment of yet another Backward Classes Commission. The State government then appointed third Backward Classes Commission, under the chairmanship of by M.P. Damodaran, in October 1967. This Commission submitted its report in June 1970. This Commission found the following factors responsible for social backwardness for the purposes of Article 16(4): (a) absence of requisite educational attainments (test of education); (b) Absence of money or wealth (economic test); (c) absence of ability to appropriate an adequate number of appointments (test of appropriation of appointments); and (d) caste disability, occupational stigma, and social taboos acting as obstacles in the field of education.

Madhya Pradesh

Mahajan Commission, 1980: The State government appointed a Backward Classes Commission under the chairmanship of Ramjee Mahajan in November, 1980, for drawing list of Backward Classes and suggests measures for their betterment. The Commission identified 254 castes and sub-castes as Backward Classes and suggested reservation of 35 per cent of the seats for them in educational institutions. It also wanted the same percentage of government and semi-government services to be reserved for them. In year 1984, the State Government announced reservation of 25 per cent of the jobs for the Backward Classes instead of 35 per cent as suggested by the Commission. The anti-reservationists took the matter to the streets. They also appealed to the judiciary. The Bhopal High Court asked the State Government to refrain from bringing the reservation policy. If the government plan for reservation was executed, it would mean 65 per cent on the basis of caste; SCs: 22.5 per cent, STs: 7.5 per cent and OBCs: 35 per cent. The government also proposed to reserve four per cent for the economically backward, five per cent for ex-servicemen, three per cent for freedom fighters and 'technical' hands and one per cent for miscellaneous categories. On a whole, it was 78 per cent reservation of posts and seats. It was not adequate and just on the part of government to leave only 22 per cent seats and posts for open competition. In 1993, the Government of Madhya Pradesh declared that 50 per cent posts will be filled through open competition.

Maharashtra

Deshmukh Committee, 1961: In November 1961, the State Government appointed a Backward Classes Committee, under the Chairmanship of B.D. Deshmukh, to report on the reservation of Backward Classes in government jobs. This committee, in its report of January 1964, grouped Backward Classes into four categories: (i) Scheduled Castes and neo-Buddhist, (ii) Scheduled Tribes, (iii) denotified and nomadic tribes, and (iv) other backward communities. It also recommended that reservation in government services and educational institutions for different categories of Backward Classes should be linked to the percentage of their population in the State. State Government broadly accepted the recommendations and made the reservation in state services and educational institutions for four categories of Backward Classes, viz., the SCs and neo-Buddhists (13 per cent), the Scheduled Tribes (seven per cent), denotified and nomadic tribes (four per cent), and other backward communities (10 per cent). Subsequently in April, 1979 the State government issued orders that 80 per cent of all vacancies under the State government, local bodies, etc., should be reserved for Economically Weaker Sections of society.

Punjab

In the year 1951, the State Government appointed a committee on Backward Classes to identify the Backward Classes in the State. The criteria implied for the identification of Backward Classes were economic, educational and social backwardness. On the basis of its recommendations, the government declared 14 castes as OBC, consisting two per cent of the population as backward and suggested the same percentage of reservation. The government accepted the recommendations. Only two per cent seats and posts were reserved for OBCs in Punjab. Similar concessions were given in respect of admission to educational institutions.

Brish Bhan Committee, 1965: In 1965, the State government appointed an Evaluation Committee headed by Brish Bhan to review the concessions given to Backward Classes. This committee, in its report of 1966, made the following recommendations: (a) the existing list of Backward Classes should be made rational so that classes or castes which were no longer backward might be excluded. (b) the existing reservation of two per cent of the seats in educational institutions should be increased to five per cent. The committee also observed that reservation in service was not serving any useful purpose and government should give concessions mainly in matters of education.

Harcharan Singh Commission, 1975: In its fourth report in 1975-76, Punjab Vishan Sabha Committee on Welfare of Scheduled Castes, Scheduled Tribes, and the Backward Classes under the chairmanship of Harcharan Singh recommended that 15 per cent reservation should be made for OBCs in services. The government found it difficult to accept this recommendation as it had already provided for reservation upto 25 per cent for the SCs and upto 20 per cent for retired army personnel. Therefore, it continued with its policy of reserving five per cent of the seats in educational institutions and five per cent of initial appointments in public service. In 1993, reservation for OBCs increased to 23 per cent in Punjab.

Tamil Nadu

Tamil Nadu has been the pioneer in providing special concessions to OBCs. For the welfare of depressed or deprived sections of society the first such step was taken by Madras Government with the framing of Grant-in-Aid Code in 1885 to regulate financial aid to educational institutions, providing special facilities for students of depressed classes. After the separation of Andhra Pradesh, the Government of Madras ordered in 1964 that 16 per cent of all posts under the State Government should be reserved for Scheduled Castes and Scheduled Tribes and 25 per cent for Backward Classes. This scheme of reservation was struck down by the Supreme Court and subsequently the State

Government decided in 1951 that henceforth reservation should be made for Scheduled Castes and Backward Classes only.

Sattanathan Commission, 1969: In November 1969, the State Government appointed Backward Classes Commission under the chairmanship of A.N. Sattanathan. The Commission, in its report of 1970, used educational and social backwardness and the nature of the occupation continued traditionally by a majority of the members of a caste as the main criterion of backwardness. Sattanathan Commission divided the Backward Classes into two parts: (a) backward classes, and (b) most backward classes. It suggested 17 per cent reservation for the Backward Classes and 16 per cent for the Most Backward Classes. It took the population of the Scheduled Castes and the Scheduled Tribes as found during the 1971 census, and gave directions that 31 per cent of all posts in government services and seats in educational institutions be reserved for the Backward Classes and 18 per cent for the SCs and STs. In November 1980, the State Government increased the reservation for the Other Backward Classes from 31 per cent to 50 per cent.

Ambashanker Commission, 1982: Following the decision of Supreme Court, the government constituted a 21-member Backward Classes Commission under the chairmanship of J.A. Ambashanker to re-evaluate the classification of Backward Classes in the State and to re-assess their reservation quota of 50 per cent. The Commission submitted its report in February 1985, and advised for the reserved quota to be slashed to 32 per cent. The Finance Minister announced the Government's acceptance of the Supreme Court's ruling that the reservation for the Backward Classes and the Scheduled Castes and the Scheduled Tribes in total should not exceed 50 per cent. The Tamil Nadu government, however, passed orders re-affirming the reservation of 50 per cent for OBCs in July 1985.

Uttar Pradesh

In Uttar Pradesh, in 1945, the Government United Provinces of Agra and Oudh identified 37 Hindu castes and 21 Muslim groupings as backward and gave them educational concessions. In 1950, the Uttar Pradesh government reserved 10 per cent of the jobs in government services and educational institutions for the Scheduled Castes but did nothing specific for the Backward Classes. In 1955, a cabinet sub-committee drew up two lists of Backward Classes– one for the purpose of recruitment to the public services and the other for the sanction of educational concessions. The first consisted of 15 and the second of 59 backward castes.

Cheedi Lal Sethi Commission, 1975: In October 1975, a Most Backward Classes Commission was constituted under the chairmanship of Cheedi Lal Sethi to consider the position of the 'most Backward Classes of citizens' as distinguished from the 'Backward Classes' and to suggest measures for improving their conditions. The Commission used social evils like poverty, illiteracy, housing, occupation, caste, social inequality and representation in government service, industry and commerce as parameters for measuring backwardness. After two years' deliberation it gave its report in June 1977. The list that was first prepared contained 36 backward castes with little land or without land (17 per cent), the second had 18 agriculturalist castes (10 per cent) and the last one was exclusively for the Backward Classes from the Muslim community (2.5 per cent). The Commission recommended special facilities, scholarships, etc., for the caste and other sections it had designated backward.

Other States and Union Territories

Eight other States and Union Territories have notified lists on other Backward Classes without ordering a formal inquiry into their conditions. Before the implementation of Mandal Commission's recommendations some Indian states like Assam and Union Territories like Pondicherry felt educational backwardness as the most important aspect of backwardness and reserved some seats for the educationally backward in educational institutions. They have made no such reservation in government jobs. Haryana has provided for 10 per cent reservation in government services and two per cent in professional and technical institutions for OBCs. Himachal Pradesh has reserved five per cent of all posts for OBCs and also extended some educational concessions to backward class students. Before 1993, in Delhi, Meghalaya, Orissa, and

Rajasthan, the Backward Classes were not getting any preferential treatment in the context of appointment to public jobs and admission to educational institutions. But, they do enjoy certain concessions regarding school fees, books, mid-day meals, etc. In 1961, both Delhi and Orissa which had earlier drew the list of OBCs on the ground of caste opted for the economic criterion in place of the caste criterion and dispensed with the lists of Backward Classes prepared on caste basis. This situation almost continued till 1993. Many other states like Arunachal Pradesh, Mizoram, Nagaland, Sikkim, Tripura and West Bengal had not made any list of other Backward Classes till 1993. None of the Union Territories has done so. These states do not consider Backward Classes as calling for State action in respect of their socio-economic conditions. The Backward Classes have never come up as a political force in these states. Nor that there is no Backward Class lobby, but it has not acquired and perceptible influence so far. There, OBCs remained out of touch of special treatment. Now 27 per cent jobs have been reserved for them in the Central services which prepared background for reservation in all states. It has taken this position even during the Chief Ministers Conference or various other platforms.

References

Aggarwal, Patrap. Caste and Social Stratification among Muslims in India. Manohar, 1978.

Ansari, Ghaus. Muslim Caste in Uttar Pradesh: A Study of Culture Contact. Lucknow, 1960.

Ambedkar, B.R. (1935). "The Untouchables who were they and why they become Untouchables?" http://www.ambedkar.org/.

Anand A. Yang, Bazaar India: Markets, Society, and the Colonial State in Bihar, University of California Press, 1999.

Arvind Narayan Das, Agrarian movements in India: Studies on 20th century Bihar (Library of Peasant Studies), Routledge, London, 1982.

Acharya Hazari Prasad Dwivedi Rachnawali, Rajkamal Prakashan, Delhi.

"Annual Report, 2007-2008". National Commission for Backward Classes, Government of India. 2009. http://www.ncbc.nic.in/Pdf/annual.pdf.

Aggarwal, Pratap, Caste and Social Stratification among Muslims in India. Manohar, 1978.

Ambedkar, Bhimrao. Pakistan or the Partition of India. Thackers Publishers.

Ambedkar, B.R. (1946). The Untouchables: Who Were They and Why They Became Untouchables? as reprinted in Volume 7 of Dr. Babasaheb Ambedkar Writings and Speeches, published by Government of Maharashtra 1990; Complete Writings.

Ambedkar, B.R. (1946), who were the Shudras.

Atal, Yogesh (1968) "The Changing Frontiers of Caste" Delhi, National Publishing House, 1968.

Atal, Yogesh, "Changing Indian Society" Chapter on Varna and Jati. Jaipur, Rawat Publications, 2006.

Austin, Granville, The Indian Constitution: Corner Stone of a Nation, Oxford, 1966, p. 50.

Baines, Jervoise Athelstane (1893). General report on the Census of India, 1891, London, Her Majesty's Stationery Office.

Blunt, E.A.H. (1931). The Caste System of Northern India, republished 1964, S. Chand & Co., Delhi.

Bayly, Susan. Caste, Society and Politics in India from the Eighteenth Century to the Modern Age. Cambridge University Press, 1999.

Burman, B. K. Roy, Beyond Mandal and After – Backward Classes in Perspective, Mittal Publications, New Delhi, 1992.

Baldev Upadhyaya, *Kashi Ki Panditya Parampara,* Sharda Sansthan, Varanasi, 1985.

Bates, C., "Race, Caste and Tribe in Central India: The early origins of Indian anthropometry". Edinburgh Papers In South Asian Studies (3). 1995. http://www.sps.ed.ac.uk/__data/assets/pdf_file/0005/38426/WP03_BATES_RaceCaste_and_Tribe.pdf.

Berreman, Gerald D., Race, Caste, and Other Invidious Distinctions in Social Stratification. University of California, Berkeley, 1972.

Crooke, William (1896). Tribes and Castes of the North-Western Provinces and Oudh, 4 Vols.

Constituent Assembly Debates, Vol. VII, Government of India (New Delhi), 1947, pp. 696-97.

"Constitution of India". Ministry of Law, Government of India. http://lawmin.nic.in/olwing/coi/coi-english/coi-indexenglish.htm. Retrieved 2012.

Christopher Alan Bayly, Rulers, Townsmen, and Bazaars: North Indian Society in the Age of British Expansion, 1770–1870, Cambridge University Press, 1983.

Chalam, K.S., "Caste Reservation and Equality of Opportunity in Education", Economic and Political Weekly, Vol. XXV, No. 41, Oct. 13, 1990.

Desai and Kulkarni, "Changing Educational Inequalities in India in the Context of Affirmative Action". Demography 45 (2): 245–270, May, 2008, PMC 2474466. PMID 18613480.

Duiker/Spielvogel. The Essential World History Vol. I: to 1800. 2nd Edition 2005.

Dumont, Louis. Homo Hierarchicus: The Caste System and Its Implications. Complete English edition, revised. 540 p. 1970, 1980 Series: (Nature of Human Society).

Eric Stokes, "The First Century of British Colonial Rule in India: Social Revolution or Social Stagnation?", Past and Present 58: 136–160. JSTOR 650259, February 1973.

E.A.H. Blunt, The Caste System of North India, first edition in 1931 by Oxford University Press, new edition by S. Chand Publishers, 1969.

"Early Evidence for Caste in South India," pp. 467-92 in Dimensions of Social Life: Essays in honour of David G. Mandelbaum, Edited by Paul Hockings and Mouton de Gruyter, Berlin, New York, Amsterdam, 1987.

Forrester, Duncan B., "Indian Christians' Attitudes to Caste in the Nineteenth Century," in Indian Church History Review 8, No. 2 (1974): 131-147.

Forrester, Duncan B., 'Christian Theology in a Hindu Context,' in South Asian Review 8, No. 4 (1975): 343-358.

Forrester, Duncan B., 'Indian Christians' Attitudes to Caste in the Twentieth Century,' in Indian Church History Review 9, No. 1 (1975): 3-22.

Forrester, Duncan B., Caste and Christianity: Attitudes and Policies on Caste of Anglo-Saxon Protestant Missions in India (London and Atlantic Highlands, NJ: Curzon Press and Humanities Press, 1980).

Gwyer and Appadorai, Speeches and Documents on Indian Constitution, 1921, Vol. 1, Oxford Publisher, 1957, pp. 261-265.

Genetic Evidence on the Origins of Indian Caste Populations — Bamshad *et al.* 11 (6): 994. Genome Research.

Ghurye, G.S., Caste, Class and Occupation. Popular Book Depot, Bombay, 1961.

Ghurye, G.S., Caste and Race in India, Popular Prakashan, Mumbai 1969 (1932).

Galanter, Marc, Competing Equalities: Law and Backward Classes in India, Oxford (New Delhi), 1984, p. 159.

Galanter, Marc. "Who are the OBCs? An introduction to a Constitutional Puzzle", EPW, 1978.

Ghosh, Partha S. "Positive Discrimination in India: A Political Analysis", Ethnic Studies Report, Vol. XV, No. 2, July 1997.

Gupta, Dipankar, "Do Muslims Need Reservations?", The Economic Times, 26/7/2004.

Hooda, Sagar Preet, "Contesting Reservations", Rawat Publications, New Delhi, 2001.

Harold Coward- Hindu-Christian Dialogue: Perspectives and Encounters, Motilal Banarsidass, 1993, ISBN 81-208-1158-5, pp. 14-20 [1].

Indra Sawhney vs. *Union of India,* Supreme Court, 16, November, 1992.

Jogendra Nath Bhattacharya, Hindu Castes and Sects, Munshiram Manoharlal, Delhi, first edition 1896, new edition 1995.

Jaffrelot, Christophe, India's Silent Revolution: The Rise of the Lower Castes, C. Hurst & Co., 2003.

J. John; Sociology, Prentice Hall, 10th ed., 2004, ISBN: 0-13-184918-2, pp. 249-251.

Kamble, J.R., Rise and Awakenning of Depressed Classes in India, National Publisher, New Delhi, 1979, pp. 67-68.

Kane, Pandurang Vaman: History of Dharmasastra: (ancient and mediaeval, religious and civil law) — Poona: Bhandarkar Oriental Research Institute, 1962–1975.

Khan, M.S., Current Problems of Indian Economy, Ashish Publishing, New Delhi, 1994.

Kohli, Atul, India's Democracy: An Analysis of Changing State-Society Relations, Orient Longman, New Delhi, 1991, p. 15.

Lal, K.S. Growth of Scheduled Tribes and Castes in Medieval India (1995).

Lata Sinha, Origin of Caste System of India, Just another worldpress.com.

Louis, Prakash, "Scheduled Castes and Tribes, the Reservation Debate", EPW, June 2, 2003, pp. 2478.

Mathur, M.L., Encyclopaedia of Backward Castes (In 4 Volumes), Reservation (Volume 1), Kalpaz Publications, Delhi, 2004.

Mathur, M.L., Encyclopaedia of Backward Castes (In 4 Volumes) (Judgements: Before and After Mandal Judgement, Volume 4), Kalpaz Publications, Delhi, 2004.

Mathur, M.L., Encyclopaedia of Backward Castes (In 4 Volumes), Commissions (Vol. 2), Kalpaz Publications, Delhi, 2004.

Murray Milner, Jr., Status and Sacredness: A General Theory of Status Relations and an Analysis of Indian Culture, New York: Oxford University Press, 1994.

Mathur, M. L., Encyclopaedia of Backward Castes (In 4 Volumes), Reservation (Volume 1), Kalpaz Publications, New Delhi, 2004.

Manu ((Lawgiver)); Manu; Patrick Olivelle, The law code of Manu. Oxford University Press, 2004, pp. 185–.ISBN 978-0-19-280271-2. http:/ /books.google.com/books?id=RGPSEuNsPLEC&pg=PA185.

"Meira Kumari, a Dalit leader is the new Lok Sabha Speaker". NCHRO. 2009. http://www.nchro.org/index.php?option=com_co ntent& view=article&id=6863:meira-kumar—dalit-leader-is-the-new-lok-sabha-speaker&catid=5:dalitsatribals&Itemid=14.

Michaels, Axel, Hinduism: Past and Present 188-97 (Princeton 2004) ISBN 0-691-08953-1.

M.N. Srinivas, Social Change in Modern India, Orient Longman, Delhi, 1995.

Mahavir Prasad Dwivedi essays.

M.A. Sherring, Hindu Tribes and Castes as Reproduced in Benaras, Asian Educational Services, New Delhi, First edition 1872, new edition 2008.

Mookherjee, Dulal, The Essence of Bhagavad Gita. Academic Publishers, 2002, pp. 472. ISBN 978-81-87504-40-5.

Mishra, R.G. and Kaur, Gurvinder, Reservation Policy and Personnel Selection, Uppal Publishing House, New Delhi, 1990, p.14.

National Front: Lok Sabha Election Manifesto, 1989, p. 36.

OBC Quota Law held valid, News Panorama of India and World (pp. 18-19), Vol. 20, No. 8, June, 2008.

Padhy, K. S. and Mahapatra, Jayashre, "Reservation Policy in India", Ashish Publishing House, New Delhi, 1985.

Panandiker, V.A. Pai, (ed.), The Politics of Backwardness, Reservation Policy in India, Konark Publishers Pvt. Ltd., Delhi.

Prasad, A., "Reservational Justice to OBCs, Theoretical and Practical issues", Deep and Deep Publications, New Delhi, 1997.

Padhy, K. S. and Mahapatra, Jayashree, Reservation Policy in India, Ashish Publishing House, New Delhi, 1988, p.17.

"Profile: Mayawati Kumari". BBC News. 16 July 2009. http://news.bbc.co.uk/2/hi/1958378.stm.

Raj, Papia and Aditya Raj, "Caste Variation in Reproductive Health of Women in Eastern Region of India: A Study Based on NFHS Data" Sociological Bulletin, 2004, 53 (3): 326–346.

Ranganayakamma, For the solution of the "Caste" question, Buddha is not enough, Ambedkar is not enough either, Marx is a must, Hyderabad: Sweet Home Publications, 2001.

Russell, R.V. and R.B. Hira Lal, The Tribes and Castes of the Central Provinces of India, 4 Vols. London, 1916.

Radha Krishnan, P., Job Quotas in the Private Sectors", EPW, Oct. 2, 2004.

Sharma, Dr. Shish Ram, Protective Discrimination – Other Backward Classes in India, Raj Publications, Delhi, 2002.

Singh, S.N., Reservation: Problems and Prospects, Uppal Publishing House, New Delhi, 1987.

"Scheduled Castes and Scheduled Tribes Population: Census 2001". Government of India. 2004. http://censusindia.gov.in/Census_Data_2001/India_at_glance/scst.aspx.

"Status of caste system in modern India". Dr. B.R. Ambedkar and His People. 2004. http://www.ambedkar.org/News/reservation inindia.pdf.

Srinivas, M.N., Religion and Society among the Coorgs of South India, p. 32 (Oxford, 1952).

Susan Bayly - Saints, Goddesses and Kings: Muslims and Christians in South Indian Society, pp. 243-253, Cambridge University Press, 2004, ISBN 0-521-89103-5 [2].

Singer and Cohn, Structure and Change in Indian Society. Aldine Publishing Co., 2007, ISBN 978-0-202-36138-3.

·Swami Vivekananda, The Complete Works of Swami Vivekananda (8 Vols. Calcutta). V. 1952, pp. 25–30. ISBN 978-81-85301-46-4.

Srinivas, M.N. Religion and Society among the Coorgs of South India. Oxford, 1952.

Swami Sahajanand Saraswati Rachnawali (Selected works of Swami Sahajanand Saraswati), Prakashan Sansthan, Delhi, 2003.

Second Backward Classes Commission, 1980, p. 2.

Singh, Parmanand, Equality, Reservation and Discrimination in India, Deep and Deep Publications, New Delhi, 1985, p. 80.

Singh, Shyama Nand, Reservation: Problems and Prospects, Uppal Publishing, New Delhi, 1991, p. 72.

Sharma, B. A.V. and Reddy, Madhusudhan, Reservation Policy in India, Light and Life Publisher, New Delhi, 1982, pp. 14-15.

The Constitution of India, Ministry of Law and Justice, Delhi Controller of Publications, New Delhi, 1986, p. 14.

Vidyasagar, R. and Suresh V., "Backward Classes and Reservation", EPW, Vol. 25, No. 16, April 21. 1990.

Yadav, K. C., Flaws in the Creamy Layer Concept, The Times of India, October 7, 1993.

3

Other Backward Classes in Assam

Before the implementation of Mandal Commission's recommendations some Indian states like Assam and Union Territories like Pondicherry felt educational backwardness as the most important aspect of backwardness and reserved some seats for the educationally backward in educational institutions. They have made no such reservation in government jobs. Haryana has provided for ten per cent reservation in government services and two per cent in professional and technical institutions for OBCs. Himachal Pradesh has reserved five per cent of all posts for OBCs and also extended some educational concessions to backward class students. Before 1993, in Delhi, Meghalaya, Orissa, and Rajasthan, the Backward Classes were not getting any preferential treatment in the context of appointment to public jobs and admission to educational institutions. But, they do enjoy certain concessions regarding school fees, books, mid-day meals, etc. In 1961, both Delhi and Orissa which had earlier drew the list of OBCs on the ground of caste opted for the economic criterion in place of the caste criterion and dispensed with the lists of Backward Classes prepared on caste basis. This situation almost continued till 1993. Many other states like Arunachal Pradesh, Mizoram, Nagaland, Sikkim, Tripura and West Bengal had not made any list of other Backward Classes till 1993. None of the Union Territories has done so. These states do not consider Backward Classes as calling for State action in respect of their socio-economic conditions. The Backward Classes have never come up as a political force in these states. Nor that there is no Backward Class lobby, but it has not acquired and perceptible influence so far. There, OBCs remained out of touch of special treatment. Now 27 per cent jobs have been reserved for them in the Central services which prepared background for reservation in all states. It has taken this position even during the Chief Ministers Conference or various other platforms. The Assam Backward Classes Commission was set-up in 1993.

CENTRAL LIST OF OBCs FOR THE STATE OF ASSAM

Entry No.	*Caste / Community*	*Resolution No. and Date*
1.	Ahom	12011/68/93-BCC(C) dt 10/09/1993
2.	Baria	12011/68/93-BCC(C) dt 10/09/1993
3.	Barui	12011/68/93-BCC(C) dt 10/09/1993 12011/21/95-BCC dt 15/05/1995
4.	Barjubi	12011/68/93-BCC(C) dt 10/09/93
5.	Baroi	12011/68/93-BCC(C) dt 10/09/1993
6.	Chutia, Chutiya	12011/68/93-BCC(C) dt 10/09/1993
7.	Choudang	12011/68/93-BCC(C) dt 10/09/1993
8.	Ganak in Districts of Cachar, Karimganj and Hailakandi	12011/68/93-BCC(C) dt 10/09/1993 2011/21/95-BCC dt 15/05/1995
9.	Ghosh, Gop, Gowala, Gawala, Goal, Goala	12011/68/93-BCC(C) dt 10/09/1993

10.	Kumar, Rudra Paul of districts of Cachar, Karimganj and Hailakandi	12011/68/93-BCC(C) dt 10/09/ 1993 12011/21/95-BCC dt 15/05/1995
11.	Kupadhar, Kushiari, Parh	12011/68/93-BCC(C) dt 10/09/ 1993
12.	Mahisya Das, Mahisya	12011/68/93-BCC(C) dt 10/09/ 1993
13.	Manipuri, including Manipuri Brahmin and Manipuri Muslim	12011/68/93-BCC(C) dt 10/09/ 1993 12011/21/95-BCC dt 15/05/1995
14.	Moran, Matak	12011/68/93-BCC(C) dt 10/09/ 1993
15.	Mukhi	12011/68/93-BCC(C) dt 10/09/ 1993
16.	Napit	12011/68/93-BCC(C) dt 10/09/ 1993
17.	Nepali (i.e.) Thapa, Gurung, Lama, Gaine Rai, Chhetri, Lihu, Magar, Lohar, Dami, Sarki i.e., Cobbler)	12011/68/93-BCC(C) dt 10/09/ 1993 12011/21/95-BCC dt 15/05/1995
18.	Koch-Rajbonshi* (* The entry after restoration of caste/ community 'Koch-Rajbonshi' w.e.f. 03.04.1997 (expect for the period when ordinance regarding inclusion of the caste/community 'Koch-Rajbonshi' in the ST	12011/68/93-BCC(C) dt 10/09/ 1993 12011/2/96-BCC dt. 27/01/1996 12015/13/2010-B.C. II. dt. 08/12/ 2011

list was in force) as per advice of NCBC	
19. Sudra Das, Dey	12011/68/93-BCC(C) dt 10/09/1993
20. Saloi	12011/68/93-BCC(C) dt 10/09/1993
21. Sut, Soot	12011/68/93-BCC(C) dt 10/09/1993
	12011/21/95-BCC dt 15/05/1995
22. Scheduled Caste persons converted to Christianity	12011/68/93-BCC(C) dt 10/09/1993
23. Tantripal, Tanti, Tantri	12011/68/93-BCC(C) dt 10/09/1993
24. Tea Garden Labourers,	12011/68/93-BCC(C) dt 10/09/93
Tea Garden Tribes, ex-Tea Garden Labourers, and ex-Tea Garden Tribes as listed below	12011/21/95-BCC dt 15/05/1995
1. Ahirgoala	12011/68/93-BCC(C) dt 10/09/93
2. Arya Mala	12011/68/93-BCC(C) dt 10/09/93
3. Asur	12011/68/93-BCC(C) dt 10/09/93
4. Barhai	12011/68/93-BCC(C) dt 10/09/93
5. Basphor	12011/68/93-BCC(C) dt 10/09/93
6. Bhokta	12011/68/93-BCC(C) dt 10/09/93
7. Bauri	12011/68/93-BCC(C) dt 10/09/93
8. Bowri	12011/68/93-BCC(C) dt 10/09/93
9. Bhuyan	12011/68/93-BCC(C) dt 10/09/93
10. Bhumij	12011/68/93-BCC(C) dt 10/09/93
11. Bedia	12011/68/93-BCC(C) dt 10/09/93

12. Beldar	12011/68/93-BCC(C) dt 10/09/93
13. Bharaik	12011/68/93-BCC(C) dt 10/09/93
14. Bhatta	12011/68/93-BCC(C) dt 10/09/93
15. Basor	12011/68/93-BCC(C) dt 10/09/93
16. Baiga	12011/68/93-BCC(C) dt 10/09/93
17. Baijara	12011/68/93-BCC(C) dt 10/09/93
18. Bhil	12011/68/93-BCC(C) dt 10/09/93
19. Bondo	12011/68/93-BCC(C) dt 10/09/93
20. Binjia	12011/68/93-BCC(C) dt 10/09/93
21. Birhar	12011/68/93-BCC(C) dt 10/09/93
22. Birjia	12011/68/93-BCC(C) dt 10/09/93
23. Beddi	12011/68/93-BCC(C) dt 10/09/93
24. Chamar	12011/68/93-BCC(C) dt 10/09/93
25. Chowdhari	12011/68/93-BCC(C) dt 10/09/93
26. Chere	12011/68/93-BCC(C) dt 10/09/93
27. Chick Banik	12011/68/93-BCC(C) dt 10/09/93
28. Dandari	12011/68/93-BCC(C) dt 10/09/93
29. Dandasi	12011/68/93-BCC(C) dt 10/09/93
30. Dusad	12011/68/93-BCC(C) dt 10/09/93
31. Dhanwar	12011/68/93-BCC(C) dt 10/09/93
32. Ganda	12011/68/93-BCC(C) dt 10/09/93
33. Gonda	12011/68/93-BCC(C) dt 10/09/93
34. Gond	12011/68/93-BCC(C) dt 10/09/93
35. Ghansi	12011/68/93-BCC(C) dt 10/09/93
36. Gorait	12011/68/93-BCC(C) dt 10/09/93
37. Ghatowar	12011/68/93-BCC(C) dt 10/09/93
38. Hari	12011/68/93-BCC(C) dt 10/09/93
39. Holra	12011/68/93-BCC(C) dt 10/09/93
40. Jolha	12011/68/93-BCC(C) dt 10/09/93
41. Keot	12011/68/93-BCC(C) dt 10/09/93

42. Koiri	12011/68/93-BCC(C) dt 10/09/93
43. Khonyor	12011/68/93-BCC(C) dt 10/09/93
44. Kurmi	12011/68/93-BCC(C) dt 10/09/93
	12011/21/95-BCC dt 15/05/95
45. Kawar	12011/68/93-BCC(C) dt 10/09/93
46. Karmali	12011/68/93-BCC(C) dt 10/09/93
47. Korwa	12011/68/93-BCC(C) dt 10/09/93
48. Kol	12011/68/93-BCC(C) dt 10/09/93
49. Kalahandi	12011/68/93-BCC(C) dt 10/09/93
50. Kalihandi	12011/68/93-BCC(C) dt 10/09/93
51. Kotwal	12011/68/93-BCC(C) dt 10/09/93
	12011/21/95-BCC dt 15/05/95
52. Kharia	12011/68/93-BCC(C) dt 10/09/93
53. Kumhar	12011/68/93-BCC(C) dt 10/09/93
54. Kherwar	12011/68/93-BCC(C) dt 10/09/93
55. Khodal	12011/68/93-BCC(C) dt 10/09/93
56. Khond	12011/68/93-BCC(C) dt 10/09/93
57. Koya	12011/68/93-BCC(C) dt 10/09/93
58. Kondpan	12011/68/93-BCC(C) dt 10/09/93
59. Kohor	12011/68/93-BCC(C) dt 10/09/93
	12011/21/95-BCC dt 15/05/95
60. Kormakar	12011/68/93-BCC(C) dt 10/09/93
61. Kashan	12011/68/93-BCC(C) dt 10/09/93
62. Lahar	12011/68/93-BCC(C) dt 10/09/93
63. Lodha	12011/68/93-BCC(C) dt 10/09/93
64. Lodhi	12011/68/93-BCC(C) dt 10/09/93
65. Madari	12011/68/93-BCC(C) dt 10/09/93
66. Mahli	12011/68/93-BCC(C) dt 10/09/93
67. Mohali	12011/68/93-BCC(C) dt 10/09/93
68. Modi	12011/68/93-BCC(C) dt 10/09/93

69. Mahato 12011/68/93-BCC(C) dt 10/09/93
70. Malpatharia 12011/68/93-BCC(C) dt 10/09/93
71. Manki 12011/68/93-BCC(C) dt 10/09/93
72. Majwar 12011/68/93-BCC(C) dt 10/09/93
73. Mirdhar 12011/68/93-BCC(C) dt 10/09/93
74. Munda 12011/68/93-BCC(C) dt 10/09/93
75. Nonia, Nunia 12011/68/93-BCC(C) dt 10/09/93
76. Nagasia 12011/68/93-BCC(C) dt 10/09/93
77. Nagbansi 12011/68/93-BCC(C) dt 10/09/93
78. Nath 12011/68/93-BCC(C) dt 10/09/93
79. Oraon 12011/68/93-BCC(C) dt 10/09/93
80. Pasi 12011/68/93-BCC(C) dt 10/09/93
81. Paidi 12011/68/93-BCC(C) dt 10/09/93
82. Pan 12011/68/93-BCC(C) dt 10/09/93
83. Panika 12011/68/93-BCC(C) dt 10/09/93
84. Parja 12011/68/93-BCC(C) dt 10/09/93
85. Patratanti 12011/68/93-BCC(C) dt 10/09/93
86. Pradhan 12011/68/93-BCC(C) dt 10/09/93
87. Rajwar 12011/68/93-BCC(C) dt 10/09/93
88. Sahora 12011/68/93-BCC(C) dt 10/09/93
89. Santhal, Santal 12011/68/93-BCC(C) dt 10/09/93
90. Sarvera 12011/68/93-BCC(C) dt 10/09/93
91. Turi 12011/68/93-BCC(C) dt 10/09/93
92. Telenga 12011/68/93-BCC(C) dt 10/09/93
93. Tassa 12011/68/93-BCC(C) dt 10/09/93
94. Tantubai 12011/68/93-BCC(C) dt 10/09/93
95. Teli 12011/68/93-BCC(C) dt 10/09/93
96. Tanti 12011/68/93-BCC(C) dt 10/09/93

25. Teli 12011/68/93-BCC(C) dt 10/09/93
26. Yogi, Jogi, Jugi Nath 12011/68/93-BCC(C) dt 10/09/93

27. Maimal (Muslim Fisherman) 12011/68/93-BCC(C) dt 10/09/93
28. Maria 12011/68/93-BCC(C) dt 10/09/93

Origin and Brief History of Various Castes

Ahom

The Ahom people of Assam are the descendants of the ethnic Tai people that accompanied the Tai prince Sukaphaa into the Brahmaputra valley in 1228 and ruled the area for six centuries. Sukaphaa and his followers established the Ahom kingdom (1228-1826), and the Ahom dynasty ruled and expanded the kingdom until the British gained control of the region through the Treaty of Yandabo upon winning the First Anglo-Burmese War in 1826. The kingdom established by the Ahom people gave Assam its name.

The modern Ahom people and their culture are a syncretic blend of the original Tai culture, the indigenous Tibeto-Burmans and Hinduism. Many of the Tai followers of Sukaphaa were unaccompanied males, who subsequently married into the local communities. Some ethnic groups, including the Tibeto-Burman speaking Borahi people, were completely subsumed into the Ahom community. Members of other communities, based on their allegiance to the Ahom kingdom or the usefulness of their talents, were accepted as Ahoms. Gradually, the Indo-Aryan Assamese language replaced the Ahom language as the Ahoms converted to Hinduism and other aspects of Indian culture though one-third of the Ahom population still follow Tai original religion, Furalung. The Ahom language, till a few years ago was known by approximately 400-500 members of the Ahom priestly class. Deeply concern about the Ahom language, Tai Ahom organisations are now trying to revive Tai Ahom language again among masses of Tai Ahom people by establishing various Tai schools in Upper Assam. Many institutes like P.K. Buragohain Institute for Tai and South East Asian Studies, Guwahati, Central Tai Academy, Patsaku, etc., have come up in recent days. In coming days more Tai schools are planned to be established across Assam.

Starting in the late 20th and continuing into the early 21st century, there has been renewed interest among the Ahoms in their culture and language leading to increased study and attempts at revival. The 1901 census of India enumerated approximately 1,79,000 people identifying as Ahom. The latest available census records slightly over two million Ahom individuals however, estimates of the total number of people descended from the original Tai-Ahom settlers are as high as eight million.

History of Ahom

In the early 13th century, Mong Mao was a small kingdom of Tai people, related to the Shan, in present day Yunnan Province, China. In 1228, Sukaphaa, a prince of Mong Mao began his journey with about 9000 followers, mostly men. He crossed the Patkai hills and reached the Brahmaputra valley in 1228. He moved from place to place, searching for a seat. He decided not to attack the Morans and Borahis but befriend them instead. His followers, much depleted from the original 9000, married into the Borahi and the Moran ethnic groups. The Borahis, a Tibeto-Burman people, were sub-sumed into the Ahom fold, though the Moran maintained their independent ethnicity. Sukaphaa finally established his capital at Charaideo near present-day Sivasagar in 1253 and began the task of state formation.

The Ahom kingdom then consolidated its power, building their kingdom for the next 600 years. The first major expansion was at the cost of the Sutiya kingdom, which was annexed in 1522 under King Suhungmung. The expansion's success was not only a result of Ahom military prowess, but also of changes in the Ahom social and political outlook. Suhungmung was the first Ahom king to adopt a Hindu name: Swarga Narayan. The Sutiya region was placed under the Sadiyakhowa Gohain a new position that was created. In 1536, the Dimasa Kacharis, known to Ahoms as "Timisa", were uprooted from their capital at Dimapur. Thus, by the middle of the 16th century, the Ahoms were in control of all of present day eastern Assam. The late 17th century saw another expansion of Ahom territory. After the 1682 battle of

Itakhuli, that marked the end of the Ahom-Mughal conflicts, much of the control of Koch Hajo fell into the hands of the Ahoms. By bringing the various tribal groups and regions less than one ruler and one governing polity the Ahoms are considered the architects of modern Assam.

Ahom power declined in the latter half of the 18th century. The capital city was taken for a short period during the Moamoria rebellion. In the first part of the 19th century, the Burmese army invaded their kingdom, uprooted their capital and set-up a puppet Ahom king. The Burmese were defeated by the British in the First Anglo-Burmese War resulting in the Treaty of Yandaboo in 1826, which paved the way for the British to convert the Ahom kingdom into a principality and which marked the end of the Ahom rule. Assam was then annexed by British India, becoming a province and then a state as the Ahom identity gradually became Assamese. Now, the Ahoms are again reviving their original Tai language, culture.

Asur

Asur people are a tribal/Adivasi people living primarily in the Indian state of Jharkhand, mostly in the Gumla, Lohardaga, Palamu and Latehar districts.

The total population of Asurs is 10,712 with a decennial growth rate of 37.63 from the 1981 population as per the 1991 census. They are not a significant group in the census highlights for Sscheduled Tribes in Jharkhand. Similarly, they are an insignificant group in West Bengal, but Asurs were amongst the Proto-Australoid groups inhabiting the western regions of West Bengal in pre-historic times. In the 1981 census, their literacy rate was 10.66 per cent. Asurs are traditionally iron-smelters. They were once hunter gatherers, having also involved in shifting agriculture. However, majority of them shifted into agriculture with 91.19 per cent enlisted as cultivators as per the 2010 edition of the Encyclopaedia of Scheduled Tribes in Jharkhand.

Their indigenous technology of iron smelting gives them a distinct identity; as they claim to have descended from the ancient

Asuras who were associated with the art of metal craft. When smelting, the Asur women sing a song relating the furnace to an expectant mother encouraging the furnace to give a healthy baby, i.e., good quality and quantity of iron from the ore; and were thence, according to Bera, associated with the fertility cult (Bera 1997:32).

The Asur society is divided into 12 clans. These Asur clans are named after different animals, birds and foodgrains. Family is second prominent institution after the clan. Except in emergency cases, they use traditional herbal medicines. They have their own community council (jati-panch) where disputes are settled. They accept food from Rajputs, Oraon, Kharwar, Thakur, Ghasi, and few others; and maintain putative kinship ties with Kharwar, Munda and other neighbouring tribes. Except the burial site, they share all other public spaces with their neighbours. They live in pats (a clearing area) surrounded by the forest, and their houses are made of mud walls supported by wooden poles with a roof covered with paddy straw and self-baked khapras (tiles). Their houses consist of spaces for cattle and birds and a separate area for worship of ancestors. Utensils for cooking and storing water drawn from wells are made of iron, aluminium and eastern ware. Traditional male clothing is dhoti while the females wear tattoo marks (depicting totemic objects) upon their bodies as ornaments. The females also wear other metal and non-metal ornaments as well as glass bangles. They use common agricultural implements for cultivation; and occasionally hunt game in the forest using bows and arrows.

The modern Asur tribe is divided into three sub-tribal divisions, namely, Bir (Kol) Asur, Birjia Asur and Agaria Asur. The Birjia are recognised as a separate Schedule Tribe. The Asur religion is a mixture of animism, animatism, naturalism and ancestral worships. They also believe in 'black magic' like bhut-pret (spirits) and witchcraft. Their chief deity is Singbonga. Amongst the other deities are Dharati Mata, Duari, Patdaraha and Turi Husid. They celebrate festivals like Sarhul, Karma, Dhanbuni, Kadelta, Rajj Karma, Dasahara Karam.

Baria

The community get their name from the Sanskrit word *vari* meaning water. According to their traditions, they were the lords of the waterways. The Bari is sub-group of the Kshatriya 'Donwar' community. They are descent from Kirat Bari, a soldier in the army of Maharana Pratap Singh. The community is now found mainly in eastern and southern Uttar Pradesh and Bihar and speak the Bhojpuri in Awadhi dialect.

According to mythological texts, Bari was also known as Sharaswat Brahmins in the era of Rama of Ayodhya. They used to cook food for Rama and called as "Bar". Due to lack of education they shifted to other sub-clans which were associated with "Sisodiya" of Rajput clan in the middle age of India. In the history of Rajput, they lost life for their king in the battlefield. They also claim descent from Rupan Bari, a soldier in the army of [Alha udal]. Bari people are very reserve and spend their whole life in serving their owners and in return they never ask for land, that is why most of the Bari people were landless. Bari spent many years in forest because of fear of killings by Mugals and their subordinates in India. They adopted the art of utensil making from leaves and started making "leaf crockery" for their Kings in exile at jungles. Bari also does trading of pan leaves in state like Maharashtra and Madhya Pradesh.

The Bari is strictly endogamous community, and marry close kin. They were a landless community sometime back, and earned their living by collecting forest products. After Government land *bandobast* programme they now have abundant land in their names. A majority of the community were once daily wage labourers but times had changed and they are working in established Government and Private Sector industries. They are now able to educate their children with ease and some of them had even successfully settled in USA, Singapore, Thailand and various major Metros of India. Each of their settlement contains an informal caste council, known as a biradari panchayat. The panchayat acts as instrument of social control, dealing with issues such as divorce and adultery.

Bari classified as "Other Backward Classes" in Uttar Pradesh, Haryana and Delhi. The community use the surname i.e., Bari, Rawat, Rawal, Singh and Thakur. They are also very close to Tamboli and Baria Community of other state. Bari is known as Rajput and Kshatriya. Before few years back the main source of income of Bari samaj was on farming of 'Betel Leaves' which they also have unique quality in India. Now-a-days, Bari samaj is moving towards development cultural as well as in the living style. In Maharashtra the surname of Bari caste are like Kolhe, Aswar, Tade, Khalse, Katole, Patil, Naik, Aatbal, Varade, Bundhe, Nagpure, etc. are used. And as mentioned above biradari panchayat in Maharashtra referred as "Bari Panch (Members) Mandal", which helps people to solve their internal dispute at caste level.

Basor

The Basor are a Hindu caste found in the state of Uttar Pradesh in India. They are also known as Dumar, and have Scheduled Castes (SC) status. The Basor are a sub-division within the SC community, who were traditionally involved in the manufacture of bamboo furniture. Their name means a worker in bamboo. The Basor are found mainly in the districts of Jalaun, Hamirpur, Mahoba, Jhansi and Banda and in Chhattisgarh Basor Mohalla Sitamani Korba, Basor Mohalla Kosamanda Janjgir-Champa, Puraana Rapta Sabji Market Shiwrinarayan District. Janjgir Champa and Madhya Pradesh Bhopal, Jabalpur, Gwalior, Rewa are the district where they generally resides. They speak Bundelkhandi dialect, although most can also understand the high version of Hindi, known as Khadi Boli.

The Basor practice strict community endogamy, as well as clan exogamy, which a common practice among most North Indian Hindus. Their clans are called gotras, the main ones being the Bahmangot, Dhuneb, Katahriya, Sikarwar, Samangot, Sonach and Supa. Marriages do not occur with the Muslim Bansphor community. The Basor live in multi-caste villages, but occupy their own distinct quarters. Each of their settlement contains an informal caste council, known as a panchayat. The panchayat is headed by a pradhan, a position which is hereditary. In addition, there is an overarching panchayat of between three and four villages, which headed by a chaudhary. The panchayat resolves any intra-community dispute, as well as acting an instrument of social control. They are Hindus and have Lakshmi and Durga as their tribal deities.

The Basor are marginal farmers and share-croppers. Their traditional occupation was basket making and animal husbandry. Like other artisan castes, they have seen in their traditional occupation, with a concurrent rise in the number of daily wage labourers. Traditionally, they used to work as a labourer's and bamboo works. They also act as village musicians especially during processions, marriages and other socio-religious ceremonies. Basor community also found in Madhya Pradesh Jabalpur, Bhopal, and Gwalior are the district where they live. Now, this community also trying itself to comes in light using the weapons of education and cultural sensitivity. Arkhel, Vanshkar, Banskar, Basor, Ben, Barmaiiya are the surnames which is being used by the community long ago.

Baiga

Baiga is a tribe found in Madhya Pradesh, Uttar Pradesh, Chhattisgarh and Jharkhand states of India. The largest number of Baigas is found in Baiga-chuk in Mandla district and Balaghat district of Madhya Pradesh. They have sub-castes - Bijhwar, Narotia, Bharotiya, Nahar, Rai Bhaina, and Kadh Bhaina. Their population as of census 1981 was 248,949.

The Baiga tribes practice shifting cultivation in forest areas. They say they never ploughed the earth, because it would be like scratching the breast of their mother, and how could they possibly ask mother to produce food from the same patch of earth time and time again - she would have become weakened. That's why Baigas used to lived a semi-nomadic life, and practiced Bewar cultivation (slash and burn) - out of respect, not aggression. Until fairly recently the Baigas practiced dahiya cultivation, that is, slash and burn. Thousands of square miles of sal forests have been clean destroyed by them in the progress of their dahiya cultivation, the ground being afterwards occupied by dense scrub of low sal species springing from the stumps. The Baigas are courageous woodsman and hunters. Baigas of Central India were relucant to do work for others. The Baigas saw themselves as people of the forest, who could only live on the produce of the forest. It was below the dignity of a Baiga to become a labourer.

The Baiga tribe in Madhya Pradesh is known for its unique culture. They do not interact even with other tribals like the Gonds, believe in a hand-to-mouth existence, and do not try to access education, eat outside their community, or associate with others. After a death in the family, the Baigas just leave the house and build another. They are totally dependent on the jungle, they do not engage in tendu patta collection, which is a major livelihood provider in Madhya Pradesh.

Bedia

The Bedia a community of Bihar, they believe that they originally lived on Mohdipahar and have descended from the union of Vedbansi prince with a Munda girl. The other view is that a section of the Kurmis were outcasts and to be known as the Bedia or Wandering Kurmis. The Bedia, sometimes pronounced "Beriya", are a Hindu caste found in the state of Uttar Pradesh in India. The community has several names, like Bedia Kudmi, Choto Kudmi, Shershahbadia, Bhathia, Wandering Kurmis, Maldahiya and Badia and Bedia too, however its official name is Sharshahbadia. The word *bedia* is a corrupt form of the Hindi word *behara*, which means a forest-dweller. They are a nomadic tribe that had been notified under the Criminal Tribes Act. According to early British scholars, they were one of the many nomadic tribes found in North India, and were of the same stock as the Rajputs. According to their own traditions, they were originally Rajputs, who lost status, after their defeat at the hands of the Mughals. The community was connected with some bad works, as well as petty theft. They speak Awadhi and are found mainly in the districts of Bahraich, Barabanki, Basti, Agra, Faizabad, Gonda and Kanpur. After independence, they were denotified in 1952, when the Criminal Tribes Act was repealed.

Beldar

The community are the traditionally natives of North India, and are similar to the Oad communities, who are the navies of west India. They also claim common ancestry with Kewat community, both of whom refer to themselves as Oads.

In Maharashtra, the Beldar are found mainly in the districts of Nasik, Pune, Amravati, Akola, Yawatmal, Ahmednagar, Sholapur, Kolhapur, Sangli, Satara, Ratnagiri and the city of Mumbai. The Beldar claims to have immigrated from Rajasthan some five centuries ago. They still speak Rajasthani among themselves and Marathi with outsiders. The community is strictly endogamous, and consists of a number of exogamous clans. Their main clans are the Narora, Davawar, Kharola, Jailwar, Faatara, Horwar, Chhapawar, Tuse, Pannewar, Mahore, Basniwar, Bahr, Gorala and Udainwar. They have there personal history towards shifting from one place to another. Moreover, they are categorise themselves like in a form of sub-section of Beldar caste. Some categorisations are Mangal, Sadhra, Nadhra and many more.

Beldar is a Scheduled Castes of northern part of India. The Beldar caste is still engaged in their traditional occupation of navvies. Mostly, Beldars are employed in road constructions and digging of well and river by the government.

According to some legends, Beldar caste is said to have descended from Prithviraj Chauhan. Beldar community is the traditional navvies of northern India. They are very similar to Oad community, the construction workers of western India. Both these communities claim common lineage with Lonia community. In Hoshangabad District, some Muhammadan Beldars are also found. Regarding the origin of Beldar caste, it is also believed that probably the bulk of the Beldars and its allied castes have originated from non-Aryan tribes. The Murhas of northern districts of the country seem to be a subsidiary of the Bind tribe; further, those known as Matkuda or earth-digger are usually considered as offshoots of Gond tribe. While the Sansias and Larhias of Chhattisgarh seem to have originated from the Kols, Bhuiyas and Oraon tribe. The term Raj, meaning a mason, is also used for the Beldars in the northern regions. The Murha,

Nunia and Sansia castes are also frequently known as Beldars. Interestingly, they cannot be evidently distinguished from the main caste of Beldars. The Beldar caste of Saugor claims that their ancestors were mostly engaged in refining salt. They also have a rich culture and their music and dance play an integral part of their life. Drums, fireworks accompany the wedding processions of Beldar community. Divorce is allowed in their society. The Beldar community has several indigenous customs, which they follow faithfully. They are religious by nature.

Bhatta

Bhat, Bhatt, Bhatta or Bhatra meaning a priest or scribe in Sanskrit, is a surname common in most parts of India. This is title given to learn Brahmins. A predominantly Hindu last name, it is found most commonly in the states of Rajasthan, Gujarat, Haryana, Jammu and Kashmir, Punjab, Madhya Pradesh, Uttarakhand, Uttar Pradesh, Bihar and in West Bengal (as Bhattacharya) and some parts of Karnataka. Among the communities in India with this last name are the Nagar Brahmins, Bhattmewada Brahmins, Audichya Brahmins, Gouda Saraswat Brahmins, Gurjargaur Brahmins, Konkanastha and the Smartha Brahmins. Some families in Karnataka also share the surname belong to Havyaka, Shivalli (and/or) madhva and even Daivajna.

In the olden days, the kings used to have the presence of Brahmins for various purposes. People who belonged to the class of Brahmins mainly gave highly influential judgements on the right and wrong decisions in the court, later came to be known as 'Bhatt'. It is believed that because of this, these people possess excellent communication, judgement and logical argument skills in them. Bhatts was known to keep genealogies of Rajput kings.

The earliest reference of Bhatt can be found in Chandragupta's empire. In Mudrarakshasa, while describing different divisions in Chandragupta's army, a reference can be found to Bhatt-Bala. Here Bala means a division; hence Bhatt-Bala would mean a division composed of Bhatt.

Bhil

Bhils are primarily an Adivasi people of Central India. Bhils are also settled in the Tharparkar District of Sindh, Pakistan. They speak the Bhil languages, a sub-group of the Western Zone of the Indo-Aryan languages. Bhils are listed as Adivasi residents of the states of Gujarat, Madhya Pradesh, Chhattisgarh, Maharashtra and Rajasthan – all in the western Deccan regions and Central India – as well as in Tripura in far-eastern India, on the border with Bangladesh. Bhils are divided into a number of endogamous territorial divisions, which in turn have a number of clans and lineages. They mostly speak a dialect of Hindi. The Ghoomar dance is one well-known aspect of Bhil culture.

In feudal and colonial times, many Bhils were employed by the ruling Rajputs in various capacities, e.g., as Shikaris because of their knowledge of the terrain. Many had even become warriors in armies. Bhils respected their motherland and were ready to defend it if anybody tried to occupy it. They were in the Mewar army of Maharana Pratap and they were experts in guerilla warfare which the Mughal Empire had so much trouble handling. Today, there is a Mewar Bhil Corps.'

In Hindu mythology, popular Bhil figures are Shabari, who offered Rama and Lakshmana half-eaten jujubes when they were searching for Sita in the forest. Matanga was a Bhil sage who became a Brahmana. According to a Brahman parohit of the Ahirias at Hodal, the Baurias and Ahirias are descended from Goha, a Bhil who married a Thakur, and the children were Baurias and Ahirias where the Ahirias are very mixed and the pure unmixed Bhils are the Baurias.

Chutia

The Chutiya kingdom was established by Birpal in 1187 in north-eastern Assam, with the capital at Sadiya. The Sutiya are an indigenous ethnic group that spoke a Tibeto-Burman language, but now they speak Assamese language. According to tradition, Birpal at first became the chief of sixty families.

The most illustrious of the Sutiya kings was Gauri Narayan (Ratnadhwajpal), son of Birpal. He brought many other Sutiya groups into his kingdom. In 1224, Ratnadhwajpal defeated Bhadrasena, the king of Swetagiri. Then he went on to subjugate Nyayapal and marched toward Kamatapur, where he formed an alliance with the Kamata ruler by marrying a princess. Then he marched to Dhaka, and camped some distance away from the city. Though records exist of this expedition, there is no account of a war at Dhaka.

The hostilities with the Ahoms began in 1376 when the Ahom king, Sutuphaa, was killed by the Sutiya king during a friendly encounter. The simmering dispute often flared till 1522, when the Ahoms finally took Sadiya and killed the then king Nityapal. The Ahoms established their rule by instituting the position of Sadiyakhowa Gohain, the governor in charge of Sadiya. But the Sutiya had dispersed to frontier regions, and continued raids against the Ahoms. This finally stopped in 1673 when the Sutiyas finally accepted Ahom overlordship.

Das

Das is a common last name in India and Bangladesh, among adherents of Hinduism, Sikhism, Jainism, and Buddhism. It is a derived from the Sanskrit word Dasa (Sanskrit: Das) meaning servant of God, "devotee," or "votary". "Das" may, most accurately, be inferred as one who has surrendered to God. The people with the last name "Das" belong to the Kayastha Varna (Hinduism) in Bengal, Bihar, Assam, and Orissa. Additionally, the Das suffix was attributed to many a higher caste Kayastha, who worshiped Lord Krishna during the middle ages. The prefix of their name consisted of one of the many names of Lord Krishna and a suffix Das was added to that. Presently, initiated male followers of the ISKCON tradition adopt the last name Das or Dasa upon formally entering the ISKCON community. The present day usage of Dasa or Das in Hinduism is respectful and is not considered derogatory.

Das is also a last name (with a different meaning and etymology; Das means "badger" in Dutch, from PIE *teks) found amongst the Dutch of the Netherlands.

Ganak

Ganak is a caste of traditional astrologers from Assam, India. They are also known as Ganak Brahmins, Acharya, and Graha Bipra. They claim that they are descendants of Sakaldwipiya Brahmins, but other Brahmin clans consider them to be a lower rank. The common surnames used by this group are Sarma/ Sarmah, Changkakoti, and Bordoloi, etc.

Condemnation of Ganak people occurred around 400 BC, and was believed to be lost their supreme sacerdotal Brahminical status since that period.

During 1509-1686 AD, 11 talented Brahmins came to Assam from Kanauj, Uttar Pradesh. They were (i) Sathibar Pandey (1616 AD), (ii) Acharya Gopaldev Bhatta Chaturvedi (1586 AD), (iii) Umananda Chaturvedi (1671 AD), (iv) Keshavananda Pandey (1671 AD), (v) Acharya Gadadhara Pandey (1509 AD), (vi) Dharmmangada Trivedi (1681 AD), (vii) Gadadhara Upadhyay (1656 AD), (viii) Rangacharana Mishra (1661 AD), (ix) Bhisagacharya Ishwaragiri (1655 AD), (x) Kamalalochana Trivedi (1638 AD) and (xi) Swarupananda Dwivedi (1686 AD). Chaturvedi, Trivedi, Dwivedi, Pandey, Upadhayay and Mishra were the highest category Brahmin (under Yajurveda, Kandwa Branch and Mihirayan Gotra) in national level. During the rule of Ahom King, Shiva Singha, one Brahmin came from Simala Gaon, Nadiya District, Bengal name Krishnananda Bhattacharyya and got the royal support. The King divided the whole Brahmin community in two groups as Surya-vipra and Chandra-vipra. The above mentioned 11 families were given the status of Surya-vipra Brahmin or Ganak. (ref page no 70, Assam Buranji, Harakanta Baruah sadaramin).Thus, Ganak Brahmin status was given by the local king in Assam.

Ghosh

Ghosh is an Indian family surname found mostly amongst Bengali Kulin Kayastha Hindus. The word Ghosh is possibly derived from Ghosha, an ancient Indian female philosopher mentioned in the Vedas, or from Emperor Ghosha of the Sunga Empire, an ancient Indian kingdom.

Goala

In the Hindi belt, "Ahir," "Gwala," and "Yadav" are often used synonymously. Yadav refers to a grouping of traditionally non-elite, pastoral communities, or castes, in India and Nepal that since the nineteenth and twentieth centuries has claimed descent from the mythological King Yadu as a part of a movement of social and political resurgence.

The term 'Yadav' now covers many traditional pastoral castes such as Ahirs of the Hindi belt, the Gavli of Maharashtra, the Goala of Andhra and the Konar of Tamil Nadu. The Yadav are included in the category Other Backward Classes (OBCs) in many Indian states.

Traditionally, Yadav groups were linked to cattle-raising and, as such, were outside the formal caste system. Since the late nineteenth and early twentieth centuries, the Yadav movement has worked to improve the social standing of its constituents, through Sanskritisation, active participation in the Indian and British armed forces, expansion of economic opportunities to include other, more prestigious business fields, and active participation in politics. Yadav leaders and intellectuals have often focussed on their claimed descent from Yadu, and from Lord Krishna, which they argue confers kshatriya status upon them, and effort has been invested in recasting the group narrative to emphasise kshatriya-like valour, however, the overall tenor of their movement has not been overtly egalitarian in the context of the larger Indian caste system.

Koch Rajbongshi

Koch Rajbongshi community can be found in entire parts of Present Assam, West Bengal, Kishanganj in Bihar, Nepal, Meghalaya, Bangladesh. Koch Rajbongshi community is one of the primitive communities of the Koch Rajbongshi Kingdom being ruled by the Koch Rajbongshi Kings like King Nara Narayan, King Chilaray. The Koch Rajbongshi Kingdom is being merged with present Assam, most of the parts of the North Bengal, Parts of Nepal and Bangladesh.

People some time misunderstand and take Koch Rajbongshi as Assamese in Assam and Bengali as in West Bengal because as Koch Rajbongshis are shy by nature, they do not disclose their ancient language in public and their traditional worship pattern towards nature is a very private affair, thereby the pattern of worship is not exposed to the public or researcher and scholar in most often times with special request may be it is possible to observe such event, which is a rare golden opportunity to watch the traditional worship, they generally do not allow to do video-recording or photography of such events, they believe that nature may get offended by the act.

This behaviour of Koch Rajbongshi tribe is because of their shyness but it have also a negative effect because the world is unknown about their language and tribal culture, only the Koch Rajbongshi have the knowledge about it and they do not share it with the rest of the world. It is personal and sacred communion which they share within their brotherhood.

Kumar

The origin of Kumar can be traced back to early development of Hinduism and its origin in South Asia. The first usage of Kumar was for the Four Kumaras, the four sons of Brahma from the Puranic texts of Hinduism named Sanaka, Sanatana, Sanandana, and Sanat.

In Skanda Purana, the largest Mahapurana, a genre of eighteen Hindu religious texts, the text is devoted mainly to the leelas of Kartikeya, son of Shiva and Parvati. "Kumar" is used to refer Kartikeya.

Kurmi

The Kurmi are a Hindu agricultural Jati (community) in India and Nepal. The group has been associated with the Kunbi, though scholars differ as to whether the terms are synonymous. In 2006, the Indian government announced that Kurmi was considered synonymous with the Kunbi and Yellam castes in Maharashtra. There are differences of opinion regarding the group's classification in the traditional varna system. There are several theories regarding the etymology of the term Kurmi. It may be derived from an Indian tribal language, or may be a Sanskrit compound term krishi karmi, "agriculturalist." Another theory holds that it was derived from *kurmi,* meaning "ploughman". According to the Anthropological Survey of India, which used British Raj sources, the Kurmis of Bihar and Uttar Pradesh are divided into different sub-castes e.g., Awadhiya, Ghamalia, Konchasia, Yasawar or Joshwar, Chandel, Sindriya, Patel, etc.

With the waning of Mughal rule in the early 18th century, the Indian sub-continent's hinterland dwellers, many of whom were armed and nomadic, began to appear more frequently in settled areas and interact with towns people and agriculturists. Many new rulers of the 18th century came from such nomadic backgrounds. The effect of this interaction on India's social organisation lasted well into the colonial period. During much of this time, non-elite tillers and pastoralists, such as the Kurmi or Ahirs, were part of a social spectrum that blended only indistinctly into the elite landowning classes at one end, and the menial or ritually polluting classes at the other.

The Kurmi were famed as cultivators and market gardeners. In western and northern Awadh, for example, for much of the eighteenth century, the Muslim gentry offered the Kurmi highly-discounted rental rates for clearing the jungle and cultivating it. Once the land had been brought stably under the plough, however, the land rent was usually raised to 30 to 80 per cent above the going rate. Although British revenue officials later ascribed the high rent to the prejudice among the elite rural castes against handling the plough, the main reason was the greater productivity of the Kurmi, whose success lay in superior manuring. According to historian Christopher Bayly:

Whereas the majority of cultivators manured only the lands immediately around the village and used these lands for growing food grains, Kurmis avoided using animal dung for fuel and manured the poorer lands farther from the village (the manjha). They were able, therefore, to grow valuable market crops such as potatoes, melons and tobacco immediately around the village, sow fine grains in the manjha, and restrict the poor millet subsistence crops to the periphery. A network of ganjs (fixed rural markets) and Kurmi or Kacchi settlements could transform a local economy within a year or two.

Cross-cultural influences were felt also. Hindu tillers worshipped at Muslim shrines in the small towns founded by their Muslim overlords. The Hindu Kurmis of Chunar and Jaunpur, for instance, took up the Muslim custom of marrying first cousins, and of burying their dead. In some regions, the Kurmis' success as tillers led to land ownership, and to avowals of high status, as noted, for examples, by Francis Buchanan in the early 19th century among the Ayodhya Kurmis of the Awadh. Earlier, in the late eighteenth century, when Asaf-Ud-Dowlah, the fourth Nawab of Awadh, attempted to grant the kshatriya title of Raja to a group of influential landed Ayodhya Kurmis, he was thwarted by a united opposition of Rajputs, who were themselves (as described by Buchanan), "a group of newcomers to the court, who had been peasant soldiers only a few years before ..." According to historian William Pinch:

(The) Rajputs of Awadh, who along with brahmans constituted the main beneficiaries of what historian Richard Barnett characterises as "Asaf's permissive programme of social mobility," were not willing to let that mobility reach beyond certain arbitrary socio-cultural boundaries. ... The divergent claims to status in the nineteenth century (and earlier) illustrate the point that for non-Muslims, while varna was generally accepted as the basis for identity, on the whole little agreement prevailed with respect to the place of the individual and the jati within a varna hierarchy.

Although the free peasant farm was the mainstay of farming in many parts of north India in the 18th century, in some regions, a combination of climatic, political, and demographic factors led to the increased dependence of peasant cultivators such as the Kurmi. In the Benares division, which had come under the revenue purview of the British East India Company in 1779, the Chalisa famine of 1783, and the relentless revenue demand from the company reduced the status of many Kurmi cultivators. A British revenue agent wrote in 1790, "It unfortunately happened that during the famine aforesaid a great proportion of the Kurmis,

Kacchis and Koeris were in this district as well as in others supplanted by Brahmans ... " and bemoaned the loss of agricultural revenue in part due to, "this unfavourable mutation amongst the cultivators ... "

In the first half of the nineteenth century, economic pressures on the large landowning classes increased noticeably. The prices of agricultural lands fell at the same time that the East India Company, after acquiring the Ceded and Conquered Provinces (later the North-Western Provinces) in 1805, began to press landowners for more land revenue. The annexation of Awadh in 1856, created more fear and discontent among the landed elite, and may have contributed to the Indian rebellion of 1857. Economic pressures also opened marginal areas to intensive agriculture and turned the fortunes of the non-elite peasants, such as the Kurmi, who worked for them. After the rebellion, the landowning classes, defeated but still pressed economically in the new British Raj, attempted to treat their tenants and labourers as people of lowly birth and to demand unpaid labour from them. According to historical anthropologist Susan Bayly, in some instances these were attempts to stave off decline by reinvigorating or intensifying existing forms of customary service. Elsewhere these were wholly novel demands, many being imposed on 'clean' tillers and cattle-keepers like the Ram- and Krishna-loving Koeris, Kurmis and Ahirs ... In either case, these calls were buttressed with appeals to Sanskritic varna theory and Brahmanical caste convention. ... Kurmi and Goala/Ahir tillers who held tenancies from these 'squireens' found themselves being identified as Shudras, that is, people who were mandated to serve those of the superior Kshatriya and Brahman varnas.

Mahishya

Mahishya also spelled Mahisya, is a Bengali Hindu caste, which has an Indo-Aryan lineage. Members of this caste are traditionally found in the Indian states of West Bengal and Orissa. Mahishyas are one of the predominant castes in West Bengal, especially in the southern districts of Howrah, Paschim Medinipur, Purba Medinipur, Hooghly and South-24 Parganas.

Many members are employed in the business and service sectors. Their diet and living conditions have changed over time.

Historians such as Jagabandhu Singh have referenced the Padma Purana and the Brahmavaibarta Purana to conclude that the Mahishyas and Kaivarttas (Kaibarttas) are the same caste. In general terms, a child born of a Kshatriya father and Vaishya mother is called a Kaivartta or Mahishya. If one takes the two terms to be synonymous, they are considered Kaivarttas. Mahishyas have a status between Kshatriya and Vaishya and are spread throughout Maharashtra, Chattisgarh and several other states. Bengali cultural historian Sevananda Bharati thinks that the ancient home of the Mahishya race is near present-day Ratnavati on the bank of the Narmada River (formerly known as Mahishamati). The Mahishyas migrated from Ayodhya, entering what is now Midnapore through the Chota Nagpur Plateau. Biharilal Kalye believes that the founder of the Ganga Dynasty of Orissa, Anantavarman, belonged to the Mahishya group. Others (such as Singh) disagree, believing that he belonged to Kshatriya caste of Paralakhemundi. Sir Harbert Risley agrees with Kalye, and states in *The Tribes and Castes of Bengal* that five leaders established five kingdoms in Midnapore: Tamralipta (or Tamluk), Balista (or Moynagarh), Turkee, Sujamatha and Kutabpur. The inhabitants of Tamralipta were a seafaring race, inhabiting modern Bengal and the southern coast of India.

The Mahishyas were numerically predominant in Midnapore at the turn of the 20th century as a small-landholding community. In 1896, they were identified as local aristocrats by the president of the teachers' college in Nadia, since the number of Kayasthas in Midnapore district was relatively small compared to the rest of Bengal. The Mahishyas formed a tight-knit social group; the movement to gain recognition as a caste separate from the Kaibarttas gained momentum in 1897, when the Mahishyas formed the Jati Nirdharani Samiti (Caste Assignment Forum). At the time, the Kaibarttas were divided into Jele Kaibarttas (fishermen), and Hele Kaibarttas (farmers). As the leading group in Midnapore, the 1931 census found 2.71 per cent of Mahishyas proficient in English (the language of the upwardly mobile during the British Raj). In 1921, the demand for a caste separate from the Kaibarttas was conceded, based on data which suggested that they were a socially distinct group and the predominant caste in Bengal; data from the 1921 census indicated that they were the largest Hindu caste in Bengal. In the sub-divisions of Contai and Tamluk (now comprising Purba Medinipur district), they formed 44.2 and 54.9 per cent of the population respectively. The Mahishyas (through the Mahishya Samaj) endeavoured to instill pride in their agricultural roots, since they were the cultivators of the soil. This peasant pride, along with a politically vocal leadership led by British-educated barrister Birendranath Sasmal, forged a Mahishya identity. During the Quit India Movement of the Indian independence struggle in the early 1940s, local national governments at Tamluk and Contai resisted British occupation for two years; the backbone of the resistance was the Mahishya community.

Although many are still involved in traditional work in rural areas, within a generation Mahishyas gave up agriculture in large numbers in favour of engineering and skilled labour in the urbanised areas of Howrah and Kolkata. In Howrah, the Mahishyas are the most numerous and successful business people. At the turn of the 20th century, much of the land and factories were owned by Kayasthas; by 1967, Mahishyas owned 67 per cent of the engineering businesses in the district.

Mala

Mala or Malla (different from the family/last name Malla from Andhra) is a social group or caste mostly from the south Indian state of Andhra Pradesh. Mala is derived from the Sanskrit malla, which means wrestler. They are one of the dominant Dalit castes in Andhra Pradesh, the other being Madigas.

According to Government of India census data from 2001, Malas constitute a total of 41.6 per cent (5,139,305) of the scheduled caste population of the state. They are largely concentrated in the Coastal Andhra region. During the Adi-Andhra movement of the 1930s, several Mala caste people, including few Madigas, especially from coastal Andhra called themselves as 'Adi-Andhra' and were recorded in the census with the 'Adi-Andhra' caste name akin to Adi Dravida of Tamil Nadu. (Adi-Andhra is synonym word instead of using MALA or Madiga, in Adi-Andhra Malas are 90 per cent and 10 per cent belonged to Madiga caste). In the ancient times, Malas were mostly village watchmen or hardworking labourers. They were skilled workers too and were also recruited by the British Army because of their martial skills. Presently, they don't have a specific caste profession and can be seen in many professions.

The Mahars in neighbouring Maharashtra are akin to the Malas and the two dominant dalit castes in Tamil Nadu, Paraiyar and Pallar, tend to claim the inter-relation with the Malas, Mahars and Pulayas.

Mala military exploits form an important part of Kakatiya history, culture and tradition. Mala's played a vital role in expansion of Kakatiyan kingdom. In Kakatiya military Malas are used to be called as Mohari (Telugu: mohari), the street which they lived is known as "Mohariwada". The warrior Yugandarudu who was the army chief of Prataparudra is a Mala.

The anthropological evidence shows that the Mahars or Malas seemed to have hailed primarily from the drier upland areas like the Deccan plateau. According to researchers like Ambedkar, the Mahars and similar communities like Malas were actually warriors of some defeated kingdom, they were pushed down in social status, and they were disarmed but retained as village servants.

Mala caste has got prominence during the period of Palanati Bramha Naidu (Prime Minister to Nalagam King of Macherla) (1170 to 1180 AD). The Mala Warrior Mala Kannamadasu was the first Senapathi in the history along with Kammas, Velamas and Reddies in those days. He was given high regard by Palanati Bramha Naidu, since then Macherla Chennakesava swamy became Kuladaivam to Malas in the Palnadu area.

Mala Christian

A section of the Malas also turned to Christianity but after noticing the same old caste politics in the Telugu Catholic church, shifted to Protestantism instead. They are prominent in the Andhra Evangelical Lutheran Church (AELC), Church of South India (CSI). They have made very good use of the Christian educational programmes, considerably elevating their social position and now form part of the upper middle class. These Christian Malas are commonly called Merugumala people, who came from Godavari Krishna basin. They are not considered Scheduled Castes by the Government of India but fall under the "BC-C" category (Backward castes C-category) with one per cent reservation at state-level and at national-level they come under Other Backward Class (OBC, List of OBC's; Andhra Pradesh list, Entry No. in the Central List-60 (Scheduled Castes converts to Christianity and their progeny). They have been demanding Central Government to accord them SC status on par with Dalit Buddhists, Dalit Sikhs and not to discriminate them on religious grounds for being Dalit Christians. The case is pending with the Supreme Court since 2005, when it was filed on behalf of Dalit Christians and Dalit Muslims (Pasmanda Muslim Mahaz).

Former Chief Minister Chandra Babu Naidu, from 1996 to 1997, formed the Justice Ramachandra Raju Commission to study categorisation among Scheduled Castes. The Commission's findings would eventually form the basis for the AP Scheduled Castes (Rationalisation of Reservation) Act, 2000, categorising the fifteen per cent reservation quota into four subgroups (designated "A", "B", "C" and "D"; "B" and "C" represent Madigas and Malas, respectively). The sub-categorisation policy was implemented for a four years period (2000-2004). The act, however, was first challenged by {main petitioner WPNO.11472/97} the United Forum of All Scheduled Castes, represented by that organisation's state general secretary, Dasari Srinivas.V (Present Director, Ambedkar Ias Study Circle, Sr Nagar, Hyderabad-38, 9397677681) and Dr. EV Chinnayya in WPNo. 21096/1996 mainly challenged the Justice Ramachandra Raju Commission validity under the constitutional provisions.

On SC's categorisation National Commission for SC, ST, New Delhi, called for discussions and fact findings were held from 7-7-1998 to 15-7-1998. At that time, renowned and eminent Sr Parliamentarian H Hanumanthappa (Sr Advocate in Supreme Court) was the Chairman and Bommidala Yadaiah (Telengana Mala) was also a Member in the National SC, ST Commission. On 7-7-1998 Manda Krishna hearings were noted by the commission on behalf of MRPS (Madiaga Reservation Porata Samithi) and Madiga Community.

On 9-7-98 the National Commission for SC, ST has officially invited Dasari Srinivas, V, State General Secretary, UFASC, AP, as he was the main petitioner in the case to present his case on behalf of the MALA community. On 10th July, 1998 Mallela Venkata Rao another leader in Malamahanadu and on 11th July 1998 PV Rao, President, Mala Mahanadu gave the stand on categorisation.

A.P. Scheduled Castes (Rationalisation of Reservation) Act, 2000 was vehemently opposed by Malas and Mala Mahanadu has challenged the Act in Supreme Court saying that it is against the Constitutional principles, which viewed SC's as a holistic single social group. Supreme Court on 5th Nov 2005 has struck down the Act and the verdict went in favour of Mala Mahanadu.

The apex court pronounced its judgment stating that State Government has no power to sub-categorise Scheduled Castes into groups to implement reservations in the field of education and employment in exercise of its power under Articles 15(4) and 16(4) of the Indian Constitution as public employment and education." Further it was held that the Parliament alone is competent to pass such an act under the Article 341 of the Indian Constitution.

Manipuri Brahmin

Manipuri Brahmin origins stretch as far as Gujarat to West Bengal, Bangladesh, Uttar Pradesh and Orissa. Most of the Manipuri Brahmins are pesco-vegetarians, although foods cooked during religious ceremonies and festivals are strictly lacto-vegetarian, even without onions and garlic. The most common last name or title among these Brahmins is Sharma. Sometimes females will use Devi as their title. Each Brahmin family within the community belongs to a specific gotra indicating their origin.

Manipuri Brahmins are the descendants of Indo-Aryan people. Brahmins from different parts of India such as Bengal, North India, and Orissa began to migrate to Manipur Valley in the 15th century. They started worshipping Hindu gods in Manipur by constructing temples. The appearance of Brahmins in Manipur in the 15th century may be due to the rise of Muslim power in Bengal and the subsequent repression and religious persecution of the Hindus there. In 1717, a Bengali Brahmin named Shantidas Gosai (or Shantidas Adhikari) converted King Pamheiba of Manipur to Hinduism. A particular form of Vaisnavism was also adopted and spread under the reigns of King Kyamba through King Khagemba in the 19th century. Toward the end of the 19th century, and at the advent of the 20th century, a great force of Gaudiya Vaishnavism came and spread in Manipur. Many Hindu temples were also constructed during this period and a greater number of Brahmins came to Manipur and settled as pujaris for the temples. These Brahmins, living with the Meiteis and sharing with them a corporate life by adopting Meitei ways of living and language, formed the Manipuri Brahmins.

Manipuri Muslim

The Muslim Manipuris locally known as Panghal are a cultural group and religious minority who have been living with the majority community – the Meitei who are co-valley dwellers and with hill inhabitants – Naga and Kuki who are Christians. Muslims have been living in Manipur, North East India since the nineteenth century AD. Now they form a population of 8.32 per cent of the total state population; in 2001 government census, Muslims with 190,939 persons (Pangal or Meitei-Pangal as local names).

The Mughals enthroned Chhatra Manikya (ruling 1661-66) in Tripura while Govinda Manikya too fled to Arakan where he again met Shuja. On the breach of trust by Arakan king Sanda Sudama, Shuja fled back to Tripura whose king quickly dispatched Shuja to Manipur by supplying an elephant in 1661, so that it might not antagonise the military force of Aurangzeb led by Mir Jumla. The Mughals lately came to know of the situation but Shuja was already gone. The Mughal prince Shangkusum (Shah Shuja) reached Manipur in December 1661, according to Cheitharol Kumbaba. The Mughals sent a three men embassy to Manipur in late December 1661, this time to retrieve the aggrieved family of Shuja. At that time, Shuja was taking shelter in at Haignang of Kairang (east of Imphal), now known as Shuja-lok (Shuja cave). In the meantime in Tripura, Chhatra Manikya was too dethroned and Govinda Manikya came back from Arakan to claim the throne and ruled Tripura again from 1667 to 1675. The Manipur king Khunjaoba sent back a three men embassy to the court of the Mughal emperor Aurangzeb in 1662 while a Mughal ambassador named Nur Beg was held back in Manipur by the Qazi of Manipur named Muhammad Sani, so that the retreating two Mughal messengers named Dur Beg and Rustam Beg should not tell about Shuja's existence in Manipur. Yet, Shuja was sent up to Ukhrul hill with some Muslims (already settled in Manipur) as precautionary measure from Mughal informers. Thus, Tripura and Manipur kings played crucial roles in saving the life of Shah Shuja probably because they did not like the Mughal expansionist policy of Aurangzeb.

Prince Shah Shuja had a wife named Praveen Banu (Piara Banu, Pai Ribanu), a sister namely, Sabe Banu, three sons – Zainibuddin (Bon Sultan or Sultan Bang), Buland Akhtar and Zainul Abedin, three daughters – Gulrukh Banu, Roshanara Begum and Amina Begum. Shah Shuja lost the war of succession, and bid Hindustan farewell on 6th June 1660 fleeing to Arakan via Tripura-Chittagong. Shuja carried two vessels of gold and silver, jewel, treasures and other royal appendages to Arakan. Shuja first arrived at Chittagong and stayed for some time, from where he took the land route to Arakan which is still called Shuja Road. A thousand palanquins (carriers) carried the harem ladies and Shuja prayed the Eid prayer at a place called Edgoung (Eidgah) in Dulahzara which is still in Chittagong on the way to

Arakan. Shuja undertook the land journey for 13 days and 13 nights with a troubled mind on the eastern bank of Naf River, half a mile north of Maungdaw town which is still known as Shuja village. Some of Shuja's retinues there were later retained by the British army as archers army from 1826. The final day of the sea route took Shuja to Arakan where he was received by an envoy of Arakan king Sanda Sudamma and escorted to a separate quarter for the Mughal prince. Niccolai Manucci wrote: "The date of flight (of Shuja from Dacca) was June 5, 1660 and arrived in Arakan on August 26, 1660." Harvey noted that Shuja came to Arakan as Sudamma promised to provide him some of his famous ships to take him to Mecca for pilgrimage. He broke the promise. When Shuja arrived in Arakan with half a dozen camel loads of gold and jewelry, the temptation was too great for the Arakan king. Princess Gulrukh Banu fell victim to Sudamma and she promptly died in suicide, while Sultan Bang and another brother died fighting. They ran amok, nearly succeeded in firing the royal palace of Sudamma in December 1660, while many Mughals were massacred. Arakan king's mother was against the killing of Shuja, being a guest in the first instant. The Portuguese, who were well-known there as pirates, saved Shuja but robbed him of gold and jewels. The surviving Mughals with Shuja escaped back to Tripura on 16th May 1661 with much difficulty and arrived in Manipur in December 1661. While Aurangzeb's reconnaissance men were on the hunt for Shuja and for every bit of news. Conscious of this, Shuja's men spread false news that Shuja died fighting in Arakan, while others rumoured he shipped to Mecca. There were a thousand different tales about Shuja's fate and nothing could be conclusive. After all this trauma and travesty, Shuja helped by Mughals and Pathans of Arakan.

Matak

Assam presents a picture of great variety with her people belonging to different racial groups, speaking different dialects and professing different religious rites practices. Assamese culture, being thus a composite one, the true essence of it not properly understood without a study of the history and civilisation of its different constituent elements. The Matak who formed a distinct community by themselves, developing certain cultural traits and patterns of social behaviour under the Vaishnava reformers, form one of these important constituent elements. They also played a very significant role in the political developments of the history of the entire North East, since they became politically organised towards the later part of the 18th century till the annexation of their kingdom to British India in 1893. There is a great difference of opinion regarding the origin of the word 'Matak' and its actual interpretation. According to one school of thought, the actual spelling of the term is Matek, which means men of one principle–Mat-principle, ek-one. But according to the Tai-Ahom and Assamese chronicles the Ahom named the people they met according to their physical trait and nature. Sukapha the founder of the Ahom dynasty had to face a strong resistance from the section of the Maran. It is, therefore, said that the term Matak is coined by the Ahom, meaning thereby 'powerful men', Ma-powerful tak- means weighed or examined.

According to a census carried out by Sadau Assam Matak Sanmilan, the present population of the community is more than 12 lakhs. Most of them live in the present Dibrugarh and Tinsukia district which once formed the major part of their kingdom. The rest lie scattered throughout the Brahmaputra valley, mainly, in the districts of Sibsagar, Lakhimpur, Darrang, and Nogaon.

Moran

There are a number of opinions regarding the meaning of Moran. According to certain numbers of Elders, the word owes its origin to a myth. It is said that an old lady of this community, a physician by profession, had the supernatural power of giving life to dead ones, for which she was called 'Moran', meaning one who can call back a dead. 'Mor' means die 'An' means call back. Kedar Brahmachari expresses the view that a people knows a Maurang, Muurang or Morang, migrated to Saumar area (easternmost part) of ancient Assam from Nepal and in course of time, came to be known as Morans. Benudhar Sharma has mentioned that many years before the coming of Sukapha to Saumar, a man from the Meram clan of the kingdom of Dharampala, a king of ancient Assam, became king in a place known as Lahdoi. The word Moran was coined from the name of this King. According to Endle, the original home of the Morans was in the Hukong Valley and the term Moran comes from the name of their progenitor 'Moran' who came over to Assam and settled near the Tiphuk River. J.P. Wade, one of the earliest British officers mentions the term 'Moran' to mean the rebels against the Ahom monarch. The Morans are presently found mostly in Tinsukia district of Upper Assam with some sprinkling in Arunachal Pradesh.

Nai

The Nai is a Hindu and Sikh caste or clan originating in India. It is found throughout India. The Nai belong to a caste variously called Sain, Mangali, Vostaad, Manthri, Napit, Nayi, Nayee or Valand. The Nai were traditionally barbers but had other specialised roles. They have also been associated with land-owning. They were traditionally used as messengers and go-betweens in delicate matters. They acted as ambassadors between different states. They traditionally led wedding parties or carried messages between villages and communities. They are known for keeping the secrets, following a strictly disciplined life, and for keeping their body clean, active and physically fit. In the state of Gujarat, the Nais are referred by the name Valand. The Valand have several territorial divisions, such as the Soratia, Halai, Gohil, and Jalawadi. They are further divided into clans, called ataks, the main ones being the Vaghela, Parmar and Hanani. The Valand are endogamous and practice clan exogamy. They speak Gujarati and concentrated in the urban areas. The community is involved in the different trades, with many rural Valand have given up agriculture. Some were practitioners of Ayurvedic medicine.

Nath Yogi

Yogi Nath, simply known as Yogi, is a Bengali Hindu caste descended from the Nath Sampradaya (sect). The yogis are the followers of Shaivism and primarily united with the tradition of Nath Sampradaya.

The yogis were primarily associated with the Yogic-traditions promoted by the great Nath saints, e.g., Matsyendranath,

Gorakshanath, Chauranginath, etc. Hatha yoga is considered as the prominent part of those traditions promoted by these great Nath masters. The Nath Sampradaya is considered as a development of the earlier Siddha or Avadhuta Sampradaya, an ancient lineage of spiritual masters. The yogis identify themselves in the lineage of classical followers of Shaivism. The Nath Sampradaya is heterodox in nature and does not recognise caste barrier to open their teachings and lessons. Their teachings are being followed by people from higher as well as lower castes.

The yogis had to suffer with the establishment of caste-hierarchy based elitism in Bengal. According to Satish Chandra Mitra, Ballal Sen attempted for re-establishment of Brahmanism endorsing Vedic-tradition and additionally promoted caste-based elitism while he demoted the yogis in the caste hierarchy. It can be noted that Vedic-tradition and Yogic-tradition were evolved differently. Today, both of these traditions coexist under the banner of Hinduism. The Yogic-tradition which is considered as an initiation of lord Shiva is usually believed by the historians as a pre-Vedic tradition. Any possibility of sharing same root by these two traditions at any point of time is yet to be justified by the historians. The post-Vedic Hindu-literatures are observed to be influenced with the gradual integration of both of these traditions. In Bengal during Ballal Sen, some elements with sense of intolerance between these two traditions as well as difference in opinion between elitist strategy and heterodox strategy towards caste-system were possibly the factors which didn't work well for the yogis. Conveying similar opinion with the heterodox strategy, elitism in any form is usually criticised for hampering the proper human resource development in a society, depriving a society from healthy competitions and finally directing a society in a position to survive below of its potential. According to Bipin Chandra Pal, after this establishment of elitist caste-system in Bengal, they had to face many problems with their social positions. Many of them then settled in the outlying tracts of eastern Bengal, especially in the districts of Sylhet, Tipperah, Noakhali, Chittagong, Mymensingh and Dhaka. Many of the yogis adopted weaving as profession.

According to James-wise, the yogis were an ambitious caste, who recognised the value of education. According to Santosh Kumar Kundu, they were very much inclined towards the study of Sanskrit. However, on account of their social degradation, they had to suffer serious economic hardships for their education and survival. The governments of India and West Bengal both have provided affirmative action to the non-creamy layer of the yogi-caste through inclusion of this caste in the category of Other Backward Classes (OBC) since 1994. OBC status is verified at time to time and a caste is subjected to removal from affirmative action if the social, educational and economic conditions satisfy certain threshold assessments. Social-growth is observed to be on rise among the non-creamy section of the yogi-caste. At the present time, Hatha yoga has been immensely popular in the Western countries. It works as pride-factor to the Indians and possibly intense pride-factor to the yogis.

The principles of Yoga philosophy of Nath tradition are stated in various books, e.g., Gorakshagita, Goraksha Paddhati, Siddha Siddhanta Paddhati, Amaraugha Sasana, Amaraugha Prabodha, Mahartha Manjari, Gheranda Samhita, etc., all written in Sanskrit. Hatha yoga is a holistic path of yoga which includes disciplines, postures (asana), purification procedures (shatkriya), gestures (mudra), breathing (pranayama), meditation (dhyana), samadhi.

Prominent Nath masters, Matsyendranath and Gorakshanath are also found to be greatly honoured in some areas of Buddhism as Mahasiddhas and are credited with great powers and perfected spiritual attainment. It can be noted that Buddhism, in fact, was originated from the same land of Yoga and shares similarities with different traditions of Yoga, e.g., cultivation of higher wisdom through meditation, etc. Such similarities have led some authors to refer the possibilities of associations between Buddhism and Yogic-traditions documented in later-age. Satish Chandra Mitra expressed his opinion in this regard that yogis are unconsciously Buddhists in their faith. The yogis, however, are not found to believe in any dependency with

Buddhism. Dependency of Hatha Yoga with Buddhism is not generally found to be advocated by any Yoga-expert. At present, Hatha yoga is considered as one of the important traditions of Hinduism.

Many of the yogis are observed as religious-minded people. The worship and initiation to different faiths are found to be performed by the priests belonging to own yogi-caste. They do not sacrifice during worship. Earlier the yogis used to bury their dead, by placing the corpse upright in Yogic posture. Nowadays they are also found to cremate their dead. They observe *ashaucha* for ten days.

Chhetri

Chhetri or Chhettri, synonymous with Kshetri and Khatri are all derivatives of Kshatriya, the warrior and ruler caste group or varna of Hinduism. Chhetris speak Nepali, the national language, and are part of the dominant Khasa culture and the wider Pahari Khas – Nepali population. Chhetri refers to Kshatriyas from the hills of Nepal but not from the Nepalese Terai or India.

They formed Nepal's largest caste group, 15.5 per cent of the population. Chhetris are overwhelmingly Hindu (99.48 per cent according to the 2001 Census). In Nepal's hill districts their proportion of the population rises to 41 per cent compared to 31 per cent Brahmin and 27 per cent other castes. This greatly exceeds the Kshatriya portion in most regions with predominantly Hindu populations.

The Himalaya was considered a sacred place for attaining liberation in Hindu mythology. References to Brahmins and Kshatriyas are found in Banawali (Tantric texts) on Nepal, in whose ancient setting the Kathmandu Valley was still a lake. The lake was owned by Banasura or some claims Danasur (The mix of Kirati and Assyrian or often called Ashur). Manjushree (Mongoloid or related to Kirat people) came from China and drained the water from the pond and thus the valley came into existence.

Before the Shah dynasty (1768-2008) united Nepal excluding the eastern region of Nepal from Arun onwards Limbuwan was the only federal state with whom Prithivi Narayan Shah signed treaty and continued as a federal state. The Limbuwan and Nepal treaty was renewed often till Mahendra Shah imposed 'Bhumisudhar Ain' or kind of Land reform Act. Kings of various ethnic and caste groups ruled about 50 small kingdoms. The ancient name of this Himalayan region was Khas-des. Khas peoples were the most populous and are mentioned in the histories of India and China. The Khas were Indo-European-speaking Aryan mountain dwellers, spreading from west to east across the hills of the Central Himalaya. They established many independent dynasties in early medieval times. The Khas people had an empire, the Ka?a Kingdom which included Kashmir, part of Tibet, and Western Nepal (Karnali Zone). It is also believed that during the rule of Shah Dynasty "Lahad Singh" and "Pahad Singh" were invited for making strategical war against Kasthamandap and Kritipur. Later they were renowned as "Deuwa" and then "Deuja". Their bravery let the king defeat Kasthamandap and Kritipur. Since then "Deuja" and "Shah" have had a smooth relationship.

Anthropologists believe that within the context of Indo-Aryan migration, the majority of Chhetris derive from unions between Khas and indigenous groups, as the Khas progressively encroached on indigenous homelands. Many Chhetris exhibit traits of mixed racial heritage, more so than Brahmins (called Bahun in the Nepalese hills). There are several recognised ways to enter the Chhetri caste apart from Jharra (pure) Chettri or Khas :

1. Having nothing but ancestors ultimately tracable to Kshatriyas.

2. Being the scion of a Brahman father and any other "clean" caste including Magar or other Tibeto-Burman "hill tribes".

3. The child of a Chhetri father and a woman from these lower but "clean" castes is still Chhetri.

4. An arbitrary community can start following Chhetri caste rules (especially in diet), hiring Bahuns to conduct certain rituals and even to write dubious genealogy. Over generations, these claims of Chhetri affinity become plausible to broader audiences.

Despite racial admixture, Chhetris remain strongly indo-Nepalese in culture and language.

In the early modern history of Nepal, Chhetris played a key role in the unification of the country, providing the core of the Gorkhali army of the mid-18th century. During the monarchy, Chhetris continued to dominate the ranks of the Nepalese Army, police, Nepalese government administration, and even one regiment of the Indian Army. Under the pre-democratic constitution and institutions of the state, Chhetri culture and language also dominated various ethnic groups to the disadvantage and exclusion of many minorities and indigenous peoples. The desire for increased self-determination among these minorities and indigenous peoples was a central issue in the Nepalese Civil War and subsequent democratic movement. Till the date chhetri, bahun, dasnami and dalit had allied to seek the brotherhood and protested against the federal state system and go along with the late King Mahendra's administrative structure consisting of 14 zones and 75 districts however, the five development regions introduced by late King Birendra is the mandate to be followed in the future too.

Family name of Nepali Chhetri are Baruwal, Karki (revenue officer), Bhandari (military officers and some are store keeper), Khadka (sword-bearer), Bisht (baron/distinguished), Baniya (Military Officers), Dhami, Thapa (Officer) (Tibetan: man at the border), Thada rahi Adhikari, Budhathoki, Deoja, Khatri (KC), Gharti Chhetri (GC), Budhathoki Chhetri (BC), Dangi Chhetri (DC), Kunwar, Bohara, Kathayat, Dani, Rana (Timilsina), Basnet, Chhetri (Kshatriya), Silwal.

There is some confusion about the surname Rana. This was a self-designated surname of the former hereditary prime ministers of Nepal. The first autocratic Prime Minister of Nepal, Jang Bahadur Kunwar, changed his surname to Rana to strengthen his claim and association with Rana kings in Rajasthan, the claimed origin of his ancestors.

Gurung

The Gurung people, also called Tamu, are an ethnic group from different parts of Nepal. Gurungs, like other East Asian featured peoples of Nepal such as Sherpa, Tamang, Thakali, Magar, Manaaggi, Mustaaggi, and Walunggi, are the indigenous people of Nepal's mountain valleys. They live primarily in the Gandaki zone, specifically Lamjung, Kaski, Mustang, Dolpa, Tanahu, Gorkha, Parbat and Syangja districts as well as the Manang district around the Annapurna mountain range. Some live in the Baglung, Okhaldhunga and Taplejung districts and Machhapuchhre as well. Small numbers are believed to be living in India's West Bengal and Sikkim, as well as Bhutan.

There are about more than 0.7 Million Gurungs in Nepal (2.5 per cent of the Nepali population) of which 338,925 speak the Gurung language.

The Gurung have a rich tradition of music and culture. The Gurung have established the system of Rodhi which is a little similar to modern discothèques, where young people meet and share their views in music and dancing. They have their own music and dancing history. Some musical dances such as Ghatu and Chudka are still in existence. In many Gurung villages they are still performing these types of musical dances, which are performed either solo or in a group. Gurung films have been produced which promote these musical dances.

The surname is not only found in Nepal but other countries such as Mexico, Chile, the UK, the US, and India.

Their traditional occupation was based on sheep herding, trans-Himalayan trade and farming. In the 19th and early 20th century, many Gurung were recruited to serve in the British and Indian Gurkha regiments. Today, the Singapore Police, Brunei reserve units and the French Foreign Legion incorporate ethnically Gurung members. While serving in the British Army they have earned more than six Victoria Cross awards. Gurungs are not only restricted to military occupations; many live in urban areas and are employed in all types of labour, business and professional services.

Gurungs trace their descent patrilineally, organised into two groups, or moieties of patrilineal clans.

A noted Gurung tradition is the institution of Rodhi where teenagers form fictive kinship bonds and become Rodhi members to socialise, perform communal tasks, and find marriage partners. But the institution is rarely in existence because of its notoriety in the community. 'Rodhi' literally means weaving and making of baskets.

Generally speaking, the Gurungs are divided into two castes (Jaat in the local tongue); four and the sixteen. Within the tin Jaat there exist further sub-divisions: namely, Ghale Ghotane, Lama and Lamichhaney. However, these are not an original jaats of Gurung they were given by Aryen (Hindu) after they arrived in Nepal. Their proper jaats are 'Kown, Lam, and Lem. Each of these castes has their sub-castes of own; Kown has: Lhyege Kown, Jhobro Kon, Takrey Kown, Khelag Kown and many others; Lam: Painghy Lam, Tamee Lam, Cahaiber Lam, Tuchai Lam, Kupchai Lam and many others. They have their own sub-castes including Rilde, Ghaldu, and Tamja. The Gale does not come under Gurung Jaat. They have their own history and marry amongst their subcastes. The cultural norms and values of three jaads are greatly influenced by the Tibetans. Tibetan priests perform all rituals, and tin caste gurung are mainly Buddhists. However, nauw jaat gurung did not change their ancient religion bonism and bon priest performs all rituals for them. Gurungs are very homogenous in society, whereby a Gurung is typically married to another Gurung people. This practice has existed for a long time without contention and to this day, this practice is still very ubiquitous, though less heightened.

Despite Nepali's being a South-Asian, Gurung people bear similar physical traits like Chinese, Mongoloid or Tibetans. Typically, a Gurung person have dark-brown almond eyes, double eye-lids, dark hair, high cheekbones, full lips, small jawline, light skin, and a fairly elevated nose-bridge.

A study has noted that a Gurkha mercenary in Singapore or Great Britain would typically support up to five relatives from home, despite already having to support their immediate family members. The foreign remittance of the Gurkha's pension fund as well as disposable income has benefited Nepal's Economy to some extent.

A notable Gurung person is Designer Prabal Gurung, a Singapore-born, Nepali-American Fashion Designer. His father was a Gurkha soldier who served in Singapore.

Rai

The Rais are one of the most ancient indigenous ethno-linguistic groups of Nepal. They were Raipa meaning king (Rai means King in old Khaskura). Once someone was recognised as a ruler, Hindus awarded them the title Rai. When the Nepalese Gorkha king Prithvi Narayan Shah couldn't defeat Khambu king, he somehow took them in confidence that the land is theirs forever and gave them the title Rai in around B.S. 1832. The title of Rai instead Khambu Kirant people who used to live in Wallo Kirant and Majh Kirant for particular reason. The Rai are the Khambu (people living in Mud Hut). Then the post Rai was provided to the topmost leaders of the region. They were given the power to collect land tax. That's why sometimes Rai people are called jimmi or jimmi-wal. The Rai belong to the Kirati-group or the Kirat confederation that includes Limbu, Sunuwar, Yakkha and Dhimal ethnic groups.

According to the anthropologist Dor Bahadur Bista of Tribhuvan University and late Professor Suniti Kumar Chatterji (linguist and kiratologist, Calcutta University), Kirats migrated from the east via north Burma and Assam along the mid-hills (lower mountains) with their pigs in ancient times. It specially refers to Limbu and Dhimal, who called themselves Yakthumba or Yoktumba. According to Imansing Chemjong they migrated from the Assam valley to Pallo kirant in around 600 AD.

According to Chatterji and other prominent linguists, the Rai, Limbu, and Dhimal languages are pronominalised (Austric/ Kol influence) strongly indicating earliest migratory wave of these peoples compared to other Tibeto-Burmans whose languages are non-pronominalised. The traditional homeland of the Rai extends across Solukhumbu, Okhaldhunga (Wallo Kirat or Near Kirat), home of the Nachhiring, Bahing, Wambule, Dumi (subgroups); Khotang, Bhojpur and the Udayapur Districts (Majh Kirat or Central Kirat), home of Bantawa, Chamling, in the north-eastern hilly region of Nepal, west of the Arun River in the Sun Kosi River watershed. Rais are also found in significant numbers in the Indian state of Sikkim and in the northern West Bengal towns of Kalimpong and Darjeeling.

The Rai people are divided into many different sub-groups - Bantawa, Chamling, Sampang, Dumi, Jerung, Kulung, Khaling, Lohorung, Mewahang, Rakhali, Thulung, Tamla, Tilung, Sunuwar, Wahaling, Wambule, Yakkha, Yamphu, Jero (Jerung), Puma, Syangbo. Some groups number only a few hundred members.

More than 32 different 'panoti' languages and dialects are recognised within the Tibeto-Burman languages family. Their languages are Pronominalised Tibeto-Burman languages, indicating their antiquity. The oral language is rich and ancient, as is Kiranti history, but the written script remains yet to be properly organised as nearly all traces of it were destroyed by the following rulers of Nepal, the Lichhavis and almost eradicated by the Shah dynasty.

The traditional Kiranti religion, predating Hinduism and Buddhism, is based on ancestor-worship and the placation of ancestor spirits through elaborate rituals governed by rules called Mundhum. Sumnima-Paruhang is worshipped as primordial parents. A major Rai holiday is the harvest festival, Nwogi, when fresh harvested foods are shared by all. The Bijuwa and Nakchhung (Dhami) or Priest plays an important role in Rai communities.

The Rai people do not truly belong to the caste system. The majority of Rai people have never accepted casteism and never adopted a caste. The Nepal Federation of Indigenous Nationalities and the Nepal government have recognised this fact. Because of the fiercely independent nature of the Rai community and its location at the eastern end of the consolidated Nepalese nation-state, they were given exceptional rights of Kipat autonomy and land ownership in their homeland of Majh (middle) Kirant.

Subsistence agriculture of rice, millet, wheat, corn and cotton is the main occupation of the Rai although many Rai have been recruited into military service with the Nepal army and police, and the Indian and British Gurkha regiments and Singapore Police Force.

Rai women decorate themselves lavishly with silver and gold coin jewellery. Marriage unions are usually monogamous and arranged by parents, although "love marriage", bride capture in the past and elopement are alternative methods. Music with traditional drums and string instruments such as yele, binayo, murchunga, dhol and jhyamta, dance such as Sakela or Sakewa dance, and distilled spirits (alcohol) called aaraakha, ngashi, or waasim are central to Rai culture.

Sakela or Sakewa dance is the greatest religious festival of Kirant Rai people in Nepal. The Sakela celebration is a prayer to Mother Nature for healthy crops and protection from natural calamities. Therefore, the festival is also known as "Bhumi Puja". Starting on Baisakh Purnima, Sakela Ubhauli is celebrated for 15 days in Baisakh (April/May) marking the beginning of the farming year.

Magars

The Magars are an indigenous ethnic group of Nepal whose homeland extends from the western and southern edges of the

Dhaulagiri section of the Himalayas range south to the Mahabharat foothills eastward into the Gandaki basin. Representing 7.125 per cent of Nepal's population, according to the 2011 census, they are the largest indigenous group in Nepal.

The Magars are divided into eight major groups: Shreesh, Pun, Rana, Thapa, Ale, Burathoki, Roka, and Gharti. Magar clans intermarry with one another, and are officially of equal social standing.

Genetically and physically, Magar people are Mongoloid/east Asian. They are believed to have migrated from Tibet like the Gurungs and other prominent ethnic groups, however, there is an interesting mythical story describing Magar's origins and versions of three different language groups are presented.

The Magar of the Bara Magaranth (a group of twelve Magar kingdoms east of the Gandaki River) are said to have originated in the land of Seem. Two brothers, See Magar and Chintoo Magar, fought, and one remained in Seem, while the other left, ending up in Kangwachen in southern Sikkim. The Bhutia people lived at the northern end of this region. Over time, the Magars became very powerful and made the northern Bhutia their vassals. Sintoo Sati Sheng ruled in a very despotic manner, and the Bhutia conspired to assassinate him. Sheng's queen took revenge and poisoned 1,000 Bhutia people at a place now called Tong Song Fong, meaning "where a thousand were murdered". The Bhutia later drove the Magar out, forcing them to again migrate further south. As part of this migration, one group migrated to Simrongadh, one group moved towards the Okhaldhunga region, and another group seems to have returned to the east. No dates are given.

A second Magar federation called Athar Magarat (18 Magar Kingdoms) was situated west of the Gandaki River, inhabited by Kham Magar.

The Tarali Magar are said to have originated from a woman, who fled the region of Jumla during a war between Kalyal kings. It is not known who her spouse was but she arrived at Tarakot on the verge of giving birth to a son. One day, the boy saw a strange phenomenon in the jungle lake where he went with his cattle. The lake is said to have filled with milk, and seven shining creatures, like fairies, were bathing in the waters of the lake. He was enthralled and came to observe them daily. One day he told his mother about this strange sight, and she advised him to touch the youngest of these angels; this would cause her to become human so he could marry her, and he brought the beautiful damsel to his mother. When they asked her who she was she replied in an unknown tongue which was incomprehensible for them. The Devi was offered some bread, and she uttered the words, "Tai khe nan". Slowly they began to learn the language of this woman, and Kaike was spread among them. The language was called "Kaike", meaning "language of the Gods".

The group was first mentioned in AD 1100, when the Magar King of Palpa and Butwal, Mukunda Sen, invaded and conquered the Nepal (Kathmandu) valley. It is always understood, however, that they have resided around Palpa from time immemorial and that they were probably the earliest settlers from the north. This part of the country was formerly divided into twelve districts, each under its own ruler, being known as the Barah, or twelve Magarant or twelve Thams, the members of each supposedly being of common extraction in the male line. Some records show these twelve areas as being Argha, Gulmi, Isma, Musikot, Khanchi, Ghiring, Rising, Bhirkot, Payung, Garhung, Dhor and Satung. However, it is probable that some of the latter places should have been excluded in favour of Palpa, Galkot, Dhurkot, Char Hajar, Parbat, and even Piuthan and Salyan.

The Magars of middle and western Nepal played a role in Nepal's formative history. Their kingdom was one of the strongest of west Nepal in and around Palpa District during the time of the 22 and 24 rajya principalities (17th and early 18th centuries). Hamilton, during his research in Nepal in 1802, came to a conclusion that all the kings of 24 principalities, including Sen King of Palpa in western Nepal, were Magars. Many of the Magar aristocracy joined the Thakuri caste and status. In recent years, many scholars and historians have claimed that Nepal's former Shah Rulers were the descendants of Magar kings of the Barah Magarath/Kali Gandaki region. The 18th-century king, Prithvi Narayan Shah, the founder of the modern Kingdom of Nepal announced himself as a king of Magarant. According to Hamilton, Mincha and Khancha Khan, the forefathers of former Shah Kings of Nepal, were of Magar descent. Baburam Acharya, a prominent historian of Nepal, also confirmed that Nepal's former Shah Kings were the descendents of Magar kings.

Many prominent historians of Nepal have claimed that Aramudi, an eighth-century ruler of the Kali Gandaki region, was a Magar King. "Aramudi" derives from the word for 'river' in the Magar language. 'Ari'-'Source of Water' + 'Modi'-'River'='Arimodi' or 'Aramudi', thus the literal meaning of Aramudi is 'source of river'. Jayapida [782-813 AD] also called Vinayaditta, a king of Kashmir, invaded Kali Gandaki Region, a traditional homeland of the Magars of Nepal. Aramudi resisted the invasion. After capture by Aramudi, Vinayaditta was taken to the right banks of the Kali Gandaki river, in a strongly built fort, where Aramudi imprisoned him. Jayapida was a powerful king of Kashmir who ruled for 31 years and defeated the kings of Kanyakubja (Kannauj), and Prayag/Allahabad in Uttar Pradesh, India. He was in a conquering expedition to the valley of the Ganges.

Lohar

Lohar (Lohara) is considered to be a sub-caste among Hindus and Sikhs and a clan among Muslims in Northern India, Northern Pakistan and Nepal. In India, the Lohars are also known as Vishwakarma, Sharma, Lohana or Panchals. Muslim Lohar in North India is known as Saifi. The Pakistani city of Lahore was once called Loharpur, the city of the Lohar dynasty.

Writers of the Raj period often used the term Lohar as a synonym for blacksmith, although there are other traditional smithing communities, such as the Ramgarhia and Sikligars, and numerous non-traditional communities, including the Yadavs, Kayasthas, Rajputs and even Brahmins.

The Lohar are one of the most widespread communities in Uttar Pradesh. They are divided along religious lines, with the Hindu Lohar are known as Vishvakarmas, and Muslim Lohars are known as Saifis. The Lohar are further divided into a number of exogamous groupings, the main ones being the Kanaujiya, Purbia, Bahai, Moulia and Magajia. Most Lohar are still engaged in their traditional occupation of metal fabrication, but most of the Lohar of western Uttar Pradesh are cultivators. The assimilated Lohar speak Hindi and its various dialects such as Awadhi. But others speak Ho and some speak Western Pahari.

Sadgop

The Sadgop derive their name from the Sanskrit word 'sad' meaning good and 'gopa' meaning a milkman. They claim to be descendants of the Hindu god Krishna. According to chronicles, many members are adopted Hinduism in 11th century during Eastern Ganga dynasty after the Kurukshetra War and remaining members adopt Hinduism in 15th century during Kamarupa Kingdom. Gaya and Vrindaban are their pilgrim centers. The Sadgop are divided into two groups, the Kulin and Mulika, with the former further sub-divided into the eastern and western Kulin. The western Kulin live in West Bengal, and are further sub-divided into the Ghosh and Sarhesia. The eastern Kulin left Midnapur in West Bengal, some part of East Bengal and moved to Bihar. The Sadgop speak Bengali but those of Bihar speak Hindi as well.

The Sadgop consist of a number of sub-divisions, such as the Ghosh, Kuila, Dandapat, Mahapatra, Bera, Pal, Jana, Patra, Sarkar, Mondal and Roy. They are an endogamous group and practice gotra exogamy. The Sadgop are mainly a landholding community, but many Sadgop have settled in Kolkata and other cities of West Bengal.

Tanti

The word 'tanti' is derived from the Hindi word 'tant', which means a loom. They were traditionally weavers, and are one of the many communities found in South Asia, traditionally associated with this craft. According to their traditions, they were created by the Hindu god Shiva from his tears. The community is found in south Bihar, and district of Ranchi in Jharkhand.

The Tanti are endogamous and consist of a number of totemistic clans, the main ones being the Nag, Sal and Kachchap. They are further divided into uncha or pure Tanti, and the nicha or impure Tanti. These two sub-divisions do not intermarry. They use Tanti and Tantubai as their surnames. The Tanti speak Panchpargania dialect of Hindi. Their traditions are similar to other Hindu weaving castes, such as the Koshta and Tattama.

The Tanti were victims of mechanisation, as their traditional occupation is no longer viable. They have now joined other mainstream occupations like but not limited to business, agriculture and other major industries. The community is Hindu, but incorporate many folk beliefs. They are a fairly successful community, and many have taken to modern education. Tanti is also called Tantuway in some districts of Uttar Pradesh mainly Deoria, Gorakhpur and eastern part of Bihar mainly Chhapra, Sivan, Buxar, Arrah, etc. They are not restricted to traditional weaving occupation anymore however they do own handloom mills and textile factories producing a fabric known as "Tanti Silk". There are several economical sections which include landlords, businessmen and sects who work in government and private firms.

Department of Welfare of Plains Tribes and Backward Classes

The Department of Welfare of Plains Tribes and Backward Classes is also there in Assam which is the nodal department for formulation and implementation of monies and programmes for welfare and development of the Scheduled Tribes, Scheduled Castes and Other Backward Classes in the State of Assam. The Department is responsible for implementation of Tribal Sub-Plan and Scheduled Castes and components of the State Annual Plan and Central Government and State funded programmes for the welfare of ST/SC/OBC in the State.

The Minister for WPT and BC is the Head of the Department, who provides policy direction to the department. The Administrative head of the department is the Commissioner and Secretary to Government of Assam, who is a senior officer from the IAS cadre. The other officers in the Department are Secretary, Joint Secretary(s), Deputy Secretary(s) to the Government of Assam, Under Secretary(s) and Superintendent and Senior and Junior Administrative Assistants. There is a Planning Cell headed by the Joint Director. He is assisted by Planning Officer, Research Officer and Asstt. Research Officers and branch Assistants. There are following organisations under the Department:

(a) *Directorates*

(i) The Directorate for the Welfare of Plain Tribes and Backward Classes;

(ii) The Directorate for the Welfare of Scheduled Castes;

(iii) The Directorate of Tribal Research Institute.

(b) *Corporations / Authority*

(i) The Assam Plain Tribes Development Corporation Ltd.;

(ii) The Assam State Development Corporation for Other Backward Classes Ltd.;

(iii) The Assam State Development Corporation for Scheduled Castes Ltd; and

(iv) The Assam Tribal Development Authority.

(c) *Tribal Autonomous Councils*

(i) Bodoland Territorial Council (BTC);

(ii) Mishing Autonomous Council (MAC);

(iii) Rabha Hasong Autonomous Council (RHAC);

(iv) Tiwa Autonomous Council (TAG);

(v) Deori Autonomous Council (DAC);

(vi) Thengal Kachari Autonomous Council (TKAC); and

(vii) Sonowal Kachari Autonomous Council (SKAC);

Activities and Programmes

The WPT and BC Department is the nodal Department for implementation of schemes for welfare of the SC/SC/OBC people in the State. The schemes are implemented through the Directorates of WPT and BC, Directorate of Welfare for SC, the Corporation and the ATDA. Brief descriptions of the schemes are given below:

Schemes for Welfare of Plain Tribes Implemented by the Directorate of WPT and BC

(a) Educational Developmental Programmes: Following programmes are implemented for the educational development of the tribal people:

1. Post-metric Scholarship: This scheme is meant for the ST (P) students. It is a Centrally Sponsored Scheme fully funded by the Government of India. The total budget allocation for 2005-06 was Rs 1000.00 lakh and a total of 40,000 numbers of students were awarded scholarship at the following, rates :

1. Group A	- Rs 330.00 for days scholars, - Rs 740.00 for hostellers,
2. Group B & C	- Rs 330.00 for days scholars, - Rs 510.00 for hostellers,
3. Group D	- Rs 185.00 for days scholars, - Rs 335.00 for hostellers,
4. Group E	- Rs 140.00 for days scholars, and - Rs 235.00 for hostellers.

(2) Pre-matric Scholarship: This is a State scheme where 100 per cent fund is provided by the Government of Assam.

The budget allocation for the year 2005-06 was Rs 35.00 lakh and a total of 32500 students were awarded scholarship at the following rate:

1.	Class-I to Class-IV	Rs 10.00 P.M.
2.	Class-V to Class-VII	Rs 15.00 P.M. and
3.	Class-VIII to Class-X	Rs. 20.00 P.M.

(3) Coaching and Allied Scheme for ST (P): This is a Centrally sponsored scheme on 50:50 cost sharing basis between the State and the Central Governments. This scheme aims to provide coaching facilities to ST (P) students who are going to appear in All India Level Competitive Examinations. The total budget allocation for the 2005-06 was Rs 6.00 lakh. The coaching of the ST (P) candidates is provided in the Assam Administrative Staff College with the financial assistance provided under this scheme.

(4) Book bank for Medical, Engineering and Agriculture etc: ST students studying in various technical institutions are provided books under this scheme. This is a centrally sponsored scheme on 50:50 cost sharing basis between Government of India and Government of Assam. The budget allocation for 2005-06 was Rs 6.00 lakh under the scheme.

(5) Construction of Boys and Girls Hostel: This is a centrally sponsored scheme on 50:50 cost sharing basis between Government of India and the State Government. The budget allocation for 2005-06 was Rs 75.00 lakh under the scheme. Construction of boys and girls hostels at different Schools and Colleges is undertaken under this scheme.

(6) Vocational Training Center: This is a Central sector scheme implemented through ATDA. Centers are set up for imparting vocational training for skill development. The budget allocation for 2005-06 was Rs 200.00 lakh. There are 26 Vocational Training Centres in the various districts in the State.

(7) Upgradation of merit for ST (P) Students: It is a Central Sector Scheme and the basic aim of the Scheme is to upgrade the merit of the students of ST communities through coaching

to enable them to take advantage of the better education opportunities.

(8) Stipend for craftsmen training: This is a state plan scheme and stipend is given to the students undergoing training in the various ITIs of Assam. The total budget allocation for the 2005-06 was Rs 3.00 lakh. Under the scheme 56 tribal students were provided stipend during the year in various ITIs in the State.

References

Baruah, S.L. (1993), Last Days of Ahom Monarchy, Munshiram Manoharlal Publishers Pvt Ltd, New Delhi.

Gait, Edward (1906), A History of Assam, Thacker, Spink & Co, Calcutta.

Gogoi, Nitul Kumar (2006), Continuity and Change Among The Tai-Ahom, Concept Publishing Company.

Gogoi, Padmeshwar (1968), The Tai and the Tai kingdoms, Gauhati University, Guwahati.

Sarit Kumar Chaudhuri; Sucheta Sen Chaudhuri (2005), Primitive Tribes in Contemporary India: Concept, Ethnography and Demography, Vol. 1. Mittal Publications.

Ray, Nihar Ranjan, Bangalir Itihas Adi Parba, (in Bengali), 1980 edition, Paschim Banga Niraksharata Durikaran Samiti.

Diwakar Minz and Delo Mai Hansda (2010), Encyclopaedia of Scheduled Tribes in Jharkhand, Gyan Publishing House.

People of India Gujarat Volume XXII Part One edited by R.B. Lal, S.V. Padmanabham and A. Mohideen, Popular Prakashan.

People of India Uttar Pradesh Volume XLII Part One edited by A. Hasan and J.C. Das, Manohar Publications.

Ethnographic notes on the scheduled tribes of West Bengal by Manas Kamal Chowdhuri; West Bengal (India). Cultural Research Institute.

Gait, Edward (1906). A History of Assam. Calcutta: Thacker, Spink & Co.

Essays and Lectures on the Religions of the Hindus: Religious Sects of the Hindus V1. Kessinger Publishing, LLC, 2006, p. 353.

Sharma, Suresh Kant; Sharma, Usha, eds. (2005). Discovery of North-East India: geography, history, culture, religion, politics, sociology, science, education and economy. North-East India 5. Mittal.

Susan Bayly (2001). Caste, Society and Politics in India from the Eighteenth Century to the Modern Age. Cambridge University Press.

Hutton, John Henry (1969). Caste in India: Its Nature, Function and Origins. Oxford University Press.

Rao, M.S.A. (1979). Social movements and social transformation: A study of two Backward Classes movements in India. Macmillan.

Gadkari, Jayant (1996), Society and religion: from Rugveda to Puranas. Bombay: Popular Prakashan.

Mandelbaum, David Goodman (1970), Society in India 2. Berkeley: University of California Press.

"Central List of OBCs for the State of Assam" (PDF), National Commission of Backward Classes (Government of India).

http://www.wbnorthbengaldev.gov.in/HtmlPage/rajbongshi.aspx

The Rajbansis: preliminary enquiry towards a study of a complex ethnic group of South-East Nepal and Bengal, Johan Berlie, Regmi Research Institute, Kathmandu, Nepal, 1982.

Chisholm, Hugh, ed. (1911). "Koch". Encyclopædia Britannica (11th ed.). Cambridge University Press.

Singh, Kumar Suresh (2008). People of India: Vol. 16, Part 2. Anthropological Survey of India.

Rudolph, Lloyd I.; Rudolph, Susanne Hoeber (1984). The Modernity of Tradition: Political Development in India. University of Chicago Press.

Bhattacharya, Ranjit Kumar; Das, Nava Kishor; Anthropological Survey of India.

(Ist January 1993), Anthropology of weaker sections, Concept Publishing Company.

Kanungo, Harihar (2006), "The Origin of Ganga Dynasty - A New Insight.". Orissa Historical Research Journal. XLVII (2): 15-33.

Chakrabarty, Bidyut (1997), Local Politics and Indian Nationalism: Midnapur (1919-1944). New Delhi: Manohar.

Essays and Lectures on the Religions of the Hindus: Religious Sects of the Hindus V1. Kessinger Publishing, LLC, 2006.

Sen, Sipra (1992). Tribes and Castes of Manipur: Description and Select Bibliography. A-100, Mohan Garden, New Delhi-110059: K.M. Rai Mittal for Mittal Publications.

Prakash, Ved (2007). Encyclopaedia of North-East India, Volume 4. B-2, Vishal Enclave, Opp. Rajouri Garden, New Delhi- 110027: Atlantic.

Robinson, Rowena (2004). Sociology of Religion in India. B-42, Panchsheel Enclave, and New Delhi 110 017: Sage Publications India Pvt Ltd.

S.C., Bhatt (2005). Land and People of Indian States and Union Territories. C-30, Satyawati Nagar, Delhi- 110052: Kalpaz Publications.

Gellner, David (1986). Language, caste, religion and territory: Newar identity ancient and modern. Cambridge University Press.

Nath Yogis as Established Alternatives: Householders and Ascetics Today, Daniel Gold, Journal of Asian and African Studies, 1999.

The Politics and Aesthetics of Citation: Nath Painting in Jodhpur, 1803-1843, Debra Lynn Diamond, Ph.D Thesis, Columbia University, 2000.

D.B. Bista (1991), "The Caste System in Nepal". Fatalism and Development. Orient Longman.

Northey, W. Brook and C.J. Morris (1927). The Gurkhas Their Manners, Customs and Country. Delhi: Cosmo Publications.

Vansittart, Eden. (1993)(Reprint). The Gurkhas. New Delhi: Anmol Publications.

People of India Bihar Volume XVI Part Two edited by S Gopal and Hetukar Jha, pp. 914-916, Seagull Books.

4

Status of Other Backward Classes in Assam

The evolution of the social structure during centuries of feudalism in regions not then developed by communications led to the existence of large communities that suffered handicaps and disabilities socially, economically and educationally largely due to imposition by other economically and culturally dominant groups. This backwardness is expressed in lack of adequate opportunity for group and individual self-development in areas of health, housing, education and economic opportunities upholding dignity of life. It is measured in terms of low levels of income, the extent of illiteracy, and the low standard of life demonstrated by living conditions. The chief amongst the underprivileged or especially handicapped groups are the Scheduled Castes, the Scheduled Tribes population groups which were known as criminal tribes and other groups that constituted the weaker sections. In the Indian Constitution, the 'Other Backward Classes' are described as "socially and educationally backward class".

The data for the implementation aspect of the status of the OBCs for the present study was collected by administering tool (Family Information Blank) developed by the investigator for the purpose. There were different types of items in the family information blank used for data collection. These were multiple choice, yes/no, open-closed types. The responses to each multiple choice type and yes/no type were analysed in terms of frequency of the respondents agreement or disagreement with a particular response. The frequency was further converted into percentages. The open-end type items were analysed qualitatively.

The total population in Dhubri district is 19,48,632 (2011 census) among them other Backward Classes are 3,25,616 (approximately), i.e., 16.71 per cent. There are seven blocks in Dhubri district of Assam. But the concentration of OBC population is mainly in three blocks (Agomani, Golakganj and Rupshi). So, the researcher has selected 300 OBC families for the sample of the study from all the three blocks, i.e., 100 OBC families from each block.

In this chapter, an attempt has been made to describe the educational and socio-economic conditions of the Other Backward Classes in Dhubri district of Assam. The present chapter is divided into three sections: The section - I deals with the data related to the total number of OBC family and their total population in Dhubri district of Assam. The section - II of this chapter deals with the educational conditions of the OBCs in Dhubri district and the section - III of this chapter is devoted to the analysis and interpretation of the data related to the socio-economic conditions of the OBCs in Dhubri district of Assam.

Total Number of OBCs Family and their Population

Table 4.1: Now-a-days Nuclear Family is Increasing and Joint Family is Decreasing

Members	*No. of Family*	*Total Population*
2.	10	20
3.	59	177
4.	71	284
5.	70	350
6.	60	360
7.	10	70
8.	8	64
9.	6	54
10.	1	10

(Contd.)

(Contd. Table 4.1)

Members	*No. of Family*	*Total Population*
11.	2	22
12.	2	24
13.	1	13
Total	**300**	**1448**

Number of Members in a Family

The below table provides detail information about the member-wise family and their total population in the district in 300 samples family. Here, researcher tried to find out the number of joint family and number of nuclear family. Because, now-a-days nuclear family is increasing and joint family is decreasing. So, whether among the OBCs also same is going on or not.

The population of OBCs of 300 samples is 1448, and it is found that most of the families have 3- 6 members. Five families were found where each has more than ten members. It is also mentioned that 1448 population found from 300 sampled families and there are 2,73,577 OBCs population in Dhubri district, so, there are 56,680 OBCs family in the district.

Educational Status of the OBCs

Education is perhaps the most important social indicator. It is a first step in improving the socio-economic status of an individual or a community. Literacy and numeracy are primary learning tools and they create enabling conditions to access and process of information, to articulate individual aspirations and claims on public provisions and to participate in social transformation both through contribution to benefits from the development process. It is easy to understand that a literate person is more productive than an illiterate one. A handful of well-educated scientists, for example, may know very well all about the modern methods of agriculture, but unfortunately, however, the large number of farmers on whose performance the agricultural production of the country ultimately depends, cannot put into practice the benefits of such expert knowledge of the scientists unless the farmers have a minimum of functional literacy and numeracy. Without this minimum education,

Table 4.2: Number of Literate Member in Family

No. of Literate	No. of Family	Total no. of Literate
0.	2 (0.67%)	0
1.	20 (6.67%)	20
2.	47 (15.67%)	94
3.	68 (22.67%)	204
4.	72 (24%)	288
5.	56 (18.67%)	280
6.	17 (5.67%)	102
7.	11 (3.67%)	77
8.	5 (1.67%)	40
9.	0	0
10.	1 (0.33%)	10
11.	1 (0.33%)	11
Total	**300**	**1126**

whether acquired through formal schooling or by any other way, a person cannot even do well in petty trade activities, since he will never have full control over his stocks, credits and debits.

Table 4.3: Educational Qualification/Level of Education of Household-owner

Level of Education / EQ	No. of Household
Nil	58 (19.33%)
Primary (I-IV)	70 (23.33%)
Upper Primary (V-VIII)	68 (22.67%)
High School (IX-X)	40 (13.33%)
HSLC	40 (13.33%)
HS (Arts)	13 (4.33%)
BA	10 (3.33%)
BSc	1 (0.33%)
Total	**300**

The Table 4.2 gives the clear pictures about the number of literate in the family. The study reveals that 0.67 per cent families not having a literate member in the family that means they are fully illiterate. It is also remarkable that 6.67 per cent and 15.67 per cent families having only 1 and 2 literate member respectively in the family. The 22.67 per cent families having three literate member, 24 per cent families having four literate members, 18.67 per cent having five literate members, 5.67 per cent families having six literate member, 3.67 per cent having seven literate members, 1.67 per cent having eight literate members, 0.33 and 0.33 per cent families having 10 and 11 literate members respectively in each family. The average literate members in per family are three to four members and 77.76 per cent are literate of the total OBC population.

The entire above table shows that the literacy rate of OBC people in Dhubri district is very high. In sample, only 15.15 per cent persons are found to be illiterate and another 84.85

Table 4.4: Educational Qualification/Level of Education of House-wife

Level of Education / EQ	*No. of House-wife*
Nil	82 (29.5%)
Primary (I-IV)	68 (24.46%)
Upper Primary (V-VIII)	49 (17.63%)
High School (IX-X)	40 (14.39%)
HSLC	22 (7.91%)
HS (Arts)	12 (4.32%)
BA	4 (1.44%)
BSc	1 (0.36%)
Total	**278**

percent are found literate. But it does not mean all are educated, most of them can write their names only. In 300 samples, 19.33 per cent household-owner did not receive any kind of education and other 80.67 per cent household-owner had received some formal schooling, mostly at the primary and secondary levels. It is found that only 11 household-owners are qualified graduate level. So, it is seen that the attainment of OBCs household in higher education is very less in number.

Education of the house-wife is also most important because education of the children mainly depends on an educated mother. The Table 4.4 shows that 29.5 per cent house-wife don't have any formal education. Most of the house-wife has completed only primary and upper primary level of education and some of house-wife reached up to high school level only. The study found that only five house-wife is graduate out of 278 house-wife. Here, it is seen that women are very backward in education compare to men and only 1.8 per cent house-wives attain in higher education.

Socio-economic Status of the OBCs

A family's socio-economic status is based on family income, parental education level, parental occupation, and social status in the community such as contacts within the community, group associations, and the community's perception of the family. Families with high socio-economic status often have more success in preparing their young children for school because they typically have access to a wide range of resources to promote and support young children's development. They are able to provide their young children with high-quality childcare, books, and toys to encourage children in various learning activities at

Table 4.5: Number of Members Engaged in Job in a Family

Members	*No. of Family*	*Total Job Holder*
0.	268 (89.33%)	0
1.	26 (8.67%)	26
2.	4 (1.33%)	8
3.	2 (0.67%)	6
Total	**300**	**40**

home. Also, they have easy access to information regarding their children's health, as well as social, emotional, and cognitive development. In addition, families with high socio-economic status often seek out information to help them better prepare their young children for school.

Table 4.6: Number of House Wife in Service

Response	*No. of Household*
Yes	11 (3.67%)
No	267 (89%)
Question does not arise	22 (7.33%)
Total	**300**

Employment status of a person not only determines his/her income level, but also social status as well as self-esteem. The table shows that only 32 families are found to have members who are engaged in job and the total number of job holder is 40 in 1448 population of 300 OBCs family. But most of the household, i.e., 89.33 per cent are jobless and they depend on various types of occupation and manual labour. The job holders of the family are teachers of the primary school, police, CRPF, track man (Railway), marketing officer, clerk, chowkidwar, mali, cook man, junior engineer, P.A. to Secretariat, driver (Forest Department), 7 Batillion Assam, Home Guard, Field Assistant (FA), ANM (Medical), 4th Grade (PWD), army, Helper (Irrigation

Table 4.7: Number of Household Engaged in Other Occupation

Occupation	*No. of Household*
Cultivation	89 (29.67%)
Animal husbandry	0
Skilled labour	22 (7.33%)
Manual labour/Unskilled labour	115 (38.33%)
High businessman	1 (0.33%)
Car owner	2 (0.67%)
Shop owner	17 (5.67%)
Job holder	21 (7%)
Others	33 (11%)
Total	**300**

Department), anganwadi worker, etc. Some of them are receiving very less salary like Rs 2000-3000 per month.

The Table 4.7 shows that most of the housewife i.e., 89 per cent do not having any job, but some of the housewife goes for manual labour. And only 3.67 per cent housewife engaged in job and 7.33 per cent household respond 'question does not arise' that means some of the house owner are unmarried, wife dead and female household. The housewife who engaged in job are not permanent except one housewife and the housewife those who are not permanent employee their emoluments is very less which is Rs 500-2000.

The Table 4.7 shows that over 38.33 per cent sample households are engaged in manual labour and 29.67 per cent households are engaged in agriculture or cultivation. Around two-fifth of the households reported that manual labour as their main occupation for their livelihood. Eleven per cent of household viewed that they are engaged in some other occupation like car driver, rickshaw driver, private coaching, tube well mechanic, pujari, decorators, etc.

Table 4.8: Number of Family Depends on Various Occupations

Occupation	*Number of Family*
Shop Owner	13 (4.33%)
Services and Cultivation	17 (5.67%)
Car owner (Auto)	2 (0.67%)
Manual Labour/Unskilled	111 (37%)
Skilled Labour	22 (7.33%)
Cultivation and Other	3 (1%)
Cultivation	79 (26.33%)
Tea Stall	4 (1.33%)
Cultivation and Manual Labour	6 (2%)
High Businessman	1 (0.33%)
Others (Driver, Tution, Rickshaw, Mechanics, Decorators, Rice mill, Pujari, etc.)	30 (10%)
Service	11 (3.67%)
Pension Holder	1 (0.33%)
Total	**300**

The earlier Table 4.8 regarding occupation provides the data about the engagement of household in occupation. But this table shows data about the family who depends on various occupations. The engagement and dependence in occupation may not be same because household may engaged in business and his son or brother may engaged in service but all of them stay together in one family and house owner of that family is also one. The table reveals that 4.33 per cent household depends on shop, 5.67 per cent household depends on service and cultivation, 37 per cent household depends on unskilled manual labour, 7.33 per cent household depends on skilled labour, 26.33 per cent depends on cultivation, two per cent depends on cultivation and manual labour, 0.33 per cent depends on business, 3.67 per cent depends on service, 0.33 per cent depends on pension and others 10

Table 4.9: Monthly Income from all Sources (Total Income in a Family)

Range of Income	*No. of Family*
Below Rs 5000	120 (40%)
Rs 5001-10,000	124 (41.33%)
Rs 10,001- 20,000	36 (12%)
Rs 20,001-30,000	15 (5%)
Rs 30,001-40,000	3 (1%)
Rs 40,001-50,000	0
Rs 50,001-60,000	0
Rs 60,001-70,000	0
Rs 70,001-80,000	0
Rs 80,001-90,000	2 (0.67%)
Above Rs 90,000	0
Total	**300**

percent household depends on driving car, private tution, rickshaw, tent house, rice mill, etc., for their livelihood.

Household income is the most important indicator of economic well-being of any community. In sample, 40 per cent of household viewed that their monthly income from all sources is below Rs 5000 who mainly depends on manual labour and other 41.33 per cent household viewed that their total monthly income from all sources is Rs 5000-10,000 who depends on both manual labour and they have also some portion of agricultural land like 1-2 bighas and some of them also do side business. Only 0.67 per cent household viewed that their total monthly income in family from all sources is Rs 80,000-90,000 who engaged in job and they have large portion of agricultural land and also some members in family who engaged in business.

Table 4.10: Number of Retired Person

Response	*Number of Household*
Yes	9 (3%)
No	268 (89.33%)
Question does not arise	23 (7.67%)
Total	**300**

The above Table 4.10 shows that out of 300 household three per cent household are retired from their service and the household who response 'question does not arise' they are presently employed and their number is 23, i.e., 7.67 per cent household. The household who retired from the service they are getting emolument Rs 5000-10000 per month and some of them were chowkidwar, commando, army, clerk, dak runner, assistant teacher etc.

Table 4.11: Number of Household having Additional Source of Income or Inherited or Other Property from Parents

Response	*Number of Household*
Yes	22 (7.33%)
No	278 (92.67%)
Total	**300**

Table 4.12: Monthly Income from Inherited Property and its Sources

Sources	*Range of Income*	*Number of Household*
Agricultural Land	Rs 500-1000	12
	Rs 1001-2000	5
	Rs 2001-3000	0
	Rs 3001-4000	0
	Rs 4001-5000	3
	Rs 5001-6000	1
	Rs 6001-7000	1
Total		**22**

The additional source of income indicates the income of household, who are engaged in other occupation or side business or acquired some source of income which is inherited. The Table 4.11 shows that out of 300 household 22 household i.e., 7.33 per cent household acquired some portion of agricultural land which is a source of additional income for the household. 92.67 per cent household not having any kind of inherited property from which they will get some additional source of income.

The Table 4.12 shows that only 22 household having inherited property which is agricultural land and they earn money from those land by cultivating some seasonal crops. The monthly income of the household from agricultural land is very less which is Rs 500-1000 by 12 household in each, Rs 1001-2000 by five household in each, Rs 4001-5000 by three household in each and only one household earn money Rs 6001-7000 per month from inherited property.

Number of Girls Married before 18 Years of Age

Child-marriage is a common practice in many countries around the world; however it is especially prevalent in India, where more than one third of all child brides live. According to UNICEF, 47 per cent of girls are married by 18 years of age, and 18 per cent are married by 15 years of age. These marriages are often performed without the consent of the girls involved in the marriage. Indian law has made child-marriage illegal, but it is still widely practiced across the nation. The highest rates are seen particularly in the rural states of Andhra Pradesh, Bihar, Madhya Pradesh, Rajasthan, and Uttar Pradesh. It affects both boys and girls, but statistics show that girls are far more likely to be forced into a child-marriage than boys; however the percentage of girls forced into child-marriage in India has declined in recent years. UNICEF defines child-marriage as a formal marriage or union before 18 years of age. UN Women defines child-marriage as a forced marriage before 18 years of age because they believe children under age 18 are incapable of giving their consent. Children in Scotland can marry at 16 without any parental consent. Scotland is the only developed country where child marriage is legal. Throughout the world, the problem of early, forced marriages of children is considered to be a violation of basic human rights. It has been estimated that 49 countries have a significant child bride problem.

Table 4.13

No. of Girls	*No. of Family*	*Total*
0.	277 (92.33%)	0
1.	20 (6.67%)	20
2.	3 (1%)	6
Total	**300**	**26**

Marriage at early age is also an indicator of social and health unconsciousness of any community. Poor health, early death, and lack of educational opportunities lead the list of problems attributed to child marriage or early marriage. Additionally, from having babies too young, child brides are at an extremely high risk for fistulas (vaginal and anal ruptures). Statistically, child brides have a higher risk of becoming a victim of domestic violence, sexual abuse, and murder. The Table 4.13 shows that 7.67 per cent household-owner has given their daughter marriage before 18 years of age and most of them are manual labour in occupation.

Number of Household given Dowry at the Time of their Daughter's/Sister's Marriage

A dowry is the money, goods, or estate that a woman brings to a marriage. (A dowry consisting mainly of linen and clothing, or the contents of a hope chest is called a trousseau). Dowry contrasts with bride price, which is paid by the groom or his family to the bride's parents, and with dowry, which is property given to the bride herself by the groom at the time of marriage. The same culture may simultaneously practice both dowry and bride price. Dowry is an ancient custom, and its existence may well predate records of it. Dowries continue to be expected in some parts of the world, mainly India.

Dowry system is also prevalent in the Other Backward Classes of Dhubri district. The study shows that only 1.67 per cent of household didn't give dowry in the time of their daughter marriage and 79.33 per cent of household respond 'Question does not arise' as their daughter's are not yet of marriageable age or they don't have daughter.

Table 4.14

Response	*No. of Household*
Yes	57 (19%)
No	5 (1.67%)
Question does not arise	238 (79.33%)
Total	**300**

Social Participation on behalf of Community

Social engagement or social participation is commonly used to refer to one's participation in the activities of a social group. The term has been defined by Avison, McLeod and Pescosolido

Table 4.15

Category	*No. of Household*
Member of one organisation	15 (5%)
Member of more than one organisation	3 (1%)
Wider public leader	0
Committee Head/Party Head/Chairman	4 (1.33%)
Nil	278 (92.67%)
Total	**300**

(2007), as "the extent to which an individual participates in a broad range of social roles and relationships." and by Zhang, Jiang, and Carroll as "the commitment of a member to stay in the group and interact with other members".

The social status of a person is also based on the participation in the community, group association, contacts within the community and the community's perception of the family. The study shows five per cent of the household are the member of one organisation and only one per cent of household is found they are the member of more than one organisation. It also reveals that 1.33 per cent household are committee head/party head/chairman. But 92.67 per cent household are not participated in any organisation or holding any position in the society.

Table 4.16: Information about Married Life

Information	*No. of Household*
Wife Dead	4 (1.33%)
Husband Dead	13 (4.33%)
Married for second time	7 (2.33%)
More than one living wife	5 (1.67%)
Divorced	3 (1%)
Question does not arise	268 (89.33%)
Total	**300**

The Table 4.16 shows that 4.33 per cent households are widow and 2.33 per cent house hold get married for second time. The study also shows that 1.67 per cent household has more than one living wife and one per cent household are divorced. The

Table 4.17: Number of Daughter and Wife goes for Manual Labour

Response	*No. of Household*
Yes	25 (8.33%)
No	154 (51.33%)
Question does not arise	121 (40.33%)
Total	**300**

household who response 'Question does not arise' having one living wife.

Those who response 'Question does not arise' means they may have jobs and have good business that means their economic condition is good. But other (yes/no) response indicates that they depends on manual labour but they do not send their daughter or wife for manual labour. 8.33 per cent of household viewed that their daughter goes for manual labour.

Table 4.18: Number of Household having Agricultural Land

Response	*No. of Household*
Yes	161 (53.67%)
No	139 (46.33%)
Total	**300**

Land ownership is another important indicator of the socio-economic status of a household in rural areas. Ownership of land not only provides social prestige and economic security but also reduces vulnerability of the households. Around 53.67 per cent of the OBCs households reported ownership of agricultural

Table 4.19: Number of Household having Agricultural Land in Bighas

Agricultural Land in Bighas	*Number of Household*
1-5	106
6-10	30
11-15	9
16-20	10
21-25	4
26-30	1
31-35	0
36-40	1
Total	**161**

land to some extent, i.e., 1-5 bighas. Landless was quite widespread among the household who engaged in manual labour.

The Table 4.19 provides the data regarding the agricultural land having per household. The table shows that 106 household having 1-5 bighas agricultural land in each, 30 household having 6-10 bighas, nine household having 11-15 bighas, 10 household having 16-20 bighas, four household having 21-25 bighas, one household having 26-30 bighas and one household having 36-40 bighas agricultural land.

Table 4.20: Number of Household Aware about Agricultural Loan

Response	*Number of Household*
Yes	134 (44.67%)
No	166 (55.33%)
Total	**300**

It is mentioned in the Table 4.19 that 161 household having agricultural land and most of the farmers are not educated and rich, even they don't have enough money for proper cultivation through which they can earn more. At present most of the bank providing agricultural loan to the farmer. But it is a question that how many people are aware about this agricultural loan. The Table 4.20 shows that only 44.67 per cent household are aware about the agricultural loan and 55.33 per cent household are not aware about the agricultural loan.

Number of Household Known about Kisan Credit Card

The Kisan Credit Card is a credit card to provide affordable credit for farmers in India. It was started by the Government of India, Reserve Bank of India (RBI), and National Bank for Agricultural and Rural Development (NABARD) in 1998-99 to help farmers access timely and adequate credit. The Kisan Credit Card allows farmers to have cash credit facilities without going through time-consuming bank credit screening processes repeatedly. Repayment can be rescheduled if there is a bad crop season, and extensions are offered for up to four years. The card is valid for three years and subject to annual renewals.

Withdrawals are made using slips, cards, and a passbook. All farmers, owner cultivators, tenant cultivators, share croppers and individual farmers having agreement with institution are eligible for the card. Most banks in India that offer agricultural finance offer the Kisan Credit Card. Under the scheme, Branches may issue Kisan Credit Cards to the farmers who are otherwise eligible for sanction of short-term credit for crop production, allied activities and other non-farm activities. The farmers should come from the operational area of the Branch, as per scale of finance specific to the crop and KCC norms. The interest rate is seven per cent (SI), out of which three per cent subsidy is given by Government of India if aggregate credits are more than aggregate debits in a year. The card is valid for five years, of which crop loan and working capital components have to be renewed annually. Maximum limits: Rs 50,000 for Rabi crops and Rs 50,000 for Kharif crops. Eligibility: Individual/society. Repayment period: Kharif 31 January, Rabi 31 July. 5 Collateral Security Charge on land in case loan is above Rs 10,000 and two sureties if loan is below Rs 10,000.

Table 4.21

Response	*Number of Household*
Yes	36 (12%)
No	264 (88%)
Total	**300**

Like other bank credit cards, government of India has introduced kisan credit card for the farmers. But study reveals that only few household are aware about the kisan credit card and their number is only 12 per cent household. And 88 per cent household viewed that they do not know about the kisan credit card.

Number of Household having Job Card

The Mahatma Gandhi National Rural Employment Guarantee Act (MGNREGA) is an Indian job guarantee scheme, enacted by legislation on 25th August 2005. The scheme provides a legal guarantee for at least one hundred days of employment in every financial year to adult members of any household willing to do public work – related unskilled manual work at the statutory minimum wage of Rs 120 (US$2.20) per day in 2009 prices. If they fail to do so the government has to pay the salary at their homes. The Central government outlay for scheme is 4000 billion (US$73 billion) in FY 2010-11. This act was introduced with an aim of improving the purchasing power of the rural people, primarily semi or un-skilled work to people living in rural India, whether or not they are below the poverty line. Around one-third of the stipulated work force is women. The law was initially called the National Rural Employment Guarantee Act (NREGA) but was renamed on 2nd October 2009. In 2011, the programme was widely criticised as no more effective than other poverty reduction programmes in India. Despite its best intentions, MGNREGA is beset with controversy about corrupt officials, deficit financing as the source of funds, poor quality of infrastructure built under this programme, and unintended destructive effect on poverty.

This act was brought about by the UPA-I coalition government supported by the Left parties. And has been labelled as one of the causes for voting UPA back into power as UPA-II. Dr. Jean Drèze, a Belgian born economist, at the Delhi School of Economics, has been a major influence on this project. A variety of people's movements and organisations actively campaigned for this act. The act directs state governments to implement MGNREGA "schemes". Under the MGNREGA the Central Government meets the cost towards the payment of wage, three-fourth of material cost and some percentage of administrative cost. State Governments meet the cost of unemployment allowance, one-fourth of material cost and administrative cost of State council. Since the State Governments pay the unemployment allowance, they are heavily incentivised to offer employment to workers. However, it is up to the State Government to decide the amount of unemployment allowance, subject to the stipulation that it not be less than one-fourth the minimum wage for the first 30 days, and not less than half the minimum wage thereafter. The hundred days of employment (or unemployment allowance) per household must be provided to able and willing workers every financial year.

Provisions under NREGA

- Adult members of a rural household, willing to do unskilled manual work, are required to make registration in writing or orally to the local Gram Panchayat.

- The Gram Panchayat after due verification will issue a Job Card. The Job Card will bear the photograph of all adult members of the household willing to work under NREGA and is free of cost.

- The Job Card should be issued within 15 days of application.

- A Job Card holder may submit a written application for employment to the Gram Panchayat, stating the time and duration for which work is sought. The minimum days of employment have to be at least fourteen.

- The Gram Panchayat will issue a dated receipt of the written application for employment, against which the guarantee of providing employment within 15 days operates.

- Employment will be given within 15 days of application for work, if it is not then daily unemployment allowance as per the Act, has to be paid liability of payment of unemployment allowance is of the States.

- Work should ordinarily be provided within five-km radius of the village. In case work is provided beyond five-km, extra wages of 10 per cent are payable to meet additional transportation and living expenses.

- Wages are to be paid according to the Minimum Wages Act 1948 for agricultural labourers in the State, unless the Centre notices a wage rate which will not be less than Rs 60 (US$1.10) per day. Equal wages will be provided to both men and women.

Note: The original version of the Act was passed with Rs 155/day as the minimum wage that needs to be paid under

NREGA. However, a lot of states in India already have wage regulations with minimum wages set at more than Rs 100 (US$1.80) per day. NREGA's minimum wage has since been changed to Rs 130 (US$2.40) per day.

- Wages are to be paid according to piece rate or daily rate. Disbursement of wages has to be done on weekly basis and not beyond a fortnight in any case.
- At least one-third beneficiaries shall be women who have registered and requested work under the scheme.
- Work site facilities such as crèche, drinking water, shade have to be provided.
- The shelf of project for a village will be recommended by the gram sabha and approved by the zilla panchayat.
- At least 50 per cent of works will be allotted to Gram Panchayats for execution.
- Permissible works predominantly include water and soil conservation, afforestation and land development works.
- A 60:40 wage and material ratio has to be maintained. No contractors and machinery is allowed.
- The Central Government bears the hundred per cent wage cost of unskilled manual labour and 75 per cent of the material cost including the wages of skilled and semi-skilled workers.
- Social Audit has to be done by the Gram Sabha.

Table 4.22

Response	*Number of Household*
Yes	80 (26.67%)
No	201 (67%)
Question does not arise	19 (6.33%)
Total	**300**

- Grievance redressal mechanisms have to be put in place for ensuring a responsive implementation process.

Job card is issued under the NREGA. The Mahatma Gandhi National Rural Employment Guarantee Act aims at enhancing the livelihood security of people in rural areas by guarantying hundred days of wage-employment in a financial year to a rural household whose adult members volunteer to do unskilled manual work. The Table 4.22 shows that 26.67 per cent household owner have job card and 67 per cent household owner not having job card. The household owner who response 'Question does not arise' they are service holder. But various views come regarding the number of days they get work; it is very much irregular and not even one month in a year also. Out of 80 job card holder 45 job card holders viewed that they got work only 7-15 days in the last year. The twelve job card holders viewed that they got work 15 days to one month in the last year. But seven job card holders viewed they did work 2-6 months in the last year and 16 job card holders still could not able to open their account because as they said authority asked money for opening a account which is generally Rs 500 each job card holder.

Table 4.23: Daily Wage for the Job Card Holding Labour in Working Days

Amount	*Number of Job card holder*
Rs 77 - 78	15
Rs 80	3
Rs 100	32
Contractual (Rs 1000)	14
Question does not arise	16 (unable to open their account)
Total	**80**

The Table 4.23 reveals that out of 80 job card holders 15 job card holders got Rs 77-78 per day for their labour, three job card holders got Rs 80 per day, 32 job card holders got Rs 100 per day and 14 job card holders viewed that they are bound to work in contractual basis which is generally Rs 1000. But those who

Table 4.24: Number of Members having Job Card in the Family

Number of Job Card	*Number of Family*
1.	79
2.	1
Total	**80**

response 'Question does not arise' they could not able to open their account because of corruption.

The Table 4.24 shows that out of 80 job holders 79 family having one job cards in each and only one family found that they have two job cards in a family. And out of 79 family one Gaon Panchayat member also have job card.

Table 4.25: Type of House

Type	*No. of Household*
Kutcha	231 (77%)
Pucca	33 (11%)
Mixed	36 (12%)
Mansion	0
Total	**300**

While analysing the housing conditions of the OBCs in Dhubri district, it was observed that the OBCs have lesser proportion of pucca and mixed or semi-pucca houses which is only 11 and 12 per cent respectively. The study shows that 77 per cent household live in kutcha houses with their family and the wall of the house is of bamboo fence with tin roof. Mixed or semi-pucca houses which meant the wall of the house is of half-wall and bamboo

Table 4.26: Total Number of House Excluding one Kitchen

Number of House	*Number of Household*
1.	155 (51.67%)
2.	110 (36.67%)
3.	32 (10.67%)
4.	3 (1%)
Total	**300**

fence with tin roof which are found only 12 per cent. The pictures of houses are given in Appendix-E.

The Table 4.26 reveals that out of 300 household 155 household i.e., 51.67 per cent having only one house excluding one kitchen, 36.67 per cent household having two houses excluding one kitchen, 10.67 per cent household having three houses and only one per cent household having four houses excluding one kitchen. So, it is seen that most of the household having very less number of houses excluding kitchen and it is observed that some of them even don't have kitchen also; they prepare food in the varanda.

Table 4-27: Total Number of Rooms (House-wise)

Number of House	*Number of Rooms*	*Number of Household*
1.	0	97
	2	48
	3	9
	4	1
2.	0	75
	3	18
	4	7
	5	7
	6	1
	7	1
3.	0	20
	4	8
	5	4
	6	1
4.	0	1
	5	0
	6	0
	7	1
	8	0
	9	1

This Table 4.27 provides data in details regarding total number of room in the houses. The 97 household having one houses excluding kitchen but don't have any room in the house and only nine household having one houses but three rooms in each. The 75 household having two houses but don't have any room, 18 household having two houses and having three rooms in total, seven household having two houses and having five rooms in total, 20 household having three houses but there are no rooms, eight household having three houses and they have only four rooms in total and only few household found that they have large number of rooms according to the number of houses.

Table 4.28: Availability of Electricity in Houses

Response	*No. of Household*
Yes	42 (14%)
No	258 (86%)
Total	**300**

Electricity is also an important indicator of socio-economic development which indicates the forwardness and backwardness of the society. Only 14 per cent of household viewed that they have electricity in the houses and 86 per cent household viewed that they don't have electricity in their houses. The 10 per cent of household viewed that they have television and fan in their home and only one per cent household have refrigerator in their home. But most of the household viewed that they have mobile phone those who don't have electricity also.

Table 4.29: Type of Electrical Goods Available in Houses

Type of Goods	*Number of Household*
TV/Mobile/Fan/Refrigerator	3
TV/Mobile/Fan	25
TV/Mobile	2
Mobile/Fan	7
Mobile	142
Nil	16
Total	**195**

Availability of electronic goods is also one of the indicators to judge the socio-economic conditions of the people. Electronics goods are considered to those goods which are common electronics good like Television, Fan, Mobile, Refrigerator, etc.

The Table 4.29 shows that three household having TV/Mobile/Fan/Refrigerator, 25 household having TV/Mobile/Fan, two household having TV/Mobile, seven household having Mobile/Fan and 142 household only having Mobile. But 16 household responded that they don't have any kind of electronics goods even a mobile also.

Table 4.30: Number of Electrical Goods in Family

Goods	*Number*	*Number of Household*
TV	1	28
	2	2
Mobile	1	127
	2	41
	3	8
	4	1
	5	1
	6	0
	7	0
	8	1
Fan	1	3
	2	14
	3	8
	4	4
	5	4
	6	0
	7	2
Refrigerator	1	3

The table reveals data about the number of electronic goods available in a family. It shows in the Table 4.29 that out of 300 household only 42 household having electricity at home but 195 household having electronics goods at the home. It is seen that those who don't have electricity at home they have mobile phone. The above Table 4.30 shows that 28 household having one TV in each, two household having two TV in each, 127 household having one mobile in each, 41 household having two mobiles in each, one household having eight mobiles in their family, three household having one fan in each, 14 household having two fan in each, eight household having three fan in each, two household having seven fan in each and out of 300 household only three household have refrigerator at the home.

Number of Household having Proper Drinking Water Facility in Home

Drinking water or potable water is water safe enough to be consumed by humans or used with low risk of immediate or long-term harm. In most developed countries, the water supplied to households, commerce and industry meets drinking water standards, even though only a very small proportion is actually consumed or used in food preparation. Typical uses (for other than potable purposes) include toilet flushing, washing and landscape irrigation. Over large parts of the world, humans have inadequate access to potable water and use sources contaminated with disease vectors, pathogens or unacceptable levels of toxins or suspended solids. Drinking or using such water in food preparation leads to widespread acute and chronic illnesses and is a major cause of death and misery in many countries. Reduction of water-borne diseases is a major public health goal in developing countries.

Table 4.31: Bottled Water is Sold for Public Consumption Throughout the World

Response	*Number of Household*
Yes	256 (85.33%)
No	44 (14.67%)
Total	**300**

Water has always been an important and life-sustaining drink to humans and is essential to the survival of all known organisms. Excluding fat, water composes approximately 70 per cent of the human body by mass. It is a crucial component of metabolic processes and serves as a solvent for many bodily solutes. The United States Environmental Protection Agency in risk assessment calculations previously assumed that the average American adult ingests 2.0 litres per day. However, the United States Environmental Protection Agency now suggests that either science-based age-specific ranges or an all ages level (based on National Health and Nutrition Examination Survey 2003-2006 data) be used.

The above Table 4.31 reveals that 85.33 per cent household having proper drinking water facility in home and 14.67 per cent household viewed that they don't have proper drinking water facility in home.

Table 4.32: Number of Household having Water Supply Point nearby Home

Response	*No. of Household*
Yes	40 (13.33%)
No	260 (86.67%)
Total	**300**

Pure drinking water is one of the most important factors of maintaining good health. The study reveals that only 13.33 per cent household have water supply point nearby their home but they viewed that those supply point are not functioning at present and 86.67 per cent household viewed that they don't have water supply point nearby their home.

Table 4.33: Number of Household Responses Regarding Proper Functioning

Response	*Number of Household*
Yes	13
No	27
Total	**40**

It is observed in the Table 4.33 that 40 household having water supply point nearby their house but 27 household viewed that the water supply point they have are not functioning at present and 13 household responded that the water supply point they have are functioning properly.

Number of Household having Lavatory Facility in Home

A lavatory is a sanitation fixture used primarily for the disposal of human excrement and urine, often found in a small room referred to as a toilet/bathroom/lavatory. Flush toilets, which are common in many parts of the world, may be connected to a nearby septic tank or more commonly in urban areas via "large" (3-6 in or 7.6-15 cm) sewer pipe connected to a sewerage pipe system. The water and waste from many different sources is piped in large pipes to a more distant sewage treatment plant. Chemical toilets are used in mobile and many temporary situations where there is no access to sewerage, dry toilets, including pit toilets and composting toilet require no or little water with excreta being removed manually or composted in situ. The word toilet may also be used, especially in British English to describe the room containing the fixture, for which euphemisms such as rest-room or bath-room are used in American English. Prior to the introduction of modern flush toilets, most human waste disposal was done through the use of household chamber pots, or took place outdoors in out-houses or latrines.

Today, India after celebrating its 66th Independence Day, it is very unfortunate that the rapidly-modernising India still remains home to the world's largest number of population where open defecation is practiced. A report by the WHO and the UNICEF that showed India in a poor light says that India has a shocking number of 58 per cent of all people who defecate in the open. China and Indonesia share the second place with just five per cent of their population not having toilets. Pakistan and Ethiopia are third with 4.5 per cent such people. Adding to the shame, in a stark statement, Rural Development Minister Jairam Ramesh recently described the Indian Railways as "the world's biggest open toilet". "We are the world's capital for open defecations. The sixty per cent of all open defecations in the world are in India. This is a matter of great shame," he added.

A government panel report mentions that human waste from open-discharge toilets used by passengers is damaging railway tracks as the pH value found in human urine and excreta are leading to corrosion of tracks. No matter whether you travel by roads or railways, it can be easily witnessed that India has indeed become an open defecating ground. Are we heading towards a future where we will sink under our own poop? It makes me giggle and at the same time feel awful whenever I see a modest foreigner travelling either by road or railways and gazing at the scruffy roads or railway tracks which have become open defecating ground with human faeces all over and happily presuming it to be part of 'Incredible India'. But, the question arises as to why do people relieve their innards in the open in India? Is this practice of pooping in the open a fixed behaviour pattern of certain communities? Or do people in India in general lack sanitation awareness? Many steps have been taken in this direction to keep a check on this practice; e.g., the Cabinet Committee on Economic Affairs has increased the amount of money to be spent for household toilets in rural areas, introduction of eco-friendly toilets developed by DRDO in most of the villages and launching of schemes like 'Nirmal Bharat Abhiyan' (NBA) or Total Sanitation Campaign. But, it is important to realise that this alone will in no way turn out to be a magic bullet in solving the problem. The problem is much graver. It has been observed that people change their habits for some time of not defecating in the open, but then again return to the same old practice. But why? A major reason could be that most of them don't have access to a 'Sulabh Shauchalaya' (public convenience) close to their place and hence they have to walk everyday a few miles to attend to nature's call. Yes, it happens only in India where you can easily find a shopping mall, but no place to pee. It's not just the situation in rural India; don't you and I encounter the same problem while travelling on highways as one can hardly find any public convenience and we usually end up looking out for a gas station to unburden ourselves. Another important factor is that the practice of open defecation is a fixed behaviour pattern of certain communities as in many Indian villages people still outrightly reject the idea of using a toilet. Even talking about human excreta, faeces, etc., is considered obnoxious and taboo. Mordant, isn't it? People in rural areas still prefer open fields to defecate as they think that it keeps the lands fertile. But, when this waste flows down to rivers and lakes during the time of rains, the urban India receives the same contaminated water. Now, this contaminated water spreads various water borne diseases such as diarrhoea and cholera. As per an estimate, the 'evil' diarrhoea is the cause of death of at least 800 children below the age of five in our country every year. Further, defecating places serve as 'breeding grounds' for harmful insects raising concerns for rural children as these places are playgrounds for them and hence, increasing the chances of direct contact. It has also been observed that for girls studying in rural areas, the crisis is all the more as many drop out of school midway once they reach the age of puberty because of inadequate lavatories. It has to be understood that sanitation and the sense of cleanliness will improve only when rural and urban both India are provided proper education in this respect. For this, any government led programme should not just aim at providing more number of toilets, but at the same time try to educate, motivate and communicate to people to change their behaviour with regard to open defecation. Ultimately, it is mind-set and the habits that need to be changed. On a positive front, Sikkim has become the first 'Nirmal Rajya', i.e.,100 per cent open defecation-free state in the country with Kerala and Himachal Pradesh following the same footsteps. (India's Open-toilet Crisis, Zee News, 15th August, 2012).

Table 4.34

Response	*No. of Household*
Yes	118 (39.33%)
No	182 (60.67%)
Total	**300**

The lavatory facility is also another important indicator of health consciousness. The Table 4.34 shows that only 39.33 per cent of household have lavatory in their home and other 60.67 per cent household viewed that they don't have lavatory in their home. They use their backyard to respond to the 'call of nature'.

The availability of vehicles in the family of their own also indicates that they are economically sound. The above table shows

Table 4.35: Number of Household having Two-wheeler/ Three-wheeler/Four-wheeler

Response	*Number of Household*
Yes	22 (7.33%)
No	278 (92.67%)
Total	**300**

that out of 300 household only 22 household i.e., 7.33 per cent having two wheeler/three wheeler/four wheeler and 92.67 per cent household not having any kind of vehicle in their home.

Table 4.36: Type of Vehicles

Type	*Numbers of Household*
Two-wheeler	17
Three-wheeler (Auto)	2
One motor cycle and one four-wheeler	1
Two motor cycle and one four-wheeler	1
Power trailer	1
Total	**22**

The Table 4.36 shows that 17 household having two-wheeler in each, two household having auto (three-wheeler) in each, one household having one motor cycle and one four-wheeler and another one household having two motor cycles and one four-wheeler in their family. The study also found that one household having one power trailer.

Table 4.37: Number of Household having Domestic Animal

Response	*Number of Household*
Yes	178 (59.33%)
No	122 (40.67%)
Total	**300**

The above Table 4.37 reveals the data about the number of household having domestic animal in their home. The study found that 59.33 per cent household having domestic animal and 40.67 per cent household viewed that they don't have any kind of domestic animal at home.

The Table 4.38 provides the data about the type of domestic animal which are available in the family. It shows that 93 household having cow, 14 household having goat, one household having sheep, 69 household having both cow and goat and one household having both cow and sheep in the family.

Table 4.38: Type of Domestic Animals having in the Family

Animals	*Number of Household*
Cow	93
Goat	14
Sheep	1
Both Cow and Goat	69
Both Cow and Sheep	1
Total	**178**

Table 4.39: Number of Animals in the Family

Animals	*Number*	*Number of Household*
Cow	1	22
	2	43
	3	34
	4	25
	5	20
	6	11
	7	6
	8	1
	9	0
	10	0
	11	0
	12	1
Goat	1	15
	2	23
	3	18
	4	16
	5	3
	6	4
	7	0
	8	1
	9	0
	10	1
	20	1
Sheep	1	2

The above Table 4.39 provides the clear picture about the number of domestic animals having in a family. It shows that 22 household having only one cow in each, 43 household having two cows in each, 25 household having four cows in each, 11

Table 4.40: Number of Members Suffering from Serious Disease

Response	*No. of Household*
Yes	10 (3.33%)
No	290 (96.67%)
Total	**300**

household having six cows in each, one household having 12 cows in each, 15 household having one goat in each, 23 household having two goats in each, 18 household having three goats in each, 16 household having four goats in each, four household having six goats in each, two household having eight and 10 goats respectively and one household having 20 goats in their family. The study found that the number of sheep is very less among the household and only two household having one sheep in each out of 300 household.

The above Table4.40 shows that 3.33 per cent household has their member who has been suffering from serious disease like throat cancer, blood cancer, leprosy, TB, paralysis, psyche, etc. Most of the household viewed that they cannot afford for their treatment because most of them depends on manual labour.

Number of Household having Dispensary nearby their Home

A dispensary is an office in a school, hospital or other organisation that dispenses medications and medical supplies. In a traditional dispensary set-up a pharmacist dispenses medication as per prescription or order form.

Table 4.41

Response	Number of Household
Yes	100 (33.33%)
No	200 (66.67%)
Total	300

The above Table 4.41 shows that out of 300 household, 100 household i.e., 33.33 per cent having dispensary nearby their home and 66.67 per cent household viewed that they don't have dispensary nearby their home except sub-centre.

Table 4.42: Number of Household Getting Available Medicine from the Dispensary

Response	Number of Household
Yes	0
No	100
Total	100

The above table provides the data regarding the number of household getting available medicine from the dispensary. It shows in the Table 4.42 that out of 300 families, only 100 families having dispensary nearby their home. But this table reveals that no household getting available medicine from the dispensary. The households are viewed that the medicines are always unavailable and generally, they used to buy almost of all the medicines from outside and only few tablets use to get from the hospital. But the doctors and staffs of the hospitals use to sell those medicine especially saline and injections to the outside.

5

Measures for the Other Backward Classes

Articles 15(4), 16(4), Articles 38, 46 and the set of articles in part XVI clause (i) of Article 38 makes it obligatory for the State to "strive to promote the welfare of the people by securing and protecting as effectively as it may in which justice social, economic and political shall inform all the institutions of the national life". Article 46 further contains a very significant directive regarding promotion of educational and economic interests of other weaker sections and protects them from social injustice, in all forms of exploitation. Keeping in view the betterment and welfare of the backward classes, different provincial government enunciated several special measures for them before independence especially in the field of education i.e., grants in aids to school. After independence some of these welfare measures continued in one form or the others, for example, the educational scholarship provided by the provincial government during 1949-50.

Welfare Measures for the OBCs in Various Five Year Plans

This process continued in different five year plans in independent India. During the second plan a total amount of Rs 91.0 crore were allocated for the welfare of the backward sections, out of which Rs 9.7 crore for other Backward Classes were allocated, which during seventh plan crossed the mark of Rs 1000 crore. For Backward Classes sector, i.e., SCs/STs/OBCs, the Centre/CSS outlay was Rs 281.22 crore and expenditure Rs 388.42 crore whereas for states sector it was Rs 1239.33 crore outlay and expenditure of Rs 1456.13 crore. In the nineties and twentieth century, there has been intensification of efforts to bridge the gap in the levels of development of the other backward classes, so that by the turn of the century this disadvantaged section should be brought on par with the rest of the society in all spheres of national endeavour. According to Mandal report nearly 78.0 per cent of the respondents stated various types of disabilities like free access to public utilities, social discrimination, lack of educational opportunities etc., and only 9.0 per cent were against this. Similarly due to indebtedness and shift in occupational patterns brought all types of hardship for OBCs. In this respect, the most important input for improving the social and economic status of backward communities lies in improving their access to education and assisting them by upgradation of merit through special coaching programmes.

Development of the OBCs, which made a beginning in the eighth plan continued to receive more attention during the ninth plan with many new initiatives in the field of education and economic development. The success stories related to the development of SCs have prompted the government to adopt a similar approach towards the development of OBCs, as the needs and problems of OBCs are more or less similar to those of SCs. Thus, for ensuring educational development amongst OBCs, schemes for providing scholarships for pursuing pre-matric, post-matric and other higher education, supported with hostel facilities will be introduced. Alternatively, children belonging to OBCs will also be given opportunities to enjoy the existing hostel facilities meant for SC and ST boys and girls. For OBC students to participate effectively in the competitive examinations, pre-examination coaching centres have been set up in the ninth plan. In order to provide housing and other settlement facilities to the assetless migratory communities amongst the OBCs, a new scheme of shelter for Nomadic Groups amongst the Backward Classes has been introduced in the ninth plan.

The approach paper to the 10th plan (2002-2007) also focussed attention on the socio-economic development of Other Backward Classes and minorities in the following ways:

1. Provision of special incentives and support facilities to promote educational development of these groups with a special focus on women and girl-child.

2. Promoting entrepreneurship and technical support, i.e., vocational training in modern technologies, skill upgradation. Credit and market linkages for optimising their productive capabilities especially amongst the traditional artisans and occupational groups.

   Kaka Kalelkar Commission had recommended certain welfare measures to uplift the Backward Classes which can be included under following headings:

1. Political; 2. Economic and Industrial; 3. Public Health and Rural Water Supply; 4. Communication; and 5. Rural Housings.

   Mandal Commission had also recommended some welfare measures for the Backward Classes. Those are: 1. Vocational works, 2. Educational concessions, 3. Land reforms and allied activities, etc.

   The working group on empowerment of Backward Classes for the 10th plan (2002-2007) has mooted the following objectives for their development and empowerment:

1. Removal of the educational backwardness of the Backward Classes as a whole and of each Backward Classes with the available facilities in this field.

2. Removal of the economic under development from which Backward Classes suffer.

3. Strengthening Backward Classes communities in their respective traditional occupations and securing for them control and mastery over their respective traditional fields of economy.

4. By providing training and shifting them to other occupations which are socially dignified.

5. Providing opportunities through education and training and also by taking appropriate economic measures for Backward Classes.

6. By providing supportive measures so that they can develop their own strength for their economic upliftment.

The working group on Backward Classes also recommended sound Agricultural Policy, mobile schools of high quality for NSN communities and occupationally nomadic communities, imposition of cess on investors and contractors like quary owners, fish trawler owners etc., to meet educational cost of Backward Classes, merit-based scholarships for Backward Class students and priority for most Backward Classes, etc.

In the Ninth Five-Year Plans the following schemes have been launched in the year 1998-1999 for the welfare of Other Backward Classes by the Government of India:

1. Pre-matric Scholarship for Other Backward Classes: It aims to motivate children of OBCs studying at pre-matric stage in recognised schools. Scholarship award will be sanctioned to students whose parents/guardians income does not exceed Rs 44,500 per annum. The scholarships are given to the students in class I or any subsequent class of pre-matric stage to day scholars and class II or any subsequent class of pre-matric stage to hostlers. The scholarship will terminate at the end of class X. It will be for ten months in a year, and will be applicable to the institutions recognised by the concerned State government/UT.

2. Post-matric Scholarship to the OBC Students for Studies in India: The scheme provides financial assistance to the OBC students at post matriculation/post secondary stage to enable them to complete their education. Hundred per cent central assistance for the scholarship will be provided to the State governments/UTs to which the applicant belongs. The central scholarship will be open to Indian National belonging to OBCs studying in recognised institutions. Students whose parents/guardians income does not exceed Rs 44,500 per annum will be entitled for scholarship.

Working group on empowerment Backward Classes for 10th plan (2002-2007) has examined the existing centrally sponsored schemes. Out of six schemes, three pertains to education namely, Pre- and Post-matric scholarship and hostels for Backward Class students, which are of immense importance for their upliftment. The working group has noted the following deficiencies and has suggested measures to remove it for making these schemes more effective, which has been mentioned below:

Pre-matric Scholarship for Backward Classes:

(a) Grossly inadequate outlay.

(b) Condition of 50 per cent share of the cost to be borne by the State government.

(c) Hesitation of State governments to accept the principle of committed liability beyond the IX plan period.

(d) Lack of interest and negative attitude.

According to the working group, lack of interest and negative attitude is the most important but it is true regarding all schemes and all matters pertaining to Backward Classes alongwith Schedule Castes and Schedule Tribes. All other problems listed above have to be addressed effectively by the concerned authorities for proper and effective utilisation of the scholarships meant for Backward Classes.

3. Hostels for OBC Boys and Girls: The objective of the scheme is to provide adequate hostel facilities to the target group, i.e., OBC to provide them a level playing field and to take up educational pursuits in quality education centres. The hostels are constructed for middle, secondary, college and university level students. Under the scheme 50.0 per cent central assistance is provided to the States and 100.0 per cent to UTs for such constructions. Of the hostels to be set up under this scheme, at least one-third are constructed exclusively for girls. Five per cent of the seats in these hostels are reserved for disabled students.

4. Pre-examination Coaching: The objective of this scheme is to coach/train candidates belonging to Other Backward Classes to enable them to compete on an equal terms in competitive/entrance examinations covering recruitment to services under Central and State Governments, PSUs, Bank, Defense services and admission in different technical and vocational courses. The candidates' family income should be less than one lakh rupees. The scheme is implemented through universities and national and state level professional coaching institutions of repute. Hundred per cent central assistance to the coaching institutions is sanctioned by the MSJ & E. The scheme of pre-examination coaching for OBCs as also for SCs and Minorities have since been revised and merged as centrally sponsored scheme of coaching and allied assistance for weaker sections, a combined allocation of Rs 40 crore for SCs, OBCs and Minorities have been made for 2003-04.

5. Assistance to Voluntary Organisations for Welfare of OBCs: The scheme was launched with a major objective of involving the voluntary sector for improving the educational and socio-economic conditions of the OBCs through skill upgradation and enables them to start income generating activities on their own or get gainfully employed. The Government of India may meet 90 per cent of the approved expenditure on any or all of the specified items under the scheme. The beneficiary parents/guardians income does not exceed Rs one lakh annually.

National Backward Classes Finance and Development Corporation (NBCFDC)

The lot of Backward Classes cannot be improved solely by making reservations in employment and in the educational institutions. It is also necessary to chalk out an economic programme to provide awareness for self-employment in accordance with Article 46 of the Constitution of India, so keeping in view this NBCFDC was set up by the Government of India under Ministry of Social Justice and Empowerment on 13th January, 1992 as a company not for profit under section 25 of the companies Act 1956, with authorised share capital of Rs 700 crore and paid up share capital of Rs 406.63 crore (as on 31.03.2004). Its main objective is to promote socio-economic development of those OBCs living below the poverty line by granting loans for income generating schemes.

The corporation provides financial assistance in terms of loans/grants to the eligible beneficiaries in the following sectors: agriculture and allied, artisans and traditional occupation technical trades, small business, small scale industries and transport services.

It has launched a special scheme for eligible women beneficiaries of Backward Classes under the name of *'Swarnima' Yojna,* for getting financial assistance at concessional rate of interest upto Rs one lakh. For this the annual income of the applicant should be below Rs 22,000. The SCA have been directed to ensure 30 per cent coverage of women beneficiaries under NBCFDC scheme, out of which five per cent will be covered under this scheme.

Another scheme 'Samridhi Training Grant' has been formulated for the youth (18-25 years) belonging to Backward Classes for upgradation of their technical and entrepreneurial skill. The objective is to make the target group self-dependent through appropriate technical education. Financial assistance is provided in the form of grant and the annual family income of the applicant should be less than Rs 22,000. *'Aakanksha'* another scheme, is also on the anvil for OBCs for pursuing higher professional and technical education. To avail the benefit under this scheme, the family income of the applicant should be less than Rs 60,000 and he/she has enrolled him/her self in any government recognised technical or higher professional institutions.

The NBCFDC has so far sanctioned loans amounting to Rs 643.80 crore upto 31.3.99 out of which Rs 394.82 crore were disbursed as on 25.1.2000. The corporation has put great emphasis on training and education and spent Rs 149.30 lakh as grant in aid for 4013 beneficiaries by January, 2000.

The Corporation has also achieved more than hundred per cent growth in the Ninth Plan period over the Eighth Five Year Plan in respect of disbursement, recoveries and number of beneficiaries assisted. Under the *'New Swarnima Yojna'* which started w.e.f. 2001-02 financial assistance of Rs 50,000 is provided to the beneficiary. Another scheme *'Swayam Saksham' Yojna* has been started by the Ministry of Social Justice and Empowerment, for both an amount of Rs 61.00 crore has been released in the year 2003-04.

(a) As the majority of OBCs has been traditionally engaged in the occupations like handloom weaving, pottery, metal work, artisanship, fishing, stone-cutting etc., a special thrust will be laid on upgrading their traditional skills especially of women and to provide financial support and marketing facilities in developing entrepreneurship, either in groups or as an individual. For this appropriate educational and vocational training in modern and upcoming technologies supplemented with financial and other assistance will be provided to them, so that they can enter successfully into new ventures. To achieve all this and to provide economic empowerment to the Other Backward Classes, the Ninth Five Year Plan stressed on following points to strengthen NBCFDC, which are as follows: The NBCFDC will be activated to extend necessary support for financial viable schemes/project and to upgrade the technical self-reliant.

(b) Steps will be taken to support self-employment and income generating ventures especially for nomadic and semi-nomadic communities with a view to setting them permanently at one place.

(c) The NBCFDC will be strengthened besides encouraging the voluntary organisations in the social and economic betterment of OBCs.

(d) Traditional weavers, who are going through hardship at present, will be supported with necessary financial and material support to revive the languishing industry as a sustainable venture.

(e) The much-needed modernisation of handloom operations through appropriate apprenticeship, training and supply of raw materials will be ensured.

The development programmes for OBCs started late as compared to SCs and STs and tended to be formulated in an ad-hoc manner without any perspective. The programmes formulated for Backward Classes can no longer confined to mere educational incentives and grants and subsidies for economic activities. Comprehensive development plans are required to be formulated keeping in view the special needs and problems of each of these communities. Further these programmes have to be integrated with other general programmes in the context of overall development strategy of the plan. With the establishment of NBCFDC and recommendation given by the working group on Backward Classes empowerment for inclusion in tenth plan (2002-07) for development of Backward Classes, welfare activities for Other Backward Classes have speeded up. The best can be said that the government should immediately implement the recommendations of the working group which covers all aspects and field of their development. Also voluntary organisations for Backward Classes can play an important role in mobilisation of support for their effective implementation. Their participation is creating consciousness among Backward Classes. Despite all these efforts, it is necessary to develop leadership at different level so that their urge for betterment is constantly sustained.

Suggesting Measures for the Current Situation

Skilled labour and high craftsmanship, residents of urban area, commanding sufficient capital, government service of the upper grades, having educated parents or guardians with an atmosphere of self-confidence and culture, having adequate income and resources, having a fair amount of education, belief in science or develop scientific attitude etc., are the indicators of non-backwardness. So, on the basis of this and keeping in view of various recommendations for the welfare of Backward Classes suggested by various commissions and welfare schemes taken in the Five Year Plans, at present the following steps should be taken for removing backwardness:

- Opportunity should be given through education and training and shifting them to other occupations which are socially dignified.

- Women should be given special help in education so that they may come up to the level of men, and they should be given all opportunities in public service by giving them equality of status.

- Rural areas must be made attractive by better and healthy amenities.

- Special training should be given to the unskilled labourers to improve their efficiency, and they should be encouraged to raise the standard of efficiency, precision, dexterity grace and quickness. All labour should be educated labour.

- People should not wait for the government to take initiative for the Backward Classes. Social workers should enthusiastically start work for them.

- Curriculum should be changed according to the needs and problems of the society.

- Systematic classes must be held throughout the country, and all the educational methods and psychological aids should utilised to enthuse, both social servants and the masses, for the spread of correct ideas about health, use of money, system of administration, laws of psychology, sociology, ethics and spirituality.

References

Annual Report 2003-04, Ministry of Social Justice and Empowerment, Government of India, New Delhi.

Approach Paper of Different Five Year Plans, Government of India.

Booklet of NBCFDC, Objective, Organisations and Operating Procedure, Government of India, Ministry of Social Welfare, New Delhi.

Sinha, Sushil Kumar, Backward Classes in India-various dimensions, Raj Publications, New Delhi, 2005.

Welfare of Backward Classes, Report, Government of Andhra Pradesh, Hyderabad, 1996.

Working group on Empowerment of Backward Classes, Tenth Plan (2002-07), Government of India (NCBC), New Delhi.

Bibliography

Acharya Hazari Prasad Dwivedi Rachnawali, Rajkamal Prakashan, Delhi.

Aggarwal, Patrap, Caste and Social Stratification among Muslims in India. Manohar, 1978.

Aggarwal, Pratap, Halfway to Equality, Manohar, New Delhi, 1986.

Ahmad, Imtiaz and Saxena, N.C., Caste, Land and Political Power in Uttar Pradesh (Ch. 8) in Caste and Class in India (ed.) by K.L. Sharma, Rawat Publications, Jaipur, 1994.

Alosius, G., "Caste in and Above History", In Sociological Bulletin, Vol. 48, No. 1 and 2, March-Sept, 1999, pp. 151-174.

Ambedkar, B.R. (1935). "The Untouchables who were they and why they become Untouchables?" http://www.ambedkar.org

Ambedkar, Bhimrao. Pakistan or the Partition of India. Thackers Publishers.

Ambedkar, B.R. (1946). The Untouchables: Who Were They and Why They Became Untouchables? As reprinted in Volume 7 of Dr Babasaheb Ambedkar Writings and Speeches, published by Government of Maharashtra 1990; Complete Writings.

Ambedkar, B.R., Who were the Shudras?, 1946.

Anand A. Yang, Bazaar India: Markets, Society, and the Colonial State in Bihar, University of California Press, 1999.

Anand, Arun, What is India's Population of Other Backward Classes? New Kerala.com, 2006.

"Annual Report, 2007-2008". National Commission for Backward Classes, Government of India,2009. http://www.ncbc.nic.in/Pdf/annual.pdf.

Ansari, Ghaus. Muslim Caste in Uttar Pradesh: A Study of Culture Contact. Lucknow, 1960.

Arvind Narayan Das, Agrarian Movements in India: Studies on 20th century Bihar (Library of Peasant Studies), Routledge, London, 1982.

Atal, Yogesh, "The Changing Frontiers of Caste" Delhi, National Publishing House, 1968.

Atal, Yogesh, "Changing Indian Society" Chapter on *Varna* and *Jati*. Jaipur, Rawat Publications, 2006.

Augustine, P.A., Social Equality in Indian Society, Concept Publishing, New Delhi, 1991.

Austin, Granville, The Indian Constitution: Corner Stone of a Nation, Oxford, 1966, p. 50.

Baines, Jervoise Athelstane (1893). General Report on the Census of India, 1891, London, Her Majesty's Stationery Office.

Baldev Upadhyaya, *Kashi Ki Panditya Parampara*, Sharda Sansthan, Varanasi, 1985.

Bandyopadhyay, Shekhar. Caste, Class and Politics in Colonial Bengal: A Case Study of the Namasudra Movement of 1872-1931 (Ch. 1) in Caste and Class in India (ed.) by K.L. Sharma. Rawat Publications, Jaipur, 1994.

Bates, C., "Race, Caste and Tribe in Central India: the early origins of Indian anthropometry". Edinburgh Papers in South Asian Studies (3), 1995. http://www.sps.ed.ac.uk/__data/assets/pdf_file/0005/38426/WP03_BATES_RaceCaste_and_Tribe.pdf.

Baxi, Upendra, Justice Journey for Backward Class, in Lokayan Bulletin, No. 8.4/5, 1990.

Bayly, Susan. Caste, Society and Politics in India from the Eighteenth Century to the Modern Age. Cambridge University Press. 1999. Doi: 10.2277/0521264340. ISBN 978-0-521-26434-1.

Best, John W., Kahn, James V., Research in Education, Sixth Edition, Prentice Hall of India, New Delhi, 1992.

Berreman, Gerald D., Race, Caste, and Other Invidious Distinctions in Social Stratification. University of California, Berkeley, 1972, http://reserves.fcla.edu/rsv/NC/010015586-1.pdf

Beteille, Andre, "Race and Caste". The Hindu. http://www.hindu.com/2001/03/10/stories/05102523.htm.

Beteille, Andre, Caste, Class and Power: Changing Pattern of Stratification in a Tanjore Village, University of California Press, Berkeley, 1965.

Beteille, Andre, Inequality among Men, Oxford University Press, New Delhi.

Bhashan, L.I., Casteism: A Socio-Psychological Study, New Delhi, Classical Publication Co., 1996.

Bhattacharya, Amit, Who are the OBCs?, Times of India, April 8, 2006.

Bhatty, Zarina, Social Stratification among Muslims in India (Ch.) in Caste its Twentieth Century Avtar (Ed. And Introduction) by M.N. Srinivas. Penguin Books India (P) Ltd., 1996.

Bhosale, B.V. (Ed), Mobilisation of Backward Communities in India, Deep and Deep Publications Pvt. Ltd., New Delhi, 2004.

Bibliography of Doctoral Dissertation 1989, Social Sciences, and Humanities, Association of Indian Universities, New Delhi, 1992.

Bibliography of Doctoral Dissertation 1990, Social Sciences, and Humanities, Association of Indian Universities, New Delhi, 1993.

Bisht, Bhagavan Singh, Backward Communities, Gyan Books, 1999.

Blunt, E.A.H. (1931). The Caste System of Northern India, republished 1964, S. Chand, Delhi.

Buch, M.B., Fourth Survey of Research in Education (Vol. II) 1983 – 88, NCERT, New Delhi, 1991.

Burman, B.K. Roy, Beyond Mandal and After – Backward Classes in Perspective, Mittal Publications, New Delhi, 1992.

Chalam, K.S., "Caste Reservation and Equality of Opportunity in Education", Economic and Political Weekly, Vol. XXV, No. 41, Oct. 13, 1990.

Chanchreek, K.L. and Prasad, Saroj (ed), Mandal Commission Report: Myth and Reality: A National View Point, H.K. Publishers and Distributors, Delhi, 1991.

Chanran, F., Issues in Reservation Caste Versus Economic Status, Cosmos Book Hive, New Delhi, 1990.

Christopher Alan Bayly, Rulers, Townsmen, and Bazaars: North Indian Society in the Age of British Expansion, 1770–1870, Cambridge University Press, 1983.

Constituent Assembly Debates, Vol. VII, Government of India (New Delhi), 1947, pp. 696-7.

"Constitution of India". Ministry of Law, Government of India. http://lawmin.nic.in/olwing/coi/coi-english/coi-indexenglish.htm.

Crooke, William (1896). Tribes and Castes of the North-Western Provinces and Oudh, 4 vols.

Desai, D.A. *et. al.,* Social Justice: A Dialogue, Rawat Publication, Jaipur, 1998.

Desai and Kulkarni (May, 2008). "Changing Educational Inequalities in India in the Context of Affirmative Action". Demography 45 (2): 245–270. PMC 2474466. PMID 18613480.

Desai, I.P., Should caste be the basis for recognising backwardness? Economic and Political Weekly (EPW) 14th July, 1984.

Deshpande, Satish, Caste and the Census, in Sociological Bulletin, Vol. 48, No. 1 and 2, March-Sept, 1999, pp. 257-265.

Duiker/Spielvogel. The Essential World History Vol. I: to 1800. 2nd Edition 2005.

Dumont, Louis. Homo Hierarchicus: The Caste System and Its Implications. Complete English edition, revised. 540 p. 1970, 1980 Series: (Nature of Human Society).

E.A.H. Blunt, The Caste System of North India, first edition in 1931 by Oxford University Press, new edition by S. Chand Publishers, 1969.

"Early Evidence for Caste in South India," pp. 467-492 in Dimensions of Social Life: Essays in honour of David G. Mandelbaum, Edited by Paul Hockings and Mouton de Gruyter, Berlin, New York, Amsterdam, 1987.

Eric Stokes (February 1973). "The First Century of British Colonial Rule in India: Social Revolution or Social Stagnation?" Past and Present 58: 136–160. JSTOR 650259.

Forrester, Duncan B., 'Indian Christians' Attitudes to Caste in the Nineteenth Century,' in Indian Church History Review 8, No. 2 (1974): 131-147.

Forrester, Duncan B., 'Christian Theology in a Hindu Context,' in South Asian Review 8, No. 4 (1975): 343-358.

Forrester, Duncan B., 'Indian Christians' Attitudes to Caste in the Twentieth Century,' in Indian Church History Review 9, No. 1 (1975): 3-22.

Forrester, Duncan B., Caste and Christianity: Attitudes and Policies on Caste of Anglo-Saxon Protestant Missions in India (London and Atlantic Highlands, NJ: Curzon Press and Humanities Press, 1980).

Gaikwad, S.L., Protective Discrimination and Social Change, Rawat Publication, Jaipur, 1999.

Galanter, Marc, Competing Equalities: Law and Backward Classes in India, Oxford (New Delhi), 1984, p. 159.

Galanter, Marc. "Who are the OBCs? An introduction to a Constitutional Puzzle", EPW, 1978.

Gay, I.R., Educational Research – competencies for analysis and applications, Fifth Edition, Merill, Prentice Hall, 1996.

Genetic Evidence on the Origins of Indian Caste Populations — Bamshad *et al* 11 (6): 994. Genome Research.

Ghosh, Partha S. "Positive discrimination in India: A Political Analysis", Ethnic Studies Report, Vol. XV, No. 2, July 1997.

Ghurye, G.S., Caste, Class and Occupation. Popular Book Depot, Bombay,1961.

Ghurye, G.S., Caste and Race in India, Popular Prakashan, Mumbai 1969 (1932).

Granville, Austin, The Indian Constitution: Corner Stone of a Nation, Oxford University Press, 1966.

Gupta, Dipankar, "Do Muslims Need Reservations?" The Economic Times, 26/7/2004.

Gwyer and Appadorai, Speeches and Documents on Indian Constitution, 1921, Vol. 1, Oxford Publisher, 1957, pp. 261-265.

Hammerton, J.A., An Encyclopaedia of Human Races all Over the World (7 vols.), Gyan Publishing House, 1997.

Harold Coward, Hindu-Christian Dialogue: Perspectives and Encounters, Motilal Banarsidass Publishers, 1993.

Hellwald, Von and A.N. Keane (Ed), World Encyclopaedia of Continents, Communities and Cultures (Set of 7 Vols.), Commonwealth Publishers, 1998.

Hooda, Sagar Preet, "Contesting Reservations", Rawat Publications, New Delhi, 2001.

Hutton, J.H., Caste in India: Its nature, function and origins.' Oxford University Press, London, 1963.

Indra Sawhney vs *Union of India,* Supreme Court, 16, November, 1992.

Ishwaran, K. *et. al.,* Backward Classes: Sociologists, Economists and Jurists on Havanur Commission Report, Sociological Services and Research Centre, Bangalore, 1979.

Jain, Meenakshi, Backward Castes and Social Change in U.P. and Bihar (Ch.) in Caste its Twentieth Century Avtar (ed. and introduction) by M.N. Srinivas, Viking by Penguin Books India (P) Ltd., 1996.

Jaffrelot, Christophe (2003). India's Silent Revolution: The Rise of the Lower Castes, C. Hurst and Co.

Jogendra Nath Bhattacharya, Hindu Castes and Sects, Munshiram Manoharlal, Delhi, first edition 1896, new edition 1995.

J. John; (2004), Sociology, Prentice Hall 10th ed. ISBN: 0-13-184918-2, p 249-251.

Kamble, J.R., Rise and Awakenning of Depressed Classes in India, National Publisher, New Delhi, 1979, pp. 67-68.

Kane, Pandurang Vaman: History of Dharmasastra: (ancient and mediaeval, religious and civil law) — Poona: Bhandarkar Oriental Research Institute, 1962–1975.

Karlekar, Hiranmay, in The Mirror of Mandal: Social Justice, Caste, Class and the Individual, Ajanta Publications, Delhi, 1992.

Khan, M.S., Current Problems of Indian Economy, Ashish Publishing, House, New Delhi, 1994.

Khanna, S.K., Castes in Indian Politics, Commonwealth Publishers, Delhi, 1998.

Kirpal, V., Equality through Reservation, Rawat Book Sellers, Jaipur, 1999.

Kohli, Atul, India's Democracy: An Analysis of Changing State-Society Relations, Orient Longman, New Delhi, 1991, p. 15.

Lal, K.S. Growth of Scheduled Castes and Scheduled Tribes in Medieval India, 1995.

Lata Sinha, Origin of Caste System of India, Just another worldpress.com.

Leiten, G.K., Mandalisation Under British Rule in Bengal, Economic and Political Weekly, Vol. XXV, No. 25, June 22, 1991.

Louis, Prakash, "Scheduled Castes and Tribes, The Reservation Debate", EPW, June 2, 2003, p. 2478.

M.A. Sherring, Hindu Tribes and Castes as Reproduced in Benaras, Asian Educational Services, New Delhi, First edition 1872, new edition 2008.

Maheshwari, S.R., The Mandal Commission and Mandalisation: A Critique, Concept Publishing Company, New Delhi, 1991.

Mann, E.A., Boundaries and Identities: Muslims, Work and Status in Aligarh, Sage Publications, New Delhi, 1992.

Mandal's True Inheritors, The Times of India, (12.12.2006).

Manu ((Lawgiver)); Manu; Patrick Olivelle (2004). The law code of Manu.Oxford University Press. p. 185, http://books.google.com/books?id=RGPSEuNsPLEC&pg=PA185.

Mathur, M.L., Encyclopaedia of Backward Castes (In 4 Volumes), Reservation (Vol. 1), Kalpaz Publications, Delhi, 2004.

Mathur, M.L., Encyclopaedia of Backward Castes (In 4 Volumes), (Judgements: Before and After Mandal Judgment, Vol. 4), Kalpaz Publications, Delhi, 2004.

Mathur, M.L., Encyclopaedia of Backward Castes (In 4 Volumes), Commissions (Vol. 2), Kalpaz Publications, Delhi, 2004.

Mathur, M.L., Encyclopaedia of Backward Castes (In 4 Volumes), Reservation (Vol. 1), Kalpaz Publications, New Delhi, 2004.

Mazumdar, D.N., Caste and Communication in an Indian Village, Asia Publishing House, Bombay, 1956.

"Meira Kumar, a Dalit leader is the new Lok Sabha Speaker". NCHRO. 2009. http://www.nchro.org/index.php? option=com_content&view=article&id=6863:meira-kumar—dalit-leader-is-the-new-lok-sabha-speaker&catid=5:dalitsatribals&Itemid=14.

Michaels, Axel, Hinduism: Past and Present 188-97 (Princeton 2004) ISBN 0-691-08953-1.

Mishra, R.G. and Kaur, Gurvinder, Reservation Policy and Personnel Selection, Uppal Publishing House, New Delhi, 1990, p. 14.

Mookherjee, Dulal (2002). The Essence of Bhagavad Gita. Academic Publishers, p. 472.

Mukhopadhyay, Marmar; Parhar, Madhu, Indian Education-Developments since Independence, Vikas Publishing House Pvt. Ltd., 1999.

Mukherji, Partha N., The Indian State in Crisis? Nationalism and Nation-Building, in Sociological Bulletin, Vol. 43, No. 1, March, 1994.

Murray Milner, Jr. (1994). Status and Sacredness: A General Theory of Status Relations and an Analysis of Indian Culture, New York: Oxford University Press, 1994.

National Front: Lok Sabha Election Manifesto, 1989, p. 36.

NCERT, Fifth All India Educational Survey, New Delhi, 1992.

NCERT, Fifth Survey of Educational Research (Vol. I, Trend Report), New Delhi, 1997.

NCERT, Fifth Survey of Educational Research (Vol. II, Abstract), New Delhi, 2000.

OBC Quota Law held valid, News Panorama of India and World (page no. 18-19), Vol. 20, No. 8, June, 2008.

Omvedt, Gail, Kanshi Ram and Bahujan Samaj Party (Ch. 7) in Caste and Class in India (ed.) by K.L. Sharma, Rawat Publications, Jaipur, 1994.

Padhy, K.S. and Mahapatra, Jayashre, "Reservation Policy in India", Ashish Publishing House, New Delhi, 1985.

Palekar, S.A., Concept of Equality and Ideal Society, Rawat Publications, Jaipur, 1997.

Panandiker, V.A. Pai, (ed.), The Politics of Backwardness, Reservation Policy in India, Konark Publishers Pvt. Ltd., Delhi, 1997.

Pant, V.K., Backward Communities: Identity, Development and Transformation, Gyan Publishing House, New Delhi, 1999.

Prasad, A., Reservational Justice to OBCs, Theoretical and Practical Issues, Deep and Deep Publications, New Delhi, 1997.

"Profile: Mayawati Kumari". BBC News. 16 July 2009. http://news.bbc.co.uk/2/hi/1958378.stm.

Radha Krishnan, P., Job Quotas in the Private Sectors", EPW, Oct. 2, 2004.

Raj, Papia and Aditya Raj (2004) "Caste Variation in Reproductive Health of Women in Eastern Region of India: A

Study Based on NFHS Data" Sociological Bulletin 53 (3): 326–346.

Ranganayakamma, For the Solution of the "Caste" question, Buddha is not enough, Ambedkar is not enough either, Marx is a must, Hyderabad: Sweet Home Publications, 2001.

Ramaiah, A., Economic and Political Weekly Journal, Page no. 1203 – 1207, 1992.

Rao, C.S. and Francis, Development of Weaker Sections, Rawat Publications, Jaipur, 1999.

Rao, R. Sangeeth, Caste System in India: Myth and Reality, India Publishers and Distributors, New Delhi, 1989.

Rao, M.S.A., Social Movements in India, Vol. 1 (ed.), Manohar Publications, 1978.

Russell, R.V. and R.B. Hira Lal (1916). The Tribes and Castes of the Central Provinces of India, 4 vols. London.

Report of the First Backward Classes Commission (Chairman: Kaka Kalelkar), Govt. of India, 1955.

Report of the Second Backward Classes Commission of India (Chairman: B.P. Mandal), 1980, New Delhi.

Report of the Expert Committee for specifying the criteria for identification of socially and educationally Backward Classes (Chairman: R.N. Prasad), Government of India, 10th March, 1993.

Rupa, C., Reservation Policy – Mandal Commission and After, Steering Publishers Pvt. Ltd., 1992.

Roy Burman, B.K., Beyond Mandal and After: Backward Classes in Perspective, Mittal Publications, New Delhi, 1992.

Samaddar, Ranbir, Caste and Power in West Bengal (Ch. 2) in Caste and Class in India (ed.) by K.L. Sharma, Rawat Publications, Jaipur, 1994.

Sangwan, Om Prakash (Ed), Dalit Society and Vice Challenge of Development, Commonwealth Publications, 1996.

"Scheduled Castes and Scheduled Tribes Population: Census 2001". Government of India. 2004. http://censusindia.gov.in/Census_Data_2001/India_at_glance/scst.aspx.

Second Backward Classes Commission, 1980, p. 2.

Sen, Sipra, Tribes and Castes of Assam, Gyan Publishing House, Delhi, 1999.

Sharma, Arjun, Caste, Class and Politics in Rural India: A Comparative Study of Village Panchayats, Bihar and West Bengal, Khama Publisher, New Delhi, 1993.

Sharma, Dr. Shish Ram, Protective Discrimination – Other Backward Classes in India, Raj Publications, Delhi, 2002.

Sharma, K.L., Caste and Class in India (Reprint), Rawat Publications, Jaipur, 1998.

Sharma, Shish Ram, Protective Discrimination, Raj Publications, Delhi, 2002.

Sharma, B.A.V. and Reddy, Madhusudhan, Reservation Policy in India, Light and Life Publisher, New Delhi, 1982, pp. 14-15.

Shashi, S.S., Encyclopaedia of Indian Tribes (12 Vols), Anand Publication, Delhi, 1994.

Sherring, M.A., Hindu Tribes and Castes, Cosmo Publications, Delhi, 1987.

Shourie, Arun, The Mandal Report – This Way Lies Not only Folly, but disaster, Indian Express, 25th August, 1990.

Singh, S.N., Reservation: Problems and Prospects, Uppal Publishing House, New Delhi, 1987.

Singh, S.N., Reservation Policy for Backward Classes, Rawat Publications, Jaipur, 1996.

Singh, Parmanand, Equality, Reservation and Discrimination in India, Deep and Deep Publications, New Delhi, 1982, p. 80.

Singh, Shyama Nand, Reservation: Problems and Prospects, Uppal Publishing, New Delhi, 1991, p. 72.

Singer and Cohn, Structure and Change in Indian Society. Aldine Publishing Co., 2007, ISBN 978-0-202-36138-3.

Sinha, Sushil Kumar, Backward Classes in India – Various Dimensions, Raj Publications, New Delhi, 2005.

Srinivas, M.N., Social Change in Modern India, Orient Longman, Delhi, 1995.

Srinivas, M.N., The Pangs of Change, Frontline 14 (16), 1997.

Srinivas, M.N., Religion and Society among the Coorgs of South India, p. 32 (Oxford, 1952).

Srinivas, M.N., Caste in Modern India and Other Essays, Asia Publishing House, Bombay, 1962.

Srinivas, M.N. (ed), Caste Its Twentieth Century Avtar, Viking by Penguin Books India (P) Ltd., New Delhi, 1996.

"Status of caste system in modern India". Dr B.R. Ambedkar and His People. 2004. http://www.ambedkar.org/News/reservationinindia.pdf.

Sundaram, Natraj, Welfare of Other Backward Classes an article in the Encyclopaedia of Social Work in India, Vol. III, Ministry of Welfare, Government of India, New Delhi, 1987.

Susan Bayly - Saints, Goddesses and Kings: Muslims and Christians in South Indian Society, pp. 243-253, Cambridge University Press, 2004.

Swami Vivekananda (1952). The Complete Works of Swami Vivekananda (8 Vols. Calcutta). V. pp. 25–30. ISBN 978-81-85301-46-4.

Swami Sahajan and Saraswati Rachnawali (Selected works of Swami Sahajanand Saraswati), Prakashan Sansthan, Delhi, 2003.

The Constitution of India, Ministry of Law and Justice, Delhi Controller of Publications, New Delhi, 1986, p. 14.

Topo, S.R., Caste – A Social Evil, Rajat Publications, New Delhi, 2000.

Trivedi, Bijal P. (2001-05-14). "Genetic evidence suggests European migrants may have influenced the origins of India's caste system". Genome News Network (J. Craig Venter Institute). http://www.genomenewsnetwork.org/articles/05_01/Indo-European.shtml.

Venugopal, C.N., "G. S. Ghurye on Culture and Nation Building" in Sociological Bulletin, Vol. 42, Nos. 1 and 2, March-Sept, 1993.

Verma, H. S. (Ed), The OBCs and the Ruling Classes in India, Rawat Publications, Jaipur, 2005.

Vidyasagar, R. and Suresh V., "Backward Classes and Reservation", EPW, Vol. 25, No. 16, April 21. 1990.

Yadav, K.C., Flaws in the Creamy Layer Concept, The Times of India, October 7, 1993.

Yadav, K.C., India's Unequal Citizens – A study of Other Backward Classes, Manohar Publishers, 1994.

Index

I

J

K